What people are saying about *Driving Operational Excellence*...

Driving Operational Excellence provides key insights to understand the linkages between business financial performance, customer advocacy and loyalty, and the culture of empowered high performance employees. It delivers tactical advice for companies of all sizes and in every business on the inflections and practices needed to develop and implement specific policies and processes that produce superior business outcomes. It should be required reading for every business decision maker.

> – **Robert Doran, Loyalty Performance Manager, Nissan North America**

Driving Operational Excellence confirmed to me what I have always believed – improvement mainly involves *people*...This book gets to the heart of this noble goal. Ron Crabtree has made a valuable contribution to the management body of knowledge with this book – a must read for managers seeking a way to get results.

> – **Gary Cokins, CPIM, Manager, Performance Management Solutions, SAS and author of** *Performance Management – Integrating Strategy Execution, Methodologies, Risk, and Analytics*

You can choose to read each of the 24 chapters in this book as separate items, in no particular order, and come away with a much keener grasp of the various strategies, methodologies and tools available to organizations pursuing Lean, Six Sigma or Operational Excellence initiatives. Each of the contributors tackles a particular issue or challenge, and offers a clear and current perspective on what a company can expect in the way of measurable performance gains. However, if you take the longer view and read the book sequentially, you'll find that it offers a virtual lesson in continuous improvement, as each chapter builds upon the previous ones. This book's contributors offer best practices and lessons learned with the aim of steering you away from pointless navel-gazing exercises, and instead guiding you, the reader, toward achievable results.

> – **David Blanchard, editorial director/associate publisher of Penton Media's Supply Chain Group and author of** *Supply Chain Management Best Practices* **(Wiley)**

Driving for Operational Excellence offers a remarkable array of expertise. The book is not only a good reference for essentially all of the fundamental topics found in Six Sigma & Lean methodology but it also goes beyond by offering new insights and valuable suggestions on subjects usually avoided or only briefly covered by others. The many case studies and examples will be of interest to every business leader irrespective of their experience in Operational Excellence.

> – **James Lamprecht, management consultant and Six Sigma Master Black Belt**

There are many books to consider when researching concepts like improvement. Many of these books offer simple concepts in an exaggerated way in order to fill the pages. This book is not like those. Ron has taken the thoughts of many experts and aptly rolled them into a fine book which will prove most useful to the reader. This book is a solid addition to any professional's library.

> – **Erik V. Myhrberg, author and CEO/cofounder of Moorhill International Group, Inc.**

Reading this [book] will stimulate any executive or manager to find ways to operationally move toward excellence.

> – **Miles Kierson, Consultant**

No one in business today can likely read this book without seeing some old familiar techniques and approaches, while getting introduced to some new and very useful ones. I was pleased to see a decided emphasis on people and culture change, and not just managerial or process techniques

> – **Chuck Halper, Automotive Executive**

Driving Operational Excellence

Successful Lean Six Sigma Secrets
to Improve the Bottom Line

Ron Crabtree, Editor

MetaOps
Livonia, MI

Driving Operational Excellence
Successful Lean Six Sigma Secrets to Improve the Bottom Line

ISBN:

Paperback: 978-0-9827871-0-6

Printer: McNaughton & Gunn
Managing Editor: Darcie S. Torres
Layout Design: Pen & Pestle
Marketing: Todd Roth

Editor: Ron Crabtree
Cover Design: Chautona Havig
Project Manager: Kim Crabtree

Table of Contents

Introduction

Strategy

Chapter One: Peeling the Onion for Higher Performance

Chapter Two: Lean Thinking 101: What is Lean?

Chapter Three: Integrated Enterprise Excellence: A Systems Approach to Improvement

Chapter Four: Value Realization Methodology

Chapter Five: How to Start Making Improvements Last: Demystifying Strategy Deployment

Chapter Six: Proven Solutions for Success in Healthcare

Methodology

Chapter Seven: Daily Management: The Foundation for High Performance Organizations

Chapter Eight: Change Management Street Smarts

Chapter Nine: Driving Value through Project Selection

Chapter Ten: Managerial Accounting for the Lean Enterprise

Chapter Eleven: QPE: A LSS Approach to Process Management & Sustainability

Chapter Twelve: Operational Excellence in Non-Profits

Universal Tools

Specific Tools

The Future

Introduction

Ron Crabtree

A Personal Journey into Excellence

What do you get when you bring together 24 Lean Six Sigma (LSS), Operational Excellence (OpEx) and other Continuous Improvement experts and consultants?

A book – *this* book. Along with a lot of great, cutting-edge ideas about how to create sustainable improvement programs that actually impact a business's bottom line.

As you might expect from a group of experts in the field, we decided to start this project by getting the voice of potential customers for our new book. We reached out to over 1,000 people we knew to ask for help with our book. Over 350 people responded. They represented a diverse group with 42% being business owners and executives, 44% in management and supervision, and the remainder being individual contributors and consultants. This group came from both large and small companies, with more than 20 industries represented.

We asked our respondents to score their knowledge and skills on OpEx/LSS on a scale of 1 to 5, with 5 being 'expert.' Fifty-five percent of the respondents saw themselves as a level three or lower – ranging from 'no knowledge' to 'knowing something about it' to 'I've been involved and have a LOT more to learn.' A large portion (32%) felt they 'know a great deal,' and the balance consider themselves as experts. To be fair, this data is a bit skewed to the high side for expertise compared to the general population of professionals. This is mainly due to the fact that we only reached out to those we knew personally and to those who subscribe to my e-zine, *www.OperationalExcellenceEdge.com.*

We next asked about how far along each respondent's organization is in implementing OpEx/LSS on a scale of 1 to 5, with 5 being, 'We have mastered it.' I was quite surprised with what we learned from this section of the survey. It turns out that a whopping 75% of respondents rated themselves at a level 3 or lower: 18% were 'doing nothing yet,' 25% 'have some activities going on,' and 32% said they were 'implementing – but have much more work to do.' Only 13% ranked their organizations as 'proficient – but not yet expert,' and the balance of 11% indicated they had 'mastered' it.

Given the fact that the vast majority of organizations have attempted some form of implementation of 'improvement' programs in the last 20 years, this data suggests my hypothesis is not very far off, with almost 90% of organizations reporting they 'have a ways to go' in mastering OpEx/LSS.

We then turned to isolating the important topics revolving around continuous improvement. The results were as follows:

- Providing better quality – 91.8%,
- Improving customer service – 90.2%,
- Managing change more effectively – 89.6%,
- Reducing cost of operations – 86.6%,
- Getting employees more engaged – 85.7%,
- Getting better high-performing teams and culture – 81.4%,
- Educating the workforce – 81.4%, and
- Developing better metrics – 80.7%.

Not surprisingly, half of the topics relate to managing change and people-centered issues. This reflects what many of us see in the field: **The biggest challenge we face in implementing improvement programs is obtaining buy-in from all levels of the corporate structure, from the executives all the way down to the entry-level worker**.

Our survey also dug down into the main reasons for program failures, as seen by our respondents. The top five choices, in descending order, are: 1) ineffective communications, 2) poor metrics and unclear goals (accounting and management measurement does not support needed change), 3) not considering the entire organization as a system, 4) lacking buy-in and understanding of the workforce/middle management, and 5) failing to achieve high levels of teamwork and cooperation across the board.

With this information in mind, we, as a group, set out to answer some of the most pressing questions on the minds of our audience. The goal of this book is to answer the following questions:

1. What is Lean and what can it do for my organization?

2. Why are my improvement projects failing? Why can't I see improvement to my bottom line?

3. Which LSS or Op Ex tools can give me the most bang for my buck?

Continuous Improvement is a Never-ending Journey

Toyota failed. Toyota's quality train wrecked in 2009.

It was a shock wave that hit many Lean fanatics like an atomic bomb. For decades, Toyota has represented everything that was right about continuous improvement programs. Toyota Production System (TPS) was the epitome of Lean Six Sigma methodology: success, leading to an ever-expanding market share and profits.

But something happened. In Toyota's journey to become and remain the number one car maker in the world, there was a disconnect somewhere along the line. Experts have varied in their explanations for how and why Toyota Production System failed. Some blame Japanese culture and it's reticence to deliver bad news; some blame the corporate culture Toyota has developed, which they claim instills a huge gap in communications between the worker (who knows what is going on) and upper management. Akio Toyoda himself stated that the company failed to "connect the dots" between problems in Europe and those in North America.[1] I think it can be best summarized in one simple analogy: Toyota's Board of Directors set the objective of being the world's largest car maker. They forgot one little thing: did their customers care about that? Obviously, they did not. In the quest to be the biggest, Toyota outgrew their ability to sustainably execute.

The 64,000-dollar question circulating around the industry has become: Did Toyota fail its own system, or did the system fail Toyota?

Everyone wants an easy answer. People have picked sides and are staunchly defending their positions. The majority of the current literature falls under the opinion that Toyoda and the upper management team failed to listen to the metrics coming out of the system, choosing to live in a state of denial. Contrary to the way TPS is designed to work, they ignored the evidence coming in for decades and chose a firefighting approach to small batches of accelerator and brake problems: a recall here, a recall there, but no overall systemic fix to the problem.

Yet, there is a growing belief in the industry that perhaps it is the system that should be blamed. One argument is that continuous improvement methodologies inherently fail under recessionary periods because there is pressure throughout the enterprise to remain employed: No one wants to be the message bearer that gets shot for delivering bad news. Another argument arising within the industry is that TPS and other continuous improvement systems are incapable of sustaining the massive global enterprise Toyota is trying to forge. In such an organizational system, the theory goes, there are too many places for communication to fail. This, does, in fact seem to fit the facts of the Toyota case. Huge communication disconnects over a long period are evident in hindsight.

Unfortunately, all of these explanations fail to acknowledge the interrelation between people and the system within which they work. There is no denying that Toyota management was deaf and blind to the overwhelming evidence coming in. However, the system was built around the assumption that large, systemic problems *could not* occur because TPS was designed and built specifically to prevent, diagnose and fix defects long before they became massive problems like those Toyota has experienced. The system simply was not designed to cope with large-scope defects that actually reach the consumer. TPS failed in this situation because it was incapable of expecting and dealing with the unexpected events that rolled over them like a tsunami.

Toyoda has been lambasted by US government officials and the media for his lack of response and his denial. In his defense, I must again say that the system around which Toyota built its empire was simply incapable of producing a response to this situation. *No one* at Toyota had the tools in place to respond – the system had not created the right tools to that point.

Of course, we can analyze the Toyota situation to death and point to a myriad of disconnects and failures within their systems, but this ignores the most important question of all: **How do we all avoid becoming like Toyota and refrain from falling into the same traps**? Some think we need to rid ourselves of all current continuous improvement systems and start over from scratch with something new. This is foolhardy at worst and ill-advised at best.

Instead, we need to build upon what's good about our systems and shore up failure points in how we use OpEx/LSS thinking. For instance, two missing links in current management school teachings are a) valuing the importance of immediate, practical application of new skills, and b) knowing where to focus the organization's people in applying the new skills to get maximum results. For more details on these issues, please visit my blog at *www.AskRonCrabtree.com.*

The main purpose of this book is to help readers understand the one principle of continuous improvement that too many have failed to grasp:

Tools do not work without a broad, all-encompassing system that is embedded in the very culture of a company. Tools need people and people need tools. People, tools and systems are so interrelated in any continuous improvement program that a failure of one leads to a failure of all. Our book emphasizes this critical concept and presents ideas for improving enterprise performance in all three areas.

This book is for those who wish to build long-term success based upon operational excellence by embracing a culture that is never satisfied with the current state and continually expands the application of LSS and other proven methods. We do not abandon a system that has proven time and time again that excellence can be achieved. We simply expand and improve upon it to help companies and individuals apply the principles in a way that is flexible, fits their own needs, and accounts for the environment in which we find ourselves in the 21st century and beyond.

On the Path to Excellence: A Guide to Reading This Book

The book is broken down logically with respect to building a continuous improvement system. You can pick and choose the chapters that interest you most, or you can read the book front to back. Each chapter is designed to stand alone, but the overall presentation of the material builds logically upon previous chapters. First, we address the idea of *strategy* – creating a total system that drives the philosophy of excellence deep into the heart of company culture. Here you will find the chapters that form the foundation for creating a responsive, flexible system. Words underlined in the chapters are defined in the Glossary at the end of the book.

Charles Shillingburg peels back the myths and inaccuracies currently surrounding the idea of Lean Six Sigma – what it is and what it is not. Charles redefines LSS as a total strategy for turning your organization into a High Performance Enterprise.

Bill Artzberger dives down into the concept of Lean, distinguishing between Lean *thinking* (a systemic approach) and Lean tools. Bill outlines six rules to creating a Lean enterprise in which learning is a way of life and problem solving serves to challenge the creativity and ingenuity of the people who work within a Lean system.

Forrest W. Breyfogle III introduces you to his Integrated Enterprise Excellence® (IEE) system. This system focuses on combating many of the systemic problems experienced by companies trying to implement continuous improvement strategies. IEE emphasizes the importance of utilizing truly predictive metrics that alleviate the need to firefight problems and accurately reflect true organizational performance.

Kendall Scheer presents a guide to instituting Value Realization Methodology (VRM): a system of tools and metrics for diagnosing the current condition of a company and identifying the best areas for increased value generation growth opportunities. Kendall demonstrates a wide variety of VRM tools and metrics necessary for building a quality VRM system in your organization.

David Goodman takes us into the heart of Toyota's past success: Strategy Deployment (SD). SD, or *hoshin kanri*, is the integration of an organization's strategic and business plans with its vision, mission, value proposition, core competencies, and each individual's annual work plan. It is a process that facilitates the creation of results-oriented business processes with sustained improvements that result in long-term competitive advantages in quality, delivery, cost and growth. David outlines the basics of Strategy Deployment and provides a key lesson for those implementing a continuous improvement program: *No one* is above the system – without buy-in at all levels, no system will ever succeed.

Sheree Lavelle shows how Lean and Six Sigma can be jointly applied to real-life situations in industries beyond manufacturing. To help us visualize and understand this process, Sheree puts the heart back into LSS by focusing on applying Lean Six Sigma to the healthcare industry, outlining the practical benefits achieved by using this improvement strategy at the clinic and hospital levels.

In the next section, our book introduces six chapters on methodologies used in various continuous improvement systems. These methodologies challenge the reader to take Lean, Six Sigma and OpEx into all levels of the organization and expand their use across all industries.

David Dubinsky leads us on a journey into daily management. David presents the case for change and outlines the ten foundational methods of Daily Management. He goes beyond the technical side of process improvement to reach deep into the human side, presenting ten soft-skill solutions for driving change in any organization.

Jeff Cole expands on the human side by demonstrating nine street-smart rules for changing behavior throughout an entire organization. These savvy tips transcend immediate circumstances and help organizations become future-focused enterprises that manage change methodically and systemically.

Steve Pfeiffer outlines the importance and methods associated with successful project selection practices. Steve recognizes and addresses the concepts of limited resources and the time value of money, exploring the four key elements critical to every project selection process. He also takes you through an initial benefits estimation to show you how you can identify the projects that will give you the most bang for your buck.

Ron Chandler shows why traditional thinking in accounting fails to meet the needs of enterprises employing Lean strategies and the misconceptions and errors that can result in faulty decision making. Ron will show you how to build a Lean accounting model to identify opportunities for improvement and prioritize and track their success. He will also demonstrate how to use Lean accounting to rationalize your product base and create a quote system consistent with Lean principles.

Matt Stewart demonstrates the use of Quantify, Prioritize and Eliminate (QPE), the LSS methodology for making improvements and/or repairs to business processes through the DMAIC approach. Matt shows how a traditional shotgun approach to fixing problems only leads to more defects, more problems – and in the end – more work. Matt illustrates how LSS tools can be methodically applied to problem solving to provide the quickest, most cost-effective solutions for your organization.

Ira Weissman takes us into the oft-neglected world of non-profit corporations, showing how these organizations can benefit from the methodological approach to waste elimination and process improvement that Lean Six Sigma can provide. Ira provides a great example of how LSS methods can benefit *any* organization in *any* industry.

Next, we approach the subject of continuous improvement tools. We begin by outlining five universal tools that can be applied by any organization in any industry. These tools are the mainstays of successful LSS implementation.

Karen Young begins by showing us the basics of the DMAIC approach to waste elimination and process improvement, applying it to the healthcare setting. Karen shows us the practical side of DMAIC and how to run through the process in real life in the context of a service provider.

Gary Wickett explains the fundamentals of eliminating waste in your organization. He outlines the eight types of waste and their common sources. Gary will show you how to drill down through the waste and defects to uncover the root causes of problems in your processes.

Mike Bresko outlines the most important tool you need to change the mindset and culture in your organization: the Continuous Improvement Routine. Mike explains the transformation imperative and transformation tipping point, outlining the five primary reasons most companies fail to achieve this goal. Mike then explains the eight steps necessary for achieving the transformation tipping point in your organization.

Lorraine Marzilli Lomas discusses one of the most fundamental and critical tools serious students of LSS/OpEx must master: Voice of the Customer. Lorraine explains why accessing the voice of your customers is important, which tools glean the information you need, and how to go about obtaining that information to produce reliable and useable results. She shows how VOC can turn around a failed project or product to re-ignite customer loyalty.

Pam Gladwell demonstrates how to use Value Stream Mapping (VSM) to identify process constraints and wastes and then improve the flow of your processes. Pam does an excellent job of showing how to use VSM in non-manufacturing settings and applying it to transactional processes. Pam takes you through a real-life healthcare clinic to show you how VSM can work for any situation.

Next, we turn to some of the more specific tools employed in LSS/OpEx. These chapters take us into a detailed examination of several key "tools" in the continuous improvement toolbox, such as: facilitating, supply chain, measuring financial impact, and sales.

Joann Parrinder shows how you can apply Lean thinking to your idea development lifecycle through the 5 S's. She first outlines the basics of the cycle every idea should go through and then demonstrates how Lean principles and tools can sort out the good from the bad, scrub it down, standardize it and sustain it throughout the organization.

Steve Cimorelli takes DMAIC beyond the basics to show you how ANOVA and process maps can identify problems and solutions in your supply chain. Steve presents advanced statistical techniques and tools in an easily understandable format to help you identify the critical areas and weaknesses in your supply chain processes. Steve demonstrates a comprehensive formula any organization can use to reliably and accurately identify problems and then implement successful solutions that drive results to the bottom line.

Andres Slack presents a challenging, detailed chapter on Financial Impact Analysis (FIA) to help you identify how change and improvements impact your bottom line. Andres not only outlines why proper FIA is important, he outlines the prerequisites for performing it and then takes you through the process step by step with graphical examples that drive home the techniques involved in successful analysis.

Steven C. Leggett brings us an in-depth review of FMEA and how to use FMEA tools appropriately to identify and correct defects *before* they actually occur. By using a preventative approach to problem solving, Steve shows us how we can prevent costly defects instead of trying to firefight after the fact.

Chuck Overbeck shows us that sales is a numbers game – but not like most people think. Chuck deftly and creatively applies LSS principles and tools to the sales process through the Ideal Customer Matrix for creating the yardstick against which we qualify our sales leads, freeing up the most important resource in any sales department: time.

Finally, we wrap up the book with a few thoughts about the future with respect to LSS, OpEx and other continuous improvement strategies.

James Hardin explores the potential benefits that can be achieved by instituting continuous improvement programs in the educational setting. Little work has been done to date with respect to applying LSS to education. James discusses the far-reaching implications this has on our society and economy as a whole, and challenges the reader to support bringing continuous improvement into our educational systems.

The book ends with a conclusory chapter tying together the principles, the methodologies and the tools of continuous improvement. I address some of the challenges we all face in taking continuous improvement to the next level. We must still figure out a way to bring Lean, Six Sigma and Operational Excellence into the 21st century and create a systemic approach that is flexible enough to deal with today's challenges, as well as respond to the problems we will face in the future.

A Final Note about Lean

The concept of continuous improvement, by whatever name you call it, is a *process*. Like any process, continuous improvement does not end – *ever*. There is never a point in our business lifecycle where we can sit back and say to ourselves, "There, everything is perfect. I can rest now." Change is continuous and unrelenting, and our methods must be similarly so. Waste and defects are insidious; they are forever looking for a way to creep back into our organizations whenever our vigilance lapses. For this reason, it is critical we begin our journey by creating an enterprise-wide system that continuously monitors our processes for us.

Successful strategies rely on the whole organization to remain vigilant, not just our LSS Black Belts or Champions.

This book is about bringing together the best practices from all continuous improvement strategies. You cannot take on today's challenges without starting with the basic concept of Lean. It is fundamental to everything we do. Without Lean thinking, systems, approaches and tools, we ignore the most fundamental problems with business operations today.

Likewise, we also cannot ignore Six Sigma tools and strategies. As with waste, mistakes and defects eat away at our bottom line. The failure I see in many organizations with respect to implementing Six Sigma programs is the failure to implement the tools Six Sigma provides within a *system* that drives the very concept into the heart of the company culture to produce a philosophy that manages day-to-day activities across the entire organization. Six Sigma and Lean Six Sigma tools cannot be used piecemeal and still produce results. True results only come through systematic implementation over the long haul. Lean Six Sigma is not about quick fixes – it is about creating long-lasting, sustainable improvements that actually produce financial benefits over time.

Finally, Operational Excellence brings in the human element that is often left out of these approaches. Operational Excellence focuses on teamwork and the people who form those teams. One of the shortcomings we recognize in this book is our failure to address employee empowerment and satisfaction. Without this key element, without addressing the needs of those who must actually employ these continuous improvement strategies, methodologies and tools, we leave ourselves open to miscommunication, dissatisfaction and the risk that program implementation will fail. While senior management buy-in is critical to the success of any improvement program, buy-in from the masses is just as important. I do, however, promise that this topic will be covered extensively in the next book.

On that note, I will leave you now so that you can begin or continue your journey into the world of continuous improvement. I will meet you on the other side of your journey, and hopefully, I will be able to provide a few more words of sage advice to help you continue the process in the years to come.

---

[1] Kevin Voigt. "Toyota president: 'We failed to connect the dots.'" CNN. February 22, 2010. *http://www.cnn.com/2010/BUSINESS/02/10/money.toyoda.op-ed/index.html*

Strategy

All men can see these tactics whereby I conquer, but what none can see is the strategy out of which victory is evolved.

– Sun Tzu

Chapter One

Peeling the Onion for Higher Performance

Charles Shillingburg

Overview

Organizations of all types and sizes would like to become <u>High Performance Enterprises</u> – organizations that are more predictable, controllable, innovative, flexible and able to grow profitably and sustainably in both good and bad times; organizations that are totally aligned to beat their competition. But, how do you do this? And, in today's market, how can you do it *now*?

Most leaders and managers are operating based on what they have observed or been taught. They have not challenged the underlying assumptions behind these methods or the results on customer and organizational outcomes. Many work under the assumptions that "things just have to be this way," "what others are doing doesn't affect me," "my actions (or department) don't affect anyone else," and "there are no alternatives to the methods we are using, so what else can I do?" In this chapter, you will learn to peel your organization's onion back to reveal the answers to these questions.

This chapter will help you to:

- Recognize the breadth of organizational issues that need to be addressed and the consequences of not resolving them.
- Uncover underlying causes inhibiting your organization's performance.
- Challenge yourself to change many underlying assumptions.
- Reveal proven and effective methods and practices.

Everything Including the Kitchen Sink

An umbrella for a host of best practices, Lean Six Sigma has been successfully used for many years by large enterprises on the factory floor, for supply chain management, and/or cost saving projects. But the Lean Six Sigma discipline is a comprehensive, enterprise-wide system that can be used *every day* by organizations of every size and type and in every functional area. Lean Six Sigma is being adopted everywhere because it not only identifies problems, but provides comprehensive, proven ways to solve them. It is just good common sense, and best of all, it works!

The more you understand Lean Six Sigma and its advantages and benefits, the more you will want to embrace it. You will want to use these methods to identify your organizational weaknesses, get down to the root causes, initiate needed changes and adopt continuous improvement methods and practices to make your organization more successful and productive. In today's demanding world, you can't wait until you are in crisis. The sooner you adopt Lean Six Sigma's high performance methods, the easier it will be to manage your future, and the more adaptable, innovative and competitive your organization will be – not just to survive, but to *thrive*.

So what is Lean Six Sigma? What's in it for you, your organization, your customers and employees? Most generally, LSS is defined as *creating customer value* by *eliminating <u>waste</u> to increase flow and reduce <u>variability</u>*. But, Lean Six Sigma embodies much more than this. It is a way of *thinking* and operating on a daily basis. While you can think of it as a cultural mindset, Lean thinking is really an *action* mindset; it is one that engages everyone in your organization in new, scientific, systematic thinking that is customer centric and solutions based. It is a philosophy and action set that engages all employees, functional areas and suppliers in the end goal of better satisfying your customers. It emphasizes delivering more value in a way that is more predictable, efficient, and effective. Embracing Lean thinking and Lean Six Sigma methodologies produces an organization that is more innovative, responsive and adaptable to change, yet more under control at the same time. Employees are more satisfied because there is transparency, and they feel more empowered and more engaged. They know what they are doing, why they are doing it, and how their actions connect to their organization's success. Moreover, employees actively contribute to improving their organization's performance.

Get Out the Peeler

At the heart of your success or failure is your ability to align everybody and every system and process to a common, customer-centric purpose. You must identify and effectively deal with difficult issues. To become a High Performance Enterprise, you will need to ask and answer some hard questions and then make the changes necessary to effectively align your organization's operations and methodologies.

Aligning your company's vision, mission, sales and processes requires you to peel through your company culture and operations to find out what lies at the heart. Too many times we simply assume we know the answers and find it difficult to take a good, hard look at what lies beneath the surface. Following are a set of questions you will need to answer and address if you want to peel away waste, constraints and ineffective processes to become a High Performance Enterprise.

Mission

Do you know who your customers are? What do they want and need? If you don't know the answers to these two important questions, it will be difficult for you to outline your company mission, goals and strategies. Without customers, you have no business. Ultimately, your entire enterprise revolves around your customers – how to get them, how to keep them, and how to anticipate their ever-changing needs. Find out what your company is doing right and what it is doing wrong. A constant, customer-centric focus is the heart and soul of becoming a High Performance Enterprise.

Methods

How do your business methods relate to meeting your customer's requirements? What is the relationship in your organization between employees, management and senior executives, from department to department, between your organization and its suppliers, and even accounting? What are your measurement and reward systems and your training programs, and how do they move you further toward delivering on your customers' requirements?

You need to view your organization's performance from a *systems perspective*. This approach views the business as a group of independent but interrelated elements comprising a unified whole. Many organizations aren't even cognizant of their underlying systems and processes (or lack thereof), let alone the effect they have on organizational outcomes. High Performance Enterprises see and understand and control systemic symptoms that limit quality, value, product flow, and customer satisfaction. The rest of the pack perceives events as randomly caused by individuals or outside events beyond their control. They treat symptoms by applying Band-Aids and firefighting techniques instead of digging down and solving the root causes.

Follow this simple checklist to determine whether your company is ahead of the curve or behind it.

High Performance	Low Performance
Proactive	Reactive
Do it right the first time	Constant use of firefighting tactics to solve problems
Open Communication Policy	Need-to-know basis of communicating
Focus on continuous improvement	If it ain't broke, don't fix it
Employees are key to improvement	Employees are part of the problem

If you circled *any* of the methods on the right-hand side of the checklist, you are not operating your business at its highest potential, and you will benefit from implementing many of the methods and philosophies contained in this book and/or by seeking further assistance from the skilled experts who are a part of this Lean project.

Management

How do you define "management" in your organization? Do you think of management as a collaborative group who orchestrate employees to accomplish strategy-driven goals and who are open to observations, constructive criticism and advice? Or do you view management as *bosses* whose objectives are to make others blindly follow orders without question and who view subordinates as employees that are to be seen and not heard? Most importantly, do you treat your managers as trusted members of a team responsible for moving the company forward and meeting your strategic goals, mission and vision?

Synthesis

Does everyone in your organization and those connected to it clearly understand how their roles and responsibilities relate to the company's overall success? Does everyone feel and hold themselves accountable for your organization's ultimate success? Does your organization operate cross-functionally, cooperatively and proactively toward better satisfying your customers? Is everyone on the same page and all speaking the same language? Are you all focused on the same end outcomes?

Aligning all the players, both internal and external, with corporate strategies, goals and vision is absolutely critical to forming a harmonious synthesis that moves your entire organization toward becoming the High Performance Enterprise you want it to be. Do you believe achieving higher customer and employee satisfaction, loyalty and advocacy adds costs rather than saves money? Customer advocacy, employee satisfaction, and profitability result from the increased quality, capacity and throughput that comes from better utilizing resources and reducing time and effort.

Figure 1-1: High Performance in Action

How Much of that Onion Are You Throwing Away?

You can begin to reveal and remedy problems using the Lean Six Sigma methodology. As a starting point for exposing your organizational weaknesses, Lean Six Sigma identifies eight wastes. By identifying these wastes in your own organization, you can begin to understand how to effectively transform your enterprise. You will get down to the root causes of inefficiencies and structural weaknesses and begin your continuous improvement journey to reap the benefits it offers. These Lean Six Sigma wastes can be identified by the acronym DOWNTIME:

1. Defects
2. Overproduction
3. Waiting
4. Non-productive use of people
5. Transportation
6. Inventory
7. Motion
8. Excess processing

Defects. Are you producing defects and defective products and services? Why? Dig down and root out and correct the causes. However, having a zero defects mentality will kill the initiative necessary for success in business and is completely unrealistic. What matters is the ability and willingness of your team to dig down to the root causes behind the defects, and the initiative and creativeness of your team to find and implement the solutions to fix and prevent future occurrences.

Overproduction and oversupply. Are parts of your organization out of balance with others or with the organization as a whole? Maybe one portion of your operation is producing too much while other parts are producing too little. Do you see excess inventory piling up anywhere? The ideal in a High Performance Enterprise is <u>Just-In-Time</u> delivery. Strive toward having just enough supplies and materials required for each function at the time they are needed. Excess quantities indicate your process flow is being blocked.

Waiting (Time). Are people waiting? Whether it's your customers, patients or your employees, waiting serves no purpose. There are two important time wastes we see time and time again, regardless of industry:

1. Waiting for decisions to be made, including diagnosis time; and

2. Supplies and people waiting, "just in case."

Non-productive use of people. Are people working at their full capacity and potential? Is your management approach based on fear, demanding compliance, rather than on positive reinforcement and employee contribution? Are your people empowered or micro-managed? Do your employees feel unimportant, unheard, or as though they have little, if any, say in what they do? Do they provide constructive feedback or input about frontline operations and practices that only they can see? If individuals do not have the authority to act on their own expertise and what they observe at the time it is occurring, you will be unable to increase your organization's knowledge, flexibility and responsiveness.

Transportation. Do you see materials or information being moved from place to place, process to process, adding needless time, effort and cost? Creating complex requirements for simple processes is indicative of waste. A process that requires a worker to track down managers and obtain three signatures on a document before work on a project can begin is one example. Unnecessary transportation is often connected with inventory retrieval, but can occur anywhere in the organization.

Inventory. Bottlenecks are a clear indication of inventory problems. These can be either human or material-related. For instance, do you see stacks of supplies waiting to be used at some later date? You might also see bottlenecks in the flow of information or project work caused by individuals or incompatible systems.

Motion. Are employees taking unnecessary steps to do their jobs? For instance, are they constantly getting up and down to get materials to finish a task? Do you have the most efficient work layout to accomplish the task. If you answered yes to any of these questions, you might want to investigate the advantages of <u>cellular design</u>.

Excess processing. Processes that take a long time to complete because there are more steps than absolutely necessary are an example of waste. Maybe the number of process steps has grown as a result of defects that have been accommodated over time and built into the process instead of being addressed at the root cause level. This may have led to multiple levels of inspection rather than looking at the entire process from a fresh perspective. Do it right the first time – destroy waste at the source.

Keep Peeling

There are other tip-offs that there is work to do in your organization. Do you have underdeveloped systems thinking or development? If you see a lot of inconsistent processes, practices and results, you need to keep peeling. The obvious place to look is in manufacturing processes and procedures, but you need to look for them in other areas of your organization as well. Inconsistent advertising and marketing results and inconsistency among sales people are key indicators that there is work to do. (See Chapter 22 on Lean sales strategies).

What about your service practices: Are customers handled the same way every time, from team to team? Do you have inconsistent medical procedures like IV administration? Whatever inconsistencies you find, you need to investigate the effects these inconsistencies have on safety, quality, customer satisfaction, advocacy, revenue and costs.

Using a systems process approach, you will understand there are either predictable or unpredictable processes, and they are either working up to their potential or not. Having a system provides an effective, reproducible method for identifying weaknesses and making improvements. It allows your employees and organization as a whole to follow a prescribed procedure to determine:

- the problems

- the root cause(s)

- possible solutions

- an appropriate action plan

- whether the action plan is being followed

- how to sustain fixes/improvements and continue to achieve more

Having transparent performance results is imperative. Even using simple information boards that can be seen and acted upon and that expose problems, measure and track performance and the achievement of your objectives will help enhance transparency, communication and the credibility of your improvement efforts.

Ensuring organizational alignment is also a key indicator of a High Performance Enterprise. Does your organization operate in silos instead of being cross-functionally focused on end outcomes to customers or clients? Are your departments vertically and horizontally aligned to deliver customer requirements? Do you have clear action plans that tie individual, team and departmental performance outcomes to customer requirements? That is, can you tie your strategies and tactics together with customer requirements?

Organizational alignment helps determine which individuals and departments are accountable and to whom. It helps ensure your reward and incentive systems are consistent with your stated outcomes to deliver on customer requirements. Employees and managers should feel accountable and be held accountable for meeting customer needs and not for just performing their functional roles.

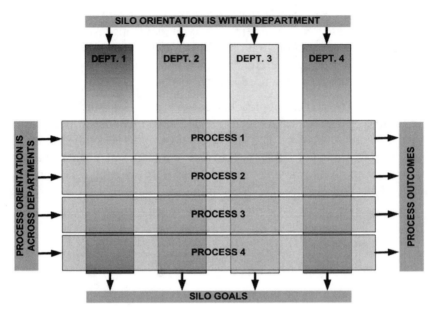

Kaizen Management Institute, LLC

Figure 1-2: Silo vs. Process Orientation

Being a High Performance Enterprise also means making sure you measure the right things. Do your customer and employee surveys measure and report appropriate variables and inputs/outputs? Your measurements and reporting systems should help you understand systemic problems and help systematically improve your operations. Disconnects between the strategic and tactical information needed to fix or improve your processes and outcomes is a sure sign of faulty methods. Do your accounting practices lead to improvements in the delivery of customer requirements by measuring the results of entire processes, or are they actually running counter to this by only measuring individual personnel, machines or departmental performance?

Are there standard operating procedures in place for the way processes are performed, or do different shifts or people perform the same tasks in very different ways? If standardization is lacking, your processes are out of control, making it impossible for you to isolate causes and effects and make effective improvements. Perhaps you over-standardize "people practices" and over automate or over script. Over-standardization can be just as harmful as having no standardization. While customers desire consistency and predictability, over-standardized, robotic treatment is not what they seek.

Some Examples to Ponder

In this chapter, we have presented numerous questions for you to ask yourself about your organization. At times, it can be mindboggling. The drive and demand for continuous improvement can be daunting to newly Lean enterprises or those who are wondering whether or not to embrace and implement a Lean strategy. At this point, it is appropriate to ask ourselves the ultimate question: Why go Lean?

Forty years ago, General Motors had a 50% market share of the U.S. automobile market. Its share of the market began declining 1-2% a year after the oil crises of the 1970s, spiraling downward to less than 20% as of April 2010.[1] GM, like other U.S. auto manufacturers, was slow to react to changing consumer requirements first brought on by the demand for more fuel efficiency, and then the demand for low cost, high quality and reliability. Japanese manufacturers, led by Toyota, steadily took over market share because there was a wide discrepancy in measurable vehicle quality between U.S. and Japanese manufacturers. Public perception of Japanese quality superiority was set at that time. Only now, with quality and reliability problems surfacing at Toyota, might this perception gap dissipate.

The lesson here is to keep abreast of changing customer requirements and rapidly meet – and ideally, exceed – customer expectations to differentiate your products and services. And, if market demand shifts abruptly, your organization needs to be open-minded and have the systems and processes in place to make it highly flexible and adaptable. With the right attitude and systems in place, an organization can respond effectively to change to remain or become a market leader.

A corollary to the story above is the quality problem Toyota currently faces. While it remains to be seen what the depth and breadth of the problems might be, it appears Toyota ultimately failed to adhere to their own principles of quality management. It is very possible that the initial systems for manufacturing, which served them so well for many years, reached the limit of their capability and capacity in Toyota's quest to become the largest automobile company in the world. Entirely new approaches may be needed to provide the highest quality and reliability at the volumes demanded in a dispersed, worldwide market. Or, as other experts believe, it may be that Toyota merely strayed from their original methods and needs to return to those principles and methods that served to make them great initially.

I worked for many years for one of the leaders in the cosmetics and toiletry industry. It was well known for making high-quality products at reasonable prices. It also had the highest profitability and growth rates in the category. The basis of its success was the utilization of innovative, systematic, scientific approaches in all aspects of its business, from product development to manufacturing and advertising. This company invented the pegboard display concept for cosmetics that is prevalent today in all retail outlets. Radically different from the way cosmetics were sold at the time (direct selling in department stores by sales agents), the pegboard system relied on advertising and product feature differentiation to drive customer demand. Using a system based on solid market research, product and advertising development and testing, the company was confident enough to launch the pegboard system in food stores and mass merchandisers – entirely new distribution points for cosmetics at the time. It not only installed the pegboards for its own product lines, but supplied pegboards for its competitors as well.

The keys to this company's success were the use of a cooperative, cross-functional management approach; scientific, systematic methods to create innovative Just-In-Time manufacturing and distribution processes; and developing, testing and differentiating its products and advertising. As a result, this company came to command up to an 80% market share in some areas.

In the automotive industry, I developed a customer satisfaction measurement system (TOPS) for the industry that identified key drivers of advocacy, loyalty and satisfaction across entire organizations. Utilizing these drivers in the sales and service areas, a survey program was developed for a major manufacturer that measured individual sales and service personnel and vehicle quality performance within individual dealerships. Based on the results, we identified several areas of opportunity within each dealership. We performed an analysis using a cross-functional dealership team to get to the root causes of deficiencies and to develop action plans to improve performance. The bulk of the improvement efforts was focused on the flow of vehicles and parts (decrease damage, improve availability) and customers (decrease waiting time in finance and insurance, access to the parts department, telephone hold times). The result was not only improved customer satisfaction and sales, but increased initial quality ratings and reduced costs to dealers and the manufacturer.

Conclusions

Transforming into a High Performance Enterprise that consistently beats the competition is paramount today. Aligning your organization to the common purpose of better satisfying customers/patients by developing competitive strengths and eliminating structural weaknesses using the Lean Six Sigma discipline helps organizations of all types and sizes become High Performance Enterprises. Employing Lean Six Sigma methodologies every day, enterprise wide, organizations can become more predictable, controllable, innovative, flexible and able to grow profitably and sustainably through both good times and bad.

Key Lessons Learned:

1. There is much to understand and address when moving your company toward becoming a High Performance Enterprise.

2. Difficult issues need to be confronted and dealt with, and improvements need to be comprehensive and systematic.

3. The organization and its systems and individuals must be aligned to achieve singular, customer-centric outcomes.

4. You need to start right now.

About the Author

Charles Shillingburg is an expert in Continuous Improvement in the service area. Building on Lean Six Sigma manufacturing approaches and his experience in Corporate Development at Noxell Corporation and J.D. Power & Associates, he developed the *Interim Outcomes, Total Brand Approach*, which is a comprehensive, flexible and adaptable approach to brand development and success. He offers education on *What Customers Value* and *Everyday Lean* that helps organizations focus their efforts on delivering critical customer values and engage everyone in Lean delivery, everyday. He brings a multi-disciplinary approach to organizational development and enterprise success. He is a Certified LSS Black Belt, LSS Sensei, customer satisfaction expert witness and measurement expert with more than 30 years experience. For more information, contact Charles through his website, *www.kaizenmi.com*.

---

[1] Tim Higgins, "Marketshare Slip Puts Pressure on GM," *Chicago Tribune*, April 29, 2010, *http://articles.chicagotribune.com/2010-04-29/news/sc-biz-0430-gm--20100429_1_automaker-s-share-chevrolet-cobalt-market-share*.

Chapter Two

Lean Thinking 101: What is Lean?

Bill Artzberger

Overview

This chapter is intended for anyone interested in learning more about Lean or improving their business operations in general. Business leaders or managers who are interested in learning how to increase profits and lower costs while improving customer satisfaction can benefit from understanding that the only way to get there is to embody the concepts involved in the philosophy of *Lean thinking*. Any organization can benefit from the application of Lean principals. However, you must first understand Lean thinking and learn the key Lean principles.

This chapter will help you to:

- Understand Lean thinking and the true meaning of "Lean."
- Understand key Lean principles to apply to your own organization.
- Get started with your Lean journey.
- Find that "one thing" you must know before you get started. Without this key, your Lean journey will not be successful.

What is "Lean Thinking"?

At its core, "Lean" is about optimizing your operations. A Lean organization consistently provides greater value to its customers while consuming fewer resources to do so. Lean organizations do not focus on a single area of their business; they focus on the entire process flow to eliminate waste and create greater customer value.

Lean organizations require less effort, less space, less capital and less time to produce lower cost goods and services with fewer defects. Lean applies in every organization, every business, and every process. It is not a tactic or simple cost-reduction program; it is a way of *thinking* and *acting* for an entire organization.

Lean does not simply mean performing <u>kaizens</u>, setting Lean focus groups, using <u>5S programs</u>, displaying Lean boards or using visual <u>pull systems</u>. Those are all Lean *tools*, which you may decide to use someday. However, these tools are not the true foundation of what it means to think and be Lean. You must do more than use a few tools and metrics to enjoy the true benefits of Lean thinking: You must create an enterprise-wide, customer-focused learning organization to be successful in creating a long-term, sustainable Lean organization. You don't get "Lean" or get "Leaned out." Lean is not a destination – Lean is a continuous journey of self-improvement that takes place every single day that you walk through the doors of your business.

The term *lean* was coined to describe Toyota's business and production system (Toyota Production System – TPS) in the late 1980s by a research team at MIT's International Motor Vehicle Program. However, the Foundation for Lean Thinking and the Toyota Production System was actually born with Henry Ford and the Ford Motor Company (as detailed in Henry Ford's bestseller, *Today and Tomorrow*, published in 1926). Henry Ford's strong belief in total process optimization and waste reduction drove Ford Motor Company to produce the highest quality automobiles of the time at affordable prices while providing the highest wages in the industry. Henry Ford made the automobile affordable for everyone, using Lean thinking and Lean techniques, before they were formalized or systematized through the Toyota Production System.

Ford's constant improvement and waste reduction focus also improved other industries and created new products and components out of scrap. Large wood planks became floor boards and body coach panels. Smaller wood pieces became steering wheels and shifter knobs. Smaller yet, scrap pieces of wood were burned to provide steam and electricity at the plant. When the scrap wood burning proved to be fairly inefficient, Ford, working with a relative, developed a method to grind, heat and compress the scrap wood to form small black nuggets. These nuggets have since become the most popular form of fuel for cooking your hamburger on the grill: charcoal. This relentless quest for process optimization and waste reduction drove Henry Ford and his brother-in-law, Edward G. Kingsford, to create the charcoal briquette industry.

The learning process is the key to process improvement and the key to Lean and Lean Six Sigma. This is *the one thing* you must know to be successful in your Lean journey. If we do not figure out how to do our jobs better, our competitors will, and we will be forced to the back of the pack.

Recall Einstein's definition of insanity: "Doing the same thing over and over while expecting different results." Organizations that have not yet accepted the concept of Lean thinking often find themselves performing the same processes day after day and wondering why none of their activities have any effect on their company's bottom line.

"We have always done it this way," is the silent killer in your organization. Complacency kills. As the world rushes by, if you're not moving with it, you're holding fast to outdated ideas and principles. This guarantees that when you do open your eyes, you will be far behind the race, and catching up will be the hardest thing you ever do. Change is imperative; but not just any change – not change for the sake of change – but the *correct* change. You need to make changes that will solve problems, make improvements, and move you forward. You need to make changes that impact your bottom line.

Example of a Successful Learning Process

When was the last time you took an airline flight? Was your flight on time or were there technical or mechanical difficulties? As a society, we tend to take airline travel and modern transportation – and the problems that go with it – for granted. As a flight instructor, I have always been intrigued by aircraft accident investigation: the painstaking reconstruction process, the analysis, the tests, and of course, the "black box." While I have a small vested interest and professional curiosity in the process, I am amazed how fascinated *everyone* seems to be with it. An airliner crash is big news. We see it on TV and read about it in the papers. But, the follow-up investigation is big news too: blow-by-blow accounts of the investigation and speculative reports are a regular staple of our media diet following a crash.

Why do we have this insatiable need to know? Many fault the investigation crews and agencies for dragging out airplane crash investigations too long, feeding the media frenzy. But these investigations begin with the sole intent of finding the root causes of failures, problems and accidents, and to prevent them from happening again. What you may not realize is that the FAA and NTSB go through similar, smaller scale processes hundreds of time each year: Seemingly small incidents and problems – an alternator problem here, an electrical problem there – are *all* researched. As a result, there are hundreds of small corrective actions taken every year by the FAA. They ground planes, issue airworthiness directives (AD's), change procedures, change training, develop new products and change current products.

As a result of all these efforts and painstaking processes, flying is now the safest form of transportation available. It is an amazing accomplishment. Just think if we could do that with auto travel! Despite similar investigations and procedures in the automobile crash sector, there are still 50,000 people killed on our roads every year, along with a quarter million injuries.

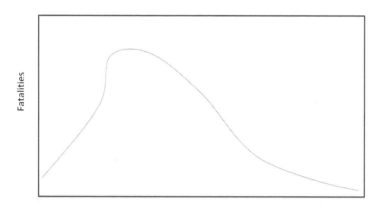

Figure 2-1: Aviation Safety Record

Stop the Blame Game

Why is it so difficult for us to institute lessons learned and self-improvement? It is for the same reason most people *think* the NTSB performs such intense accident investigations: We fear they are looking for someone to blame. We believe that if we find problems and waste in our own processes or seek out ways to improve them, we will be blamed for their existence in the first place. We can minimize or virtually eliminate this fear by focusing on the process, not on people. Standardize your methodology and your processes. Encourage and reinforce their usage and then stick with the facts.

"Creativity requires the courage to let go of certainties."

– Psychologist Erich Fromm

Many organizations cringe when problems surface in daily operations. The common reaction is simply to try to get rid of the problem as soon as possible, no matter the cost. The problem with this firefighting approach is that it only temporarily extinguishes the symptoms. When we fire fight, we get rid of the flames, which are the symptom, but if we don't eliminate the smoldering embers, the problem will simply reignite in the future. In a learning organization, systematic problem solving and optimization is not about whether organizations solve problems, but how they think about and look at those problems.

Problem solving is an important element of a learning organization that should be embraced because:

- Problems expose the gap that exists between where you are now (the current state), and where you would like to be (the ideal state).

- Problems build creative tension – pressure for a permanent solution and a better way of doing things.

- Problems should be embraced as opportunities to learn and improve.

- Only through an honest approach to problem solving will you build a culture that stops to fix problems as they occur and works to prevent them from occurring in the future.

A popular misconception took hold in the automotive industry when first exposed to the Andon cord on the assembly line: People believed it was only used to stop the line to prevent defects from moving forward. While that was one of the benefits, the primary reason for its usage was as a learning and problem-solving tool. The Andon cord allowed the assembly line worker to pause the operation when something was not functioning as expected. The team (management and assembly workers together) then had the opportunity to stop and learn, gather information to perform accurate, root-cause based problem solving. Learning was that important to Toyota. Stopping defects from moving down the assembly line is simply a side benefit of the system. If you make learning and the associated problem-solving process the key Lean principle in your organizational philosophy, you will consistently improve your business. This will drive you to consistently lower your costs, improve your quality, improve your products, improve your customer satisfaction, improve your competiveness and improve your bottom line.

It is far easier to make small, incremental changes on a daily basis than attempt large, disruptive ones. Incremental changes also tend to be much more sustainable. However, many problems, large and small, are not always obvious. Operational waste is a hidden problem that plagues all organizations. Excessive waste in your operation will strip your competiveness and rob your profits. To eliminate waste in your organization, you first must know where to look, how to recognize the waste, and then, how to eliminate it.

Key Principles and Rules for Lean Thinking

Key Lean Principle: Create a Customer-Focused Learning Organization

If you want to succeed and drive results to your bottom line, you need to create an environment where learning is at the very core of your daily operations and management. Quick fixes and turning a blind eye will not create a long-term solution. In order to create this learning environment, there are six basic Lean learning rules your organization needs to adopt and live by.

The Six Lean Learning Rules

Rule No. 1: Standardize and structure every activity.

Structured and standardized procedures allow your organization to make each process repeatable. This will also quickly expose any variations between the desired process (the standard) and the current execution. These differences provide opportunities to expose waste and eliminate it.

Rule No. 2: Simplify every activity and design them to expose deviations and problems early.

Simple is almost always better. Simple procedures are easier to follow and less likely to produce errors or defects. Error-proofing your procedures as best you can will also make them simpler and safer (*e.g.*, the part only fits one way; the gate will not close when blocked). Simplification also makes it easier to find the root cause of any defects in the process or procedure, saving time and money.

Rule No. 3: Clearly connect all activities and simplify every flow path.

We often forget how important the connections are between all the activities and procedures. It does no good to improve two operations if the product cannot get from one operation to the next. Establishing connections and clear flow paths helps correct sub-optimization in your process. We must always be concerned with the efficiency of the entire process (from raw material all the way to the customer), not just parts within it.

Rule No. 4: Practice systematic waste elimination and problem solving.

Eliminate the typical and obvious results of waste, such as bottlenecks, wait time, firefighting, finger pointing, frustration and wasted resources. Focus on the process, not the people. Without constant attention, waste will creep back into processes every chance it gets.

Rule No. 5: Improve through experimentation and change control.

Do not be afraid to experiment; try a new procedure or process. If it does not work as you expected, take it back out. Keep careful record of your changes so you can learn from them and remove them if you need to, or institute enterprise-wide changes when they are effective.

Rule No. 6: Develop and nurture a flexible, enthusiastic workforce.

Establish an open, honest learning environment in which everyone participates free from retribution or reprisals. Make everyone in your organization part of the learning environment. You will reap the benefits of empowerment, employee ownership and creative problem-solving.

Waste

All <u>non-value added</u> processes are waste. To be <u>value-added</u>, the activity must:

- Be something the customer is willing to pay for;

- The product must change in some way; and

- It must be done right the first time.

While it is not possible or even practical to eliminate *all* waste in your organization, constant vigilance will pay big dividends in eliminating *excessive* wastes and controlling costs. There are several common areas to begin scrutinizing. The seven types of waste we generally try to eliminate and keep from creeping back into our systems and processes are listed in Table 2-1, below.

How to Start a Successful, Sustainable Lean Program

You don't need to start your Lean journey all at once; although, you may decide to do this if you have a small, relativity cohesive organization. Many larger organizations find that it is more effective to start implementing a Lean program in one smaller area followed by implementations in progressively larger areas in the organization. Starting small allows you to focus your efforts in one area at a time while learning about the processes and experimenting with different approaches before you roll it out to other areas, and ultimately, throughout your entire organization. What works well in one organization may not work well in your organization.

Waste Type	Key Elements
Transportation	Any movement of material or information from one place to another.
Inventory	Any part or product that is not being processed or shipped to the customer.
Motion	Any movement by people not directly related to value-added work.
Waiting	Any time spent waiting by products or people.
Over Production	Producing more than the immediate customer needs or producing something sooner than it is needed.
Over Processing	Doing more to a product or process than the customer requires.
Defects	Any process or product defect or failure. The worst kinds of defects are those that reach the customer.

Table 2-1: The Seven Deadly Wastes

Start by informing and training each person in the selected area. Your goal is to ensure everyone understands what the process is, what the goals are, and what their role will be. It is also important that everyone understands that they can and will be expected to speak openly, honestly and freely: The focus should be on the process, not the people. Personal attacks cannot be tolerated. Learning and process improvements aren't effective without open communication. The company's long-term survivability may be at stake.

After you have everyone on board the Lean train, the next step is to gain a thorough understanding of your current operations, often referred to as the "current state." It is important that everyone understands exactly how the current processes work in their area. Process mapping (and/or value stream mapping) may help you with this process (see Chapter 17 for an in-depth treatment of this tool). Ask each person to describe exactly how they perform their work, step by step. Keep track of times spent on each activity. Document the process and compare the "real" process to the current documented process. You will most likely find quite a few differences, commonly referred to as "get arounds."

Use the group and your new understanding of your current state to develop an ideal state where you want to be. Ask yourself, if you could run each process in this division at a no-holds-barred optimal state, what would that process look like? This ideal state will be your goal. Compare your process to the Lean rules outlined above and look for hidden wastes. Even though some of the areas in your ideal state may not be practicable at the moment (or ever), it is still an important step to have a clearly defined ideal state goal in place. You may not be able to get there today or even this year, but you will be surprised how much progress you will be able to make once you have defined your goal.

The next step in your Lean journey is to define the future state of the selected process area or division. Since it is not usually possible to attain the ideal state in one step (and some of the components of the ideal state may not be possible for some time), the future state is an intermediate phase between your current and ideal states that defines your action plan and the steps you need to take toward achieving your ideal state. The steps you need to attain your future state should all be obtainable and have a defined timeline. Typically, your future state is attainable in one year or less.

During your journey, be sure to review what is working and not. Make adjustments to your plans. Keep an updated description and documentation of your current state as you accomplish each goal. Update your future state definitions as you learn and reach goals. You should always have an up-to-date understanding (across the entire team) of your current state, future state and ideal state.

Don't forget to maintain a continued focus on the learning process and your problem-solving capabilities. Post and review the goals, results, rules and wastes you've discovered throughout the company. Transparency is golden.

Continually work to expand your focus to include your entire organization and the entire end-to-end process flow. Monitor and evaluate your progress. Always capture the lessons learned and make changes based on facts.

Conclusions

In the following chapters you will learn about specific strategies, methods, tools and techniques that will help you make the correct changes in your organization. You will learn to leverage the lessons learned, spot the areas in need of improvement, and then move in swiftly for the gain. Always improving and always moving forward is the goal of Lean thinking. If you do only one thing to make a positive impact in your organization today, it should be to create a learning organization steeped in the ideals of continuous improvement and waste elimination. This is the real genius of Lean and the cornerstone to Lean thinking. All of the Lean tools and procedures you will learn to employ are simply aids to enhance and support this key principle.

Key Lessons Learned:

1. Lean is about total operational optimization.

2. You must create an enterprise-wide, customer-focused learning environment to be successful in creating a long-term, sustainable Lean organization.

3. Start your Lean journey by informing and training each person in the area selected for Lean implementation.

About the Author

Bill Artzberger is a multi-industry Lean expert with extensive corporate leadership, IT and manufacturing expertise. With demonstrated cross-functional team leadership abilities, he is adept at driving teams to deliver quality products and formulate strategic guidelines. Bill has an MBA and more than 25 years experience driving large-scale operational change programs. He has an extraordinary ability to position companies to be more competitive and efficient. Bill is a visionary innovator with a unique blend of technical expertise and business skills, as well as two patents. He is ITIL Certified, a certified Project Management Professional (PMP), and a Lean Six Sigma Black Belt. Bill is a Management Consultant at PRTM, One Towne Square, Suite 740, Southfield, MI 48076. The best way to reach Bill is through his e-mail at: *Billa@comcast.net*.

Chapter Three

Integrated Enterprise Excellence®: A Systems Approach to Improvement

Forrest W. Breyfogle III

Overview

This chapter is intended for business leaders, managers, Lean Six Sigma sponsors and project leaders who are interested in taking their business beyond traditional models and methodologies. This chapter approaches Lean Six Sigma tools through a business system viewpoint.

This chapter will help you to:

- Learn why many organizations fail at implementing Lean Six Sigma tools.
- Gain a basic understanding of the Integrated Enterprise Excellence.
- Discover the importance of value chain creation and where this process falls within the IEE business governance model.
- Develop an understanding of the importance of truly predictive metric.

Avoiding Failure

Much has been said about the gains from process improvement efforts such as Total Quality Management (TQM), Six Sigma, and Lean. However, what frequently happens when implementing these programs is that a business expends much effort establishing a function to manage this work only to terminate the efforts and perhaps lay off the function's employees when times get tough or the enterprise is looking for ways to cut costs.

To illustrate how traditional process improvement programs can be short-lived or not address the most important needs, consider how Bank of America might have been a benchmarked company in 2007 for their Lean Six Sigma deployment efforts. However, this executive bought-in process improvement effort did not help the company avoid severe problems during the financial crisis that began in 2008. In addition, during later cost reduction/downsizing efforts, the company laid off the very people they had hired to initiate the program.

Consider also Toyota. Many companies have modeled the Toyota Production System (TPS) for their process improvement efforts. However, the system that the world so widely touted did not prevent this benchmarked company from having product quality, design and other management issues, which were uncovered in 2009 and resulted in significant issues and financial loss for the company.[1] Bank of America and Toyota are only two of many companies that had issues with their continuous improvement efforts.

What went wrong?

Everyone understands that organizations need to improve or they will not survive; however, why, in general, do corporate, non-profit, and governmental process improvement efforts seem to have a finite life and a flavor-of-the-month stigma attached to them? The reason is that these efforts are not an integral part of an *overall long-lasting business management system*. Often, most process improvement project selection is determined in <u>organizational silos</u> without a business-as-a-whole assessment. The implication is that a Lean Six Sigma effort might later report 100 million dollars in savings, but nobody can find the money.

What really is needed is an overall business management *system* where process improvement efforts are pulled in from a long-lasting business measurement system that integrates big-picture analytics with innovation. The goal is to move the organization toward achieving the Three Rs of Business: everyone doing the right things, in the right way, all at the right time.

Nine-Step Business Management Governance System

The nine-step enhanced business management system described in this chapter addresses your need to do things right through the:

- Creation of non-silo performance metrics;

- Formulation of predictive measurements;

- Development of dynamic targeted strategies;

- Establishment of analytically determined performance metric improvement goals; and

- Use of a structured roadmap so everyone can follow a similar thought process when making improvements.

This unique business management system:

- Leads to healthy day-to-day behaviors;

- Reduces firefighting activities;

- Benefits the enterprise as a whole;

- Uses analytics and innovation within the business decision-making process;

- Pulls for the creation of projects that address *overall* business needs;

- Integrates the application of Lean and Six Sigma tools so that the right tool is used at the right time; and

- Provides a methodology for consistent and expedient project execution.

The financials of an enterprise are a result of the *integration and interaction of its processes*, not of individual procedures in isolation. Using a whole-system perspective, you come to realize the output of a system is a function of its weakest link or constraint. Without exercising caution, you can become focused on a subsystem that, while improved, does not impact the *overall* system. All too often, process improvement efforts are not expended in areas where the overall enterprise benefits the most.

Organizational leaders often discuss the growth in business environment complexity. Executive leadership needs to assess its business system, especially in times of economic challenge, to determine if its current management system can handle this increasing complexity. What organizations often need is an enhanced methodology that provides the framework for leadership to understand and manage its organization systematically through this ever-changing environment. (See Figure 1)

The business governance system graphically described below provides a roadmap for systematically addressing current management challenges head on.[1] This constitutes a whole-business system, not just a problem-solving, project-execution system such as Lean Six Sigma or Lean kaizen events. Because this system is different from traditional methods, it needs a name: Integrated Enterprise Excellence (IEE).

Most of the nine steps in this business system process are self-explanatory; however, the final step does not return to step one, but instead returns to step three. The implication of this type of feedback is that a long-lasting management system front end is created, which can remain structurally constant over time even through leadership, organizational, and strategy changes.

All steps of this system are important; however, focus is given to the creation of organizational metrics (Step 2) and strategy creation (Step 5).

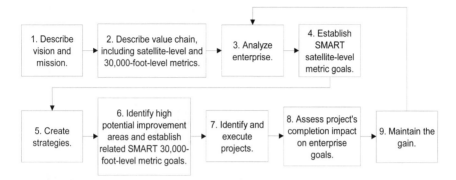

From Figure 3.6: *The Integrated Enterprise Excellence System: An Enhanced, Unified Approach to Balanced Scorecards, Strategic Planning and Business Improvement*, Forrest W. Breyfogle III, Bridgeway Books, 2008.

Figure 3-1: The Integrated Enterprise Excellence System

Step Two: Value Chain Creation

In many businesses today, the enterprise is not properly viewed as a system of <u>non-siloed</u> processes with performance measurements. Instead, organizations often report metrics in their department on a weekly, monthly, or quarterly basis relative to goals. If you aren't careful, this form of reporting can lead to firefighting, and in extreme cases, a meet-the-numbers-or-else culture that is fatal. Many companies in our current economic crisis are in this very situation. These issues can be overcome, however, when organizations view their enterprise procedures and metrics from a value-chain point of view, where the organizational chart is subordinate to the value chain itself.

Step 2 of the system requires you to describe your value chain with both <u>satellite-level</u> (financial) and the <u>30,000-foot-level</u>® (operational) metrics. An organization's value chain, as illustrated in Figure 3-2, describes what the enterprise does (rectangles) and its performance measures of success (ovals) from a customer and business point of view: cost, quality, and time.

In this value chain, the rectangular boxes would provide clickable access to process steps, functional value streams, and procedural documents. The center series of rectangular box-specified functions describe the primary business flow, and the rectangular boxes that are not in this series describe other support functions such as legal and finance.

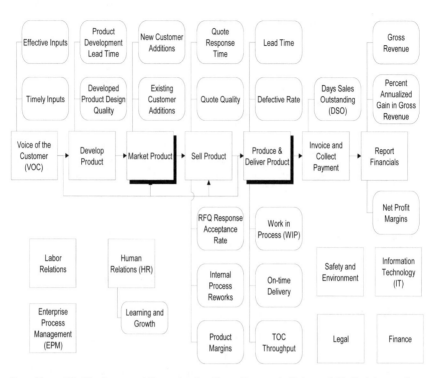

From Figure 7.3: *The Integrated Enterprise Excellence System: An Enhanced, Unified Approach to Balanced Scorecards, Strategic Planning and Business Improvement*, Forrest W. Breyfogle III, Bridgeway Books, 2008.

Figure 3-2: Value Chain with Scorecard/Dashboard Metrics

With this approach to describing your enterprise, the organization chart is properly subordinate to the value chain. The value chain is long-lasting, even through organizational changes, where process functional procedures and their metrics can change over time.

Metrics within a value chain need to be aligned with how the business is conducted. This is in contrast to creating metrics around the organization chart or strategic plan objectives, where both can significantly change over time. In addition, it is important not only to determine what should be measured, but also to have a reporting methodology that leads to healthy behavior so that the organization as a whole benefits.

Creating Good Metrics

Good metrics provide decision-making insight that leads to the most appropriate conclusion and action/non-action. The objective is to create a system that is measurable, auditable, sustainable, and consistent. Organizations can achieve significant benefits and reduce much wasted effort when a process for metric creation and improvement addresses the following areas:

- Creation of long-lasting metrics that originate from a proper assessment of which measurements will provide the most appropriate quantifiable assessment of organizational value chain functional outputs in the areas of cost, quality and time.

- Metrics that maintain basic continuity over time and are independent of changes in leadership, strategies, and organizational structure.

- Metrics need to be reported in a format that provides predictive statements when there is a recent region of stability.

- Metrics need to have peer-to-peer comparability. The reporting system needs to be consistent throughout the organization.

- The organization chart needs to be subordinate to the functional metrics so that when organizational changes occur, the basic metric structure and reporting format remains the same.

- Metrics from a corporate value chain can be drilled down throughout the organization.

- The output of a process is a function of the process' inputs and its steps ($Y=F(X)$). (See Chapter 19 for discussion). The simple setting of goals does not make it happen. This is simply "management by hope." Organizations need to have a system that analyzes their metrics collectively to establish goals for value-chain metrics that benefit the business as a whole.

- Process improvement goals for value-chain functional metrics should be established from an analytical enterprise, whole-business assessment. For example, such an assessment might lead to a marketing and sales metric improvement focus rather than manufacturing waste reduction if the organization has excess capacity and there is a financial goal to grow the business.

- Include a value chain predictive metrics assessment to determine strategies that lead to targeted projects for financial goal achievement. These strategies will lead to goals and projects that truly impact the financial goals of the whole business. This approach expands on Lean Six Sigma's DMAIC approach.

Predictive Metrics

Organizations often report performance using a table of numbers, stack bar chart or red-yellow-green reports where red indicates that a goal/specification is not being met, and green indicates that current performance is satisfactory. These reporting formats describe what has occurred in the past for some time interval but do not provide predictive statements. Without a system perspective, this reporting system can lead to firefighting behaviors.

Using a 30,000-foot-level reporting system can avoid these limitations. In 30,000-foot-level reporting, there are no calendar boundaries, and a prediction statement can be made when appropriate. For example, a current metric performance level that has been stable for the last 17 weeks at 2.2% non-conformance could be considered predictable. For predictable processes, we expect that a similar non-conformance level will continue to occur in the future unless something is done to change either the process inputs or the process execution itself.

At this level of reporting, <u>common-cause variability</u> is separated from <u>special-cause events</u>. With a 30,000-foot-level business perspective, typical micro-variability (process input differences) is considered common-cause input variability that need not be reacted to in the same manner as special-cause variability. Examples of this include variation in raw material lots, day of the week, personnel and machine differences.

Trying to determine the cause of a current problem by sending someone to "fix" it only leads to firefighting activities. More often than not in these types of situations, only minimal, if any, improvements are made from a firefighting approach since common-cause variability issues are treated as though they were special-cause. Care must be used with red-yellow-green scorecards when there is a tracking of goals throughout an organization. A red-yellow-green scorecard system can sound attractive, but it may promote firefighting activities instead.

To illustrate this point, consider the red-yellow-green scorecard shown at the top of Figure 3-3, which is from one corporation's actual scorecard system. Compare this to the 30,000-foot reporting system depicted beneath the scorecard.

This IEE metric reporting system has two steps. The first is to analyze for predictability. The second step is the formulation of a prediction statement if the process is found predictable. To determine predictability, the process is assessed for statistical stability using the 30,000-foot-level

Iampndividuals Control Chart [left], which can detect if the process response has changed over time and/or if it is stable.

When there is a current region of stability, data from this last region can be considered a random sample of the future. For this example, note how the 30,000-foot-level control chart in Figure 3-3 indicates that nothing fundamental in the process has changed, even though a traditional red-yellow-green scorecard showed the metric frequently transitioned between all three levels. For the traditional scorecard, the performance level was red 5 out of the 13 recorded times.

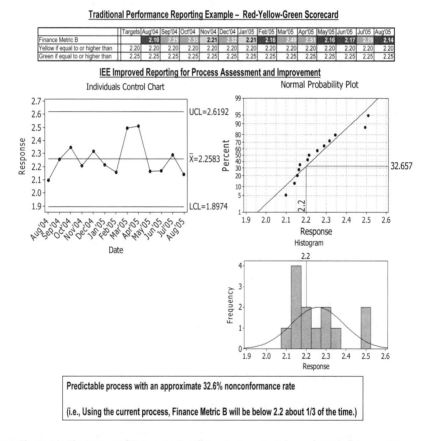

Traditional Performance Reporting Example – Red-Yellow-Green Scorecard

	Targets	Aug'04	Sep'04	Oct'04	Nov'04	Dec'04	Jan'05	Feb'05	Mar'05	Apr'05	May'05	Jun'05	Jul'05	Aug'05
Finance Metric B		2.10	2.25	2.35	2.21	2.32	2.21	2.16	2.49	2.51	2.16	2.17	2.29	2.14
Yellow if equal to or higher than	2.20	2.20	2.20	2.20	2.20	2.20	2.20	2.20	2.20	2.20	2.20	2.20	2.20	2.20
Green if equal to or higher than	2.25	2.25	2.25	2.25	2.25	2.25	2.25	2.25	2.25	2.25	2.25	2.25	2.25	2.25

IEE Improved Reporting for Process Assessment and Improvement

Predictable process with an approximate 32.6% nonconformance rate

(i.e., Using the current process, Finance Metric B will be below 2.2 about 1/3 of the time.)

From Figure 6.2: *The Integrated Enterprise Excellence System: An Enhanced, Unified Approach to Balanced Scorecards, Strategic Planning and Business Improvement*, Forrest W. Breyfogle III, Bridgeway Books, 2008.

Figure 3-3: Red-Yellow Green Scorecard vs. 30,000-foot-level® Metric

Also included in this figure is a probability plot that can be used to make a prediction statement. A probability plot can teach you a lot about a process. A closer look at this metric shows the x-axis is the magnitude of a process' response over the region of stability, while the y-axis is <u>percent less than</u>.

One very important advantage of probability plotting is that data do not need to be normally distributed for a prediction statement to be made. If the data on a probability plot closely follow a straight line, we act *as though* the data are from the distribution that is represented by the probability plot coordinate system. Estimated population percentages below a specification limit can be made by simply examining the y-axis percentage value, as shown in Figure 3-3. For example, if our specified goal is 2.2, we can estimate that we will not achieve this objective about 33% of the time, now and in the future.

With respect to business-management policy, red-yellow-green scales and 30,000-foot views produce very different behaviors. In this example, a red-yellow-green reporting policy could lead to a firefighting response one-third of the time because every time the metric turned red, management would ask the question, "Why is our performance level now red?" Yet, in actuality, the process was performing within its predictable bounds.

With performance reporting that provides a view of the bigger picture, we gain valuable insight and understanding that the variation in this example is actually from common-cause process variability. The only way to improve performance under these circumstances is through improving the process itself. Quick-fix behaviors will not solve the problem and can make things worse. Under the IEE full-view initiative, someone would be assigned to work on improving the process that is associated with this metric. This assumes that the metric identifies an improvement need that positively affects business performance as a whole. A value chain with 30,000-foot-level metric reporting can become the long-lasting front end of a system and baseline assessment from which you can create strategies and make true improvements.

Strategic Planning and Business Improvement

Consider how, with a traditional approach, organization-wide strategic statements can be very difficult to translate into specific employee actions. I encountered one organization that communicated an "expansion of production capacity" strategy. Should this strategy be applied to all produced products? For most situations, this would not be the case.

The balanced scorecard[2, 3] utilizes strategy mapping to cascade executive strategies throughout the organization. Hoshin kanri is another tool with the same effect, using a technique called catchball.

In addition, annually developed, executive retreat strategies can significantly change over time and with leadership. It is important to have strategies that transcend these changes. However, *is* it best to have strategy-building as Step One, from which all organizational metrics and operational goals are determined? With the Integrated Enterprise Excellence approach, strategies are analytically and innovatively determined in Step Five, after several very important process steps have laid a proper foundation for developing sound strategies. These well-defined strategies then lead to targeted improvement or design projects that benefit the enterprise as a whole.

Conclusions

To be competitive in an ever-changing environment, businesses need a working environment that leads to the Three Rs of business. The CEO and/or president needs to be intimately involved in the creation, orchestration and refinement of this system in order to accomplish these business objectives. This executive-developed and orchestrated system needs to integrate scorecards, strategic planning, business improvements and control, so that the enterprise as a whole benefits.

By shifting strategic planning from step one to step five of the framework, organizations can integrate leadership intuition with an analytically innovative system, providing a guiding light for achievement of the Three Rs. Within this system, we have the ability to ensure that all efforts throughout the organization are driving improvements at the top, so that the strategic plans and metrics are actually achievable with clear direction throughout the organization.

IEE provides the framework and roadmap for implementing both Deming's philosophy[4] and Collins' *Good to Great*[5] principles. Organizations can use this system as a foundation for achievement of the Malcolm Baldrige National Quality Award and Shingo Prize.

Additional Information and Resources

The above-described methodology goes beyond traditional business systems, Lean Six Sigma,[6,7] and the Balanced Scorecard methodology.[2,3] The Integrated Enterprise Excellence system is described at various levels of detail in a five-volume series, which is available from book resellers such as Amazon.com. Two of the books provide a description of the overall system.[8, 9] Volume II of the series walks step by step through the business aspects of the system,[10] while Volume III[11] and a project execution guide[12] provide the details of improvement project roadmap execution, where Lean and Six Sigma tools are truly integrated. A resource center is also available that contains more than 100 articles on this and other related topics.[13] A case study for implementing this system is described in an American Management Association article[14] and a video.[15] Executives can also attend a one-day workshop, Achieving Enterprise Excellence, to learn more about the system.

Key Lessons Learned

1. Most firms fail at implementing Six Sigma tools because they fail to first create a system in which these tools actually work.

2. Implementing the nine-step IEE system will create a solid foundation in which you can properly employ Six Sigma tools.

3. The IEE model emphasizes the importance of value chain creation and using truly predictive metrics that will help you develop sound business strategies.

About the Author

Forrest W. Breyfogle III is CEO of Smarter Solutions, Inc. and founder of the Integrated Enterprise Excellence System. He is a Professional Engineer and ASQ Fellow and received the 2004 Crosby Medal for his book, *Implementing Six Sigma*.

He has authored or co-authored thirteen books on Six Sigma and various Lean methods. His book, *Implementing Six Sigma*, is a primary body of knowledge reference for ASQ's Black Belt certification test. Five of his published books describe an Integrated Enterprise Excellence system that goes beyond Lean Six Sigma and the Balanced Scorecard.

He received the prestigious Crosby Medal from the ASQ *Implementing Six Sigma* (2ed). He has been interviewed by several TV, radio, and print publications about the application of Six Sigma, including CNNfn and CNBC Power Lunch. He founded Smarter Solutions in 1992 after a 24-year career at IBM.

Nomenclature and Service Marks

Integrated Enterprise Excellence, IEE, satellite-level, 30,000-foot-level, and 50-foot-level are registered marks of Smarter Solutions, Inc. In implementing the program or methods identified in this chapter, you are authorized to refer to these marks in a manner that is consistent with the standards set forth herein by Smarter Solutions, Inc., but any and all use of the marks shall inure to the sole benefit of Smarter Solutions, Inc. Business Way of Life and Smarter Solutions are registered service marks of Smarter Solutions, Inc.

1. "Toyota Loses its Shine," *The Economist* (December 10, 2009).
2. R. S. Kaplan and D. P. Norton, "The Balanced Scorecard – Measures that Drive Performance," *Harvard Business Review* (Jan.-Feb. 1992).
3. R. S. Kaplan and D. P. Norton, *Alignment: Using the Balanced Scorecard to Create Corporate Synergies* (Boston: Harvard Business School Press, 2006).
4. W. E. Deming, *Out of the Crisis* (Cambridge: Massachusetts Institute of Technology, 1986).
5. Jim Collins, *Good to Great: Why Some Companies Make the Leap and Others Don't* (New York: HarperCollins Publishers Inc., 2001).
6. F. W. Breyfogle III, *Statistical Methods for Testing, Development, and Manufacturing* (Hoboken, NJ: Wiley, 1992).
7. F. W. Breyfogle III, *Implementing Six Sigma: Smarter Solutions using Statistical Methods*, 2nd ed. (Hoboken, NJ: Wiley, 2003).
8. F. W. Breyfogle III, *The Integrated Enterprise Excellence System: An Enhanced, Unified Approach to Balanced Scorecards, Strategic Planning, and Business Improvement* (Austin, TX: Bridgeway Books, 2008).
9. F. W. Breyfogle III, *Integrated Enterprise Excellence Volume I—The Basics: Golfing Buddies Go Beyond Lean Six Sigma and the Balanced Scorecard* (Austin, TX: Bridgeway Books, 2008).
10. F. W. Breyfogle III, *Integrated Enterprise Excellence Volume II—Business Deployment: A Leaders' Guide for Going Beyond Lean Six Sigma and the Balanced Scorecard* (Austin, TX: Bridgeway Books, 2008).
11. F. W. Breyfogle III, *Integrated Enterprise Excellence Volume III—Improvement Project Execution: A Management and Black Belt Guide for Going Beyond Lean Six Sigma and the Balanced Scorecard* (Austin, TX: Bridgeway Books, 2008).
12. F. W. Breyfogle III, *Lean Six Sigma Project Execution Guide: The Integrated Enterprise Excellence (IEE) Process Improvement Project Roadmap* (Austin, TX: Citius Publishing, 2010).
13. Integrated Enterprise Excellence Resource Center: *http://www.smartersolutions.com/articles.php*).
14. S. Dickman and F. W. Breyfogle, "New Methods to Achieve Production and Financial Gains," *M-World*, (Winter 2008-2009), *http://www.smartersolutions.com/pdfs/online_database/asset.php?documentid=114*.
15. Integrated Enterprise Excellence (IEE), Case Study: Oracle Packaging *http://www.smartersolutions.com/casestudy/oraclepackaging/orl_asset_orlpck091808.htm*

Chapter Four

Value Realization Methodology (VRM)

Kendall Scheer

Overview

This chapter is written for those of you who have some degree of responsibility to *successfully* develop and direct business transformation. Value Realization Methodology is a unique methodology that is being deployed in a wide variety of situations, each time leading to successful transformations with measurably improved business metrics.

Businesses always change, either from coercion (competition, disruptive technology, regulation, economic shifts) or from strategy. Changes that companies undergo can be categorized as either haphazard or strategic. For example, from the perspective of a company acquired in a hostile takeover, it undergoes haphazard change because the transformation is neither planned nor expected. From the perspective of the acquiring company, the change is strategic because the transformation is planned.

Interestingly, case studies on failed acquisitions abound, proving that strategic (planned) change is all too often unsuccessful. The anticipated financial performance never materializes – a result of the value being underachieved or the cost of change ultimately exceeding the value. Well executed VRM-based transformations do not suffer this same fate.

This chapter will help you to:

- Pragmatically discover the "critical few" areas of business improvement potential.
- Determine the true costs of achieving business improvement.
- Express program initiatives in financial terms that are understood by the C-level executive suite, the board and the shareholders to obtain buy-in and continued support for program initiatives.

What is VRM?

VRM identifies and quantifies both the value of and the costs associated with transformational change. In experienced hands, VRM determines the business transformations that will yield the greatest value. It also identifies expedient paths for getting there. For those who might doubt how important that path is, think about going to see your neighbor to the east via a westerly route. It simply makes no sense. Many projects fail not because the end state has been mistakenly defined, but because the path mapped out to get there is wrong.

VRM is a collection of techniques and tools utilized to diagnose the health condition and growth opportunities of a business. Consider your business a patient and VRM as a set of medical practitioners. Some businesses are sick, meaning they are losing money, market share or customer loyalty. Some are average; they may be getting by, but not as well as the best-in-class firm in their industry segment. Some are at or near best-in-class, but still desire to improve further.

Family physicians see all types of patients. It is their job to first learn why the patient is there. For a sick patient, the goal is for the patient to return to a state of normal health. For the average patient, he or she may seek preventative services – to get a checkup so that early detection may prevent a potentially serious disease from becoming fatal. For the healthy person – an athlete perhaps – it might be to discuss an alternative diet that provides greater stamina. Regardless of the reason, a physician's first job is to understand the patient's motives for seeking the consultation: "Why are you here?"

A physician's second job is to learn the patient's base condition. This is accomplished with structured questions (essentially a guided interview), observations and tests. With increased understanding of the problem or motive, the doctor can begin to consider various treatments. Interview answers, observations and test results serve as the doctor's basis for an accurate diagnosis so that an effective treatment plan can be developed. Diagnosis is critical in this respect. If a doctor misdiagnoses a patient, proper treatment cannot be delivered. The patient will not only fail to get better or reach the desired outcome, he or she may get worse, and the doctor may need to call his malpractice insurance carrier.

Like the physician in a doctor's office, VRM enables decision makers to make informed choices on spending and benefits, compatible with a specified risk tolerance (program or project level). VRM also sponsors buy-in for transformation and sets proper expectations for returns.

VRM is deployable either alone or in conjunction with other projects and initiatives. It focuses on improving top and bottom line metrics, such as:

- Profitable sales growth
- Operating income
- Cash flow from operations
- Cost of Goods Sold (COGS)
- Productivity and efficiency

- Indirect and overhead cost

- Working capital

- Inventory and carrying costs

- Accounts Receivable

- Earnings Per Share (EPS)

- Other metrics unique to a company's Balanced Score Card

VRM Deliverables

For most people, VRM is easiest to learn by simply getting familiar with its deliverables. The exact number of deliverables from a VRM project varies, but the minimum is seven for a standalone project and ten when VRM operates with other initiatives (*e.g.*, Lean, Six Sigma, ERP blueprinting, etc.). For every VRM project, the actual number of deliverables is specifically spelled out in a Statement of Work (SOW). A selection of seven common VRM deliverables is discussed below.

Project Kickoff Materials

At the outset of a project, making your people aware of the changes to be made and obtaining their input is critical to success. Typically, there are four main documents circulated *prior* to making any change:

a.   Sponsor Letter: for client sponsor to inform and engage client team.

b.   Survey Questionnaires: questionnaires for participating regional offices, departments, plants, etc. These involve questions of a functional and financial nature to learn about current processes and performance.

c.   Shelf Data Request: a solicitation for materials that may already exist within the company, thus reducing the time involved in learning critical elements of strategy, issues, architecture(s), etc.

d.   Kickoff Presentation: a standard presentation that can be modified for specific client engagements.

An example cover letter that introduces the project and the information packet is included as Figure 4.1.

DATE
Service Provider Name
Provider Numerical Address
Provider City, State/Province
Provider Country/Code (ex., zip)

Ms. Client Manager and Client Sponsor
Client Company Name
Client Numerical Address
Client City, State/Province, Country & Code
Dear Client Manager and Client Sponsor,
All of us at Service Provider Company are excited about getting Project Name underway. In order to facilitate the VRM activities of the process, we have prepared this package of information and a list of some things that require your attention and assistance. We need you to distribute these requests for information and help us get back responses as soon as possible. The target date is by Target Date for Responses.

Enclosed you will find:
• An announcement letter for senior management
• An announcement letter for line managers and other participants
• An initial Shelf Data Request and Tracking Form (Spreadsheet)
(This is a request for existing Business Information and Key Performance Indicators - KPIs)
• An Opportunity Identification Survey and Tracking Form (Spreadsheet)
(This request is to solicit opinions about the performance of the business operations)
In preparation for the VRM activities of Project Name, please do the following:
• Edit the announcement letters and appropriate attachments, as you deem best, and distribute them ASAP. Experience has shown that the earlier we begin to engage the extended Team Members, the more successful the outcome. In addition, by properly setting expectation levels with respect to the level of involvement and effort required by each team member, we can make the most effective use of everyone's time.

• Use the enclosed Shelf Data/KPI Tracking form to maintain the status of the various data responses. Experience has taught us that the earlier hypotheses are formulated the more focused, effective and compelling the business case becomes. The Opportunity Identification Survey and Shelf Data Request are essential to our ability to formulate initial hypotheses about business improvement.

We thank you for all your help and look forward to officially starting on Project Kickoff Date.
Sincerely,
VRM Team (VRM Team Leader, VRM Team Senior Member 1, VRM Team Senior Member 2)

Figure 4-1: Sample Letter

The client manager and sponsor (who sometimes are the same person) take the enclosures and distribute them. This begins the project by informing the organization about the project and identifies the individual team members who have been selected to participate. Having the client participants begin collecting information is a helpful change management tool that gets people involved early. Within a short period after the letters go out and the data begins flowing in, a kickoff meeting occurs for all vested parties, including senior management, so that everyone gets a chance to learn and have their questions answered.

User-Identified Problems

User-identified problems is a feedback deliverable specifying the most significant issues based on interviews, shelf data reviews and survey results, which were identified early on. Results are weighted so that corrections and improvements to these problem areas will yield the greatest, and likely the quickest, financial return to the company.

The initial VRM work involves diagnosis, which begins with "patient" interaction. Here, the first step is to listen to what actual client users have to say. This is accomplished by interviewing a wide cross-section of client users using both structured and unstructured questions. By combining what we hear with information that comes in from the surveys, shelf data and other available sources, problem areas are quite quickly identified, categorized, scored and weighted. In Figure 4-2, a look at the sample interview results quickly reveals the Sales and Operations Planning (S&OP) process is the most broken of all this company's processes. To keep this project contained to a practical scope, we selected only the first six areas to "deep dive" and analyze further.

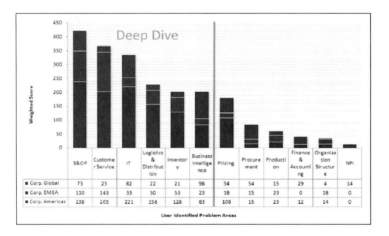

	S&OP	Custome r Service	IT	Logistics & Distribut ion	Inventor y	Business Intellige nce	Pricing	Procure ment	Producti on	Finance & Accounti ng	Organiza tion Structur e	NPI
■ Corp. Global	73	23	82	22	21	98	54	54	15	29	4	14
■ Corp. EMEA	110	143	33	50	53	23	18	15	23	0	18	0
■ Corp. Americas	238	203	221	158	128	83	108	15	23	12	14	0

User Identified Problem Areas

Figure 4-2: User-Identified Problems: Interview Results

Current State Maps

Taken together, these three current state maps yield a deeper understanding of the area of the business within the scope of the project:

> *Physical Map*: a map showing the physical reality of the company. It identifies: the inputs to the business and how these inputs come from suppliers; the value-adding activities and how they are performed;

the outputs and how they are distributed to customers, etc. This is often called the "material flow map" within industrial companies.

Virtual Map: a map of internal and external information flows. This includes IT flows and all other flows where the data being identified is used for decision making or tracking and archiving order flow. The map also shows the speed at which information is being collected and operated upon. Oftentimes, information flow speed is a huge issue. It has been repeatedly observed that when businesses physically operate faster than their "standard" information flows, they are forced to resort to awkward "expedited" information flows to run the business.

Financial Map: a map showing the P&L major categories and how financials accrue and flow to the various revenue/expense categories.

Examples of these maps are included below with additional information.

The physical map (Figure 4-3) shows how inputs come into the company and with what lead times. If lead times vary significantly, the variability is documented in this deliverable. This map shows the flows through the value-adding activities and then the distribution channels. Although the example below maps an industrial enterprise that moves material, these material flows give way to activity or transactional flows when the business deals with administrative activities, such as insurance, finance, education and government enterprises.

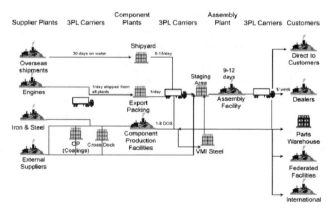

Figure 4-3: Physical Map

The virtual map (Figure 4-4) shows information flows within the organization. It documents the interaction of systems, individuals and enterprises. This map shows how the organization gathers, creates and shares critical information. The major processes are color coded to show how often the processes run. Update frequency is critical, both for inputs and processes. It is not helpful to decision makers and evaluators when an hourly process is only updated weekly.

Business Planning and Scheduling Flow

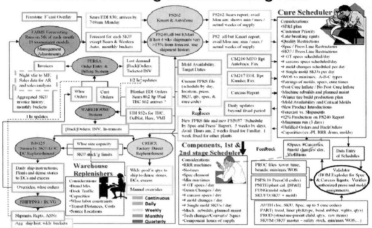

Figure 4-4: Virtual Map

The financial map (Fig. 4-5) shows how costs build up through the organization, starting with input costs (left), then costs associated with value-adding activities (both direct and indirect costs), and then adding in SG&A and profit. The VRM team works closely with the financial team to structure the map according to the expense classification scheme and chart-of-accounts used by the client. This enables the client to better relate to the resulting map. It is also a useful exercise for the VRM team because it forces them to understand how the client views and categorizes expenses. This map is extremely important because it serves as the baseline upon which to project future expenses and benefits. The map can be generated at an organizational, product or time-based level.

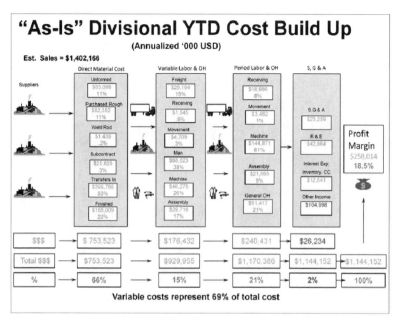

Figure 4-5: Financial Map

Five-Why Charts

These charts are generated for each of the major areas of concern remaining after user-identified problems have been sorted and weighted. In order to maintain a practical project scope, "5-why" analyses are conducted only on the most significant problem areas identified in step 2 (See Chapter 14 on 5-Why charts). This gives the VRM team sufficient time and focus to dig down into the root causes of issues in the highest value-generating areas.

There are often 10 to 12 Five-Why charts generated during any given VRM project. Each one begins with a major repetitive symptom previously identified during the early diagnostic phase. The process is designed to uncover root causes and then identify how a business process should be modified to permanently resolve the problem. If the VRM initiative is coupled with a technology project, the technology levers that address the issue are identified on the 5-Why chart. The technology project is ultimately guided down an implementation path that is most valuable to the client. This is a good example of how VRM and other initiatives are synergistic to each other.

Benefits Map

This is often called the "Ah-ha" map. Against the backdrop of the Financial Map, the financial benefits to be generated via process improvement are shown here. It is helpful to nearly all corporations to see how much and where the benefits will accrue in the P&L.

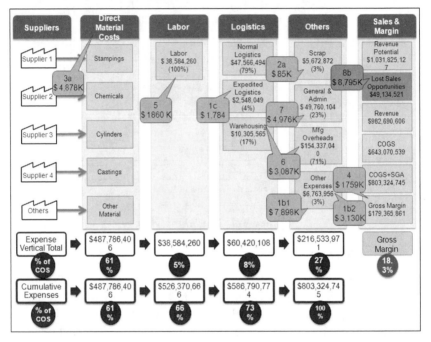

Figure 4-6: Benefits Map

The Benefits Map is a two-part deliverable. The first part is the mere listing of benefits (not shown) demonstrating the amount each benefit is worth. Included with this listing are all calculations outlining how the amounts are derived. The second part (Figure 4-6) shows where these amounts will actually accrue in the P&L. To generate both these results, the VRM team uses analytical techniques to calculate the level of financial gain associated with particular business process changes. These are arduous calculations requiring honed skills by a team well versed in the calculus of factory physics. In the spirit of the medical analogy, the Benefits Map is the projected future "healthier" state of the enterprise, based on a treatment plan (improvements that specifically target the most significant and addressable problems identified during diagnosis).

Full Financial Picture Map

This map shows the complete picture of the proposed VRM project (Figure 4-7). Not only are the benefits accounted for, but the costs of getting to those benefits are included as well. Thus, the full financial picture is depicted on a single page. The financials are presented using discounted cash-flow techniques so the results are effectively communicated to the financial team (*e.g.*, CFO, CEO and/or Board) for their understanding and buy-in. The map shows maximum investment exposure level and time of occurrence, break-even point, and Internal Rate of Return (IRR) for various periods. The Return on Investment (ROI) can be calculated from the data on this map.

Financial benefits come with a price. In other words, the treatment plan is not free. Thus, a Full Financial Picture map is generated. It shows when each of the various expenses of a program will be incurred and how they collectively accumulate. Expenses usually occur before benefits are generated. Thus, the chart depicts increasing expenses to a point of maximum investment exposure. Once the benefits begin to accrue, the project comes in to a state of payback (benefits have caught up to the expenses) and then onward to net gain. This chart is frequently known as the Rainbow Chart because of the color bands used to distinguish all the individual expenses and gains.

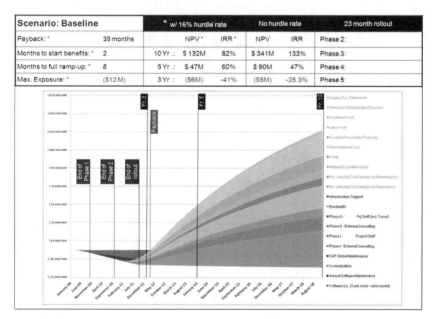

Scenario: Baseline		* w/ 16% hurdle rate		No hurdle rate		23 month rollout
Payback: *	39 months	NPV *	IRR *	NPV	IRR	Phase 2:
Months to start benefits: *	2	10 Yr.: $ 132M	82%	$ 341M	133%	Phase 3:
Months to full ramp-up: *	8	5 Yr.: $ 47M	60%	$ 90M	47%	Phase 4:
Max. Exposure: *	($12 M)	3 Yr.: ($6M)	-41%	($5M)	-25.3%	Phase 5:

Figure 4-7: Full Financial Picture Map

Financial Map – Multiple Options

A set of Financial Picture maps are developed for multiple project scenarios. For example, the customer may choose to only revamp operations at one site to keep costs low before moving the improvement project onward to other locations. Thus, the financial picture has low investment exposure, but the project is drawn out over time. Conversely, the company may choose to improve several locations simultaneously, investing faster and deeper but shortening the time to cover all operations. Some customers decide to roll out their VRM program in functional sequence. Based on the roll out scenario, a program/project path is then selected. Common criteria for selection are investment risk, team size, greatest rate of return and payback speed. The fastest payback approach is extremely useful for cash-strapped companies because the cash generated from the first initiative bootstraps subsequent phases. Many companies have successfully taken on huge VRM projects with only a minimal outlay of up-front cash.

Because there are many different paths, timeframes and approaches that can be used to reach an improved end-state, it is important to view these options in a way that makes it easy to compare them and ultimately select the one that is most compatible with company objectives. If the company is cash poor, it may be constrained to take on only a small but hard-hitting and valuable project that costs little and returns a lot. A cash-rich firm may take on a multi-faceted project requiring a large initial investment. The multiple options are depicted as several Full Financial Picture Maps, each being a unique scenario. The financials for each scenario can be viewed side-by-side. Then the firm decides which way forward is most suitable to its strategy, objectives and constraints. With help and advice from the VRM team, the most attractive options are reviewed and sorted until a particular way forward is finalized.

VRM Frequently Asked Questions (FAQs)

This section serves to address some of the more commonly asked questions about VRM.

> 1. *"How flexible is VRM as a methodology? If you ask our firm for shelf data or data-flows, we have very little to share. Does that doom the methodology?"*

Probably the greatest feature of VRM is its flexibility. Just as a family practice doctor has to deal with a vast array of patients, some who will tell the doctor a lot and some who say very little, the doctor still finds ways to obtain the information needed. The reason VRM goes after multiple channels of information (interviews, surveys, shelf data, architectural diagrams, etc.) is to come at this information issue from multiple angles to get what *is* available. VRM fills in for the lack of data with assumptions when required. These assumptions are validated with the client, and experience has proven that validated assumptions are reasonably accurate 90% of the time. So, even if the data looks like Swiss cheese (full of holes and missing elements), VRM is flexible enough to deal with the situation.

2. *"It sounds like VRM gets into a lot of detail to make calculations. We are a large corporation; to get into detail on all of our processes, plants and regions would be a large, time-consuming and expensive task. We need something simple and affordable."*

Think of VRM as a zoom camera. It can use a wide-angle lens to get a big, overall picture, or it can zoom in to pick up fine detail on a much narrower scope. VRM has been applied at the multi-national corporate level (spanning the entire enterprise), and it has been applied to a single line within a factory. The VRM process steps remain the same. It is simply the scope of the data and analyses that change.

Think again of the medical analogy. The family doctor sometimes deals with the entire person's body, trying to find out why the patient is not feeling well. At other times, the doctor focuses in on only the throbbing finger because the symptoms are specific and the data clearly points to the cause. VRM has been successfully scoped to deal with all sizes of situations. The Statements of Work (SOWs) are where the scoping is established. Furthermore, the methodology develops early hypotheses on where the greatest value will be found. The methodology is designed to identify the few "relevant and valuable" areas that should be deep-dive analyzed. There is no intention of analyzing "everything." That would be akin to trying to "boil the ocean."

3. *"You seem to imply that VRM can be all things to all people. How can this be true?"*

Saying that VRM is very flexible and can be used in all kinds of companies and situations does not mean that it intends to *do* everything. For example, in 2009, a VRM team working with a specific client found the Sales and Operations (S&OP) process was badly broken. A broken S&OP process is like having a broken locomotive on a train: Everything else follows S&OP, the process where supply is supposedly being matched to projected demand. Clearly for this client, inventory was a huge issue, as were customer responsiveness and a host of other sins. The VRM team uncovered the problem and placed value on the improvements. The team then brought in a boutique firm with a rigorous analytical tool for analyzing and fixing inventory problems. So, in the end, the VRM team brought in the specialists. In this case, starting with the specialists would have been the wrong thing to do because other serious ailments afflicting this client would not have been identified by this particular specialist – just as cardiologists are not be expected to diagnose brain cancer.

4.   *"We have already budgeted for our project. We ran a pro-forma ROI for the project. Why would we need VRM?"*

Experience has shown that projects get reviewed over time. Projects often get shelved, slowed down or canned - particularly if there is a slowdown in business or the economy. To maintain the project, it needs a rigorously defensible business case, which VRM can provide. In fact, VRM has oftentimes been an enabler for project sponsors to gain higher visibility and get more funding, or at least sustained funding, while other projects get shut down. VRM results are stated in financial terms that can be reviewed by senior executives. This allows VRM projects to get sponsorship high up in the corporation – the safest level of sponsorship to have. It can also lead to greater funding levels than usually permitted.

5.   *"We have business improvement teams, including Six Sigma teams. Why do we need the VRM team as well?"*

A majority of VRM projects have as the client-sponsor a person or persons from the client's business improvement team. Very frequently, the sponsor is a black belt or a similarly designated person. The VRM methodology is completely compatible and synergistic with Six Sigma, Lean, TQM, etc. VRM takes a holistic, large-scale view of things and then identifies and quantifies the most valuable areas to improve. Far too often, client teams do a great job of analysis and improvement, but work feverishly on things that may yield thousands of dollars in improvements when million-dollar improvements are available. VRM is good at homing in on the most valuable areas to target.

6.   *"Our company is global and operates around the world. Has VRM been used globally, and if so, how well has it worked – considering other cultures, etc?"*

VRM has evolved over more than fifteen years based on the merger of other methodologies that go back even farther. Even when it was first formed in North America in the mid-1990s, it was immediately deployed throughout Europe (Germany, UK, France, Belgium, Sweden), South America (Brazil) and Asia (Turkey, Malaysia, Singapore, Thailand and Korea). The methodology is neutral and has proven to work in all locations.

7. *"By the examples shown, it appears that VRM is primarily geared towards industrial companies. We are not an industrial company. How would VRM work for us?"*

While it is true that VRM has found its heaviest use among the industrial companies, including many Fortune 100 companies, the methodology adapts for use with either hard or soft goods. VRM simply endeavors to understand how inputs arrive, how reliably these inputs arrive, and then how they are processed and ultimately distributed. It calculates value based on business velocities, including information velocities, and other factors that relate directly or indirectly back to the top or bottom line. The VRM teams are extremely adept at flexing the methodology to the particular needs of the businesses that employ it.

8. *"It appears by the explanation of the seven standard deliverables that the VRM methodology is for planning a transformation, not for execution or maintenance. Is that true?"*

The VRM methodology has a very powerful dimension not discussed here. Indeed, VRM has the responsibility to assure the projected benefits are fully realized and maintained. In fact, some VRM projects have been entirely funded from actual realized benefits (value-based projects). VRM establishes relevant Key Performance Indicators (KPIs) that allow the organization to track, in real time, the performance of the business within the value areas identified by VRM during the analysis phase. Keeping the organization's "eye on the ball" helps assure that the projected benefits are actually achieved and maintained.

Conclusions

Based on the merger of a number of very powerful precursor methodologies, VRM has evolved into an extremely flexible and powerful tool for mining value for all types of corporate entities around the world. It works either stand-alone or in conjunction with other initiatives and methodologies. It is compatible with Lean, Six Sigma, TQM, and similar approaches. When working with other methodologies, it serves to focus energies so that the other approaches will generate maximum value for the investment of time and energy. VRM has been proven to work globally and across a wide array of industries. It does make rigorous benefit calculations but is not dependent upon a rigorous and complete data set to generate results. The best analogy is a medical one where the VRM methodology is like that of a family doctor who can assess and attend to the needs of a wide range of patients and ailments. However, when appropriate, the doctor brings in specialists. VRM practitioners similarly identify and mine value for clients but bring in specialists as required. The author has dedicated nearly sixteen of his thirty-plus years to working with the VRM methodology (and its precursor forms) because it has been found to be so truly powerful and useful.

Key Lessons Learned:

1. Value Realization Methodology is flexible and industry independent.

2. Expressing program initiatives in financial terms understood by C-level executives, the board and the shareholders so as to obtain buy-in and continued support for program initiatives is a frequently overlooked factor critical to project success.

3. VRM allows projects to be selected based on company objectives and strategies. VRM can identify which projects will give the firm the most bang for the buck.

4. VRM helps project leaders determine the best course of action, communicate that course and obtain sustained buy-in from the critical decision makers.

About the Author

Kendall Scheer is an accomplished Supply Chain, Lean and Information Technology professional. He was the 2004-2006 President of the Greater Detroit Chapter of APICS. Kendall's functionally diverse background is three dimensional: as client, vendor and consultant. This provides him a unique perspective to accurately spot realizable and justifiable transformation opportunities spanning multiple functions and varied technologies. Many "in-the trench" implementations taught him how to successfully lead diverse work teams through complex (*e.g.*, multi-site global) transformations in a streamlined and value-based manner.

Chapter Five

How to Start Making Improvements Last: Demystifying Strategy Deployment

David Goodman

Overview

This chapter is intended for everyone who has ever wondered what separates those who achieve great success with improvement initiatives from those that can't make them last. This distinction is critical for all levels of management, from supervisor to senior executive, to understand and use these methods to replace, not add to, the current process of achieving objectives. You will be unable to sustain lasting change unless all levels in a given process are modified to fit the new way of thinking.

This chapter will help you to:

- Define <u>hoshin kanri</u> (aka Strategy Deployment).
- Recognize common pitfalls in applying Lean and Six Sigma to long-term planning.
- Go through the steps to proper Strategy Deployment.
- Recognize challenges that can impede your progress.

Vision, Mission and Strategy Defined

What is the difference between a Vision, Mission and a Strategy? If they all seem similar, don't feel like you are alone. A recent study shows that many of today's business leaders do not have a clear understanding between these concepts, and the gap grows when it comes to effectively communicating those business critical headlines to the staff and company associates: executives (71%), middle managers (40%) and frontline associates (3%). This gap gets wider the larger or more global a company is and can be complicated further by cultural and language barriers. Understanding these definitions is critical before successful deployment across any organization, regardless of size, is possible.

Vision: Where are we going? What do we want to become?

Example: To become the premier, #1 supplier of electronic automotive components in the USA, and eventually, the world.

Mission: What do we do? Where do we play (markets)?

Example: To create quality automotive electrical components for automotive OEM and aftermarket.

Strategy: A detailed plan of *how* we will accomplish the Vision and Mission; how we will win in the marketplace.

Example: We will use product development and operational capabilities to under price our competition while maintaining price margins.

Strategic Planning: The process of developing and maintaining a strategic fit between the organization's goals and capabilities and its changing market opportunities. It involves defining a clear company mission, setting supporting objectives, designing a sound business portfolio, and coordinating functional strategies.

Ultimately, as illustrated in the figure below, to be successful, a series of activities needs to occur to achieve strategic goals. Consider how a plan is developed before it is deployed.

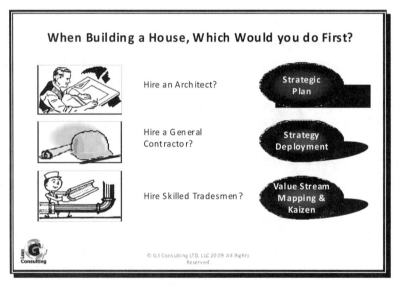

Figure 5-1: Common Sense Strategic Planning

In many instances, businesses employ actions out of sequence. How many times have you started on a path without a clear plan or map of where you want to go? Even if a map does exist, do all those pursuing a particular action know where it is and what it says? It is likely that many, if not most, do not know what or where the top leaders have stated the long- or short-term plan for achieving the company mission or vision.

Strategy Deployment (aka Hoshin Planning or hoshin kanri) is the integration of an organization's strategic and business plans with its vision, mission, value proposition, core competencies, and each individual's annual work plan. It is the process that facilitates the creation of results-orientated business processes with sustained improvements that result in long-term competitive advantages in quality, delivery, cost and growth.

A company's strategic plan and how it deploys its resources to achieve its strategic objectives are key components to its long term success. The first phase of implementing continuous improvement activities consists of performing strategic planning and Strategy Deployment. It is this crucial step that sets the stage for the success of the CI implementation and a company's success.

Why Use Strategy Deployment?

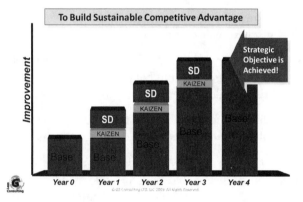

Figure 5-2: How Strategy Deployment Achieves Goals

Strategy Deployment also provides the ability to communicate key strategies to other members and help them ultimately understand how they can make an impact. The same core strategies are clear and remain aligned from the highest to the lowest levels of the organization. It is important to note that a company does not need to pursue Lean programs to implement Strategy Deployment, but the most successful companies use them hand-in-hand to maximize results to their bottom lines.

Symptoms of Typical Organizational Deficiencies

How do you know if your company's strategy is properly aligned and deployed throughout the organization? Can you even tell if things are going wrong? Here are just a few signs you need to look out for:

- The organization has a vision and mission, which serve mostly as the basis for inspirational posters, slogans, wallet cards, pocket protectors, and 'thought of the day' quizzes; all of which constitute non-value-added expenditures and activities.

- There is little or no integration between the organization's vision/mission and its strategic and business plans; little or no integration between the organization's vision/mission and the <u>Key Performance Indicators</u> (KPIs) measured on a daily basis; and little or no integration between the organization's strategic/business plans and the KPI's measured on a daily basis.

- The organization annually generates hundreds of "top priorities," while everyone recognizes the company doesn't actually have the resources to achieve even a fraction of them.

- Many themes within the organization's vision and mission statements are never measured.

- The divisions or departments within the organization can all successfully "hit their numbers," while the organization as a whole fails to make an acceptable profit.

- The organization operates on a "feed the beast" mentality, which assumes that *any* business is superior to *no* business.

- The organization employs standard or average cost accounting procedures to ensure that no one understands what business or processes are truly profitable. (See Chapter 10 for a discussion of Managerial Cost Accounting).

- True versus apparent cost and profit cannot be broken down by flow path, customer, product(s) or any critical component.

- Incentive systems that encourage the sale/production of 'any' units, versus the optimization of 'richness of product mix' sold/produced.

- Using across-the-board headcount reductions to reduce costs.

- Using headcount reductions and capital equipment investments as a first choice – rather than as a last resort – to improve profitability.

There is still a prolific misunderstanding among many organizations and senior managers trying to emulate Toyota's past success. The belief is that simply deploying Lean tools will reap rewards similar to those enjoyed by the Japanese automotive giant. Not so. Many companies already have discovered this simply isn't the case.

What Does Strategy Deployment Mean To You?

How Should You Spend Your Time?

Figure 5-3: SD Time Management

In reality, Toyota's past success derives largely from its planning and execution system. Also called *hoshin kanri*, the Strategy Deployment management system helped Toyota Production Systems remain competitive year after year by keeping the entire organization's eyes and actions focused on achieving the same goals. Other manufacturers and even whole other industries also are reaping the benefits of hoshin planning.

A Focus-Driven Alternative to Traditional Management

Strategy Deployment is a discipline intended to help an organization do several things:

- Focus on a shared goal

- Communicate that goal to all leaders

- Involve all leaders in planning to achieve the goal

- Hold participants accountable for achieving their part of the plan

So what exactly is Strategy Deployment? Broadly speaking, Strategy Deployment aims to formulate clear corporate objectives and goals, disseminating and aligning those objectives throughout all levels of the organization, and then creating plans of action to achieve them.

It's all about focus – separating the trivial problems from the truly important ones – and how they relate to the organization's overall strategy. Do the improvement actions that go on every day relate to your overall strategy? And then, what do you do about them? The process of catchball is a driving force of alignment, clarification and employee involvement. This tool translates strategies into lower-level objectives in a cause-and-effect way and gives clear annual objectives for everyone involved.

Elements of Strategic Deployment

A corporation needs to be able to clearly understand and define its vision and objectives – its need to define its "true north" in a meaningful way. It is critical a firm truly understands who it is and what it believes in.

Key considerations:

- Strategy Deployment is driven by the organization's vision, not today's problems.

- It is a system to translate vision into tangible and measurable objectives for achieving breakthroughs.

- Alignment is created by cross-functional planning to achieve short-term objectives each year.

- Strategy Deployment fosters learning through the review process: You become better planners every cycle.

- The Plan-Do-Check-Act cycle of continuous improvement is at the heart of the process.

The Strategy Deployment process is led by senior leadership but built by middle and lower management. It has two basic components. First, an annual planning process outlines what value streams need to be improved during the next 12 months, what pace of effort will be required to get the work done, and what human resources support is appropriate to achieve those objectives. This process is called "catchball." This is where goals are scrubbed and deployed downward from corporate strategy, and the actual work plans to achieve them are developed at the level where value-adding work is being done. There is some adjusting to ensure that the plan is achievable with the resources committed to it. The annual plan also includes an evaluation of the Lean maturity of the organization and the tasks that must be completed to take this stage of maturation to the next level.

The second component is a monthly meeting. This Strategy Deployment meeting is intended to maintain its focus on improvement. Meeting time is spent reviewing progress against the overall improvement plans in place and is limited to and focused on targets that are *not* being achieved. This is NOT a time set aside for congratulatory pats on the back.

Also fundamental to Strategic Deployment is the <u>PDCA</u> process – on an enterprise-wide scale. PDCA is a four-step problem-solving process, dynamic as it cycles continuously to spur greater improvements. In the *Plan* phase, management must understand its current state and develop a plan to meet its objectives. The *Do* phase translates those plans into actions at each and every organizational level. The *Check* stage involves monitoring and evaluating results against objectives. This phase may be the most difficult in that enterprise failure of PDCA most commonly occurs in this phase. The *Act* phase is about problem solving and improving the entire system.

7-Phase Strategy Deployment Process

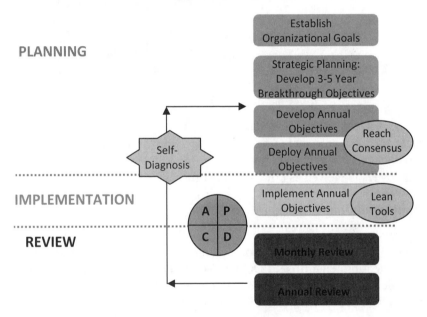

Figure 5-4: Strategy Deployment Cycle

Strategy Deployment review cycles are one of the more important, but most often overlooked, features of the process. Tactical shop floor reviews may occur weekly, while upper-level management reviews occur less frequently. These review processes bring rigor to the management process. For example, at Toyota Material Handling, each functional leader at Toyota has a midterm and an annual hoshin kanri review process for the entire company, as well as for their own areas.

The Critical Thinking Process Behind Strategy Deployment

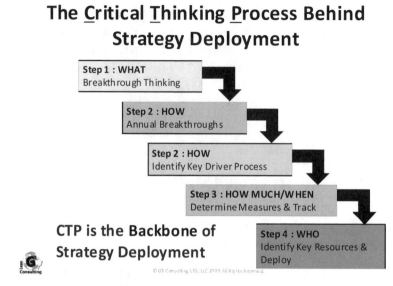

Figure 5-5: CTP – The Backbone of SD

Strategy Deployment does not operate in a "thou shalt" manner. People are not simply told what to do as in conventional planning. Instead, they are engaged in the discussion and decision processes. Participation of all employees is viewed as critical to the process itself.

Implementation Challenges

There are many possible sources of challenges to implementation. Not having enough time is one of the most frequently cited obstacles to implementing enterprise PDCA/Strategy Deployment. Reasons given include too many meetings, too much e-mail, or both. In order to free time for improvement, one key learning point is that managerial work is two-sided: There is routine work – "making the numbers" – and there is improvement work. It's important to consider that there also may be too many feedback loops in the communication process. Leaders need to maintain a balance of routine versus improvement work.

Another pitfall for organizations is the fact that those that fail often do so because they try to maintain the 'old method' in parallel with the new Strategy Deployment. The fact is, the two often conflict and take up to twice the time in an already busy schedule for those who must participate in reviews. Only one of these methods can be used to succeed, and it often requires taking the "leap of faith" that the new method will identify, clarify, assign and track all critical items it needs to address and improve. Historically, the SD method, when used properly, will address all concerns and become the daily method in which all KPI's are tracked and driven.

Additionally, it serves to provide regular communication on the status of improvements to everyone in the organization in a visual manner, to which people better relate. This allows everyone to know the status of their own contribution to helping achieve the annual and long-term targets that ensure business success, job security and long-term growth. The result is a well-informed and involved work force focused on the critical few instead of the trivial many, deftly avoiding islands of success in a sea of waste. In short, SD provides the means for achieving a world class winning team!

Conclusions

In this chapter, we discovered that the SD process is the effective planning process that follows the PDCA improvement cycle and separates those who are capable of making improvements last from those who will see only short-term success accompanied by long-term disappointment. For SD to succeed, your organization must undergo an effective analysis from both a business fundamentals and a strategic planning standpoint. It is imperative to identify the critical few issues facing your organization and select an objective to overcome the issue for a 1-3 year time frame.

Implementing SD entails seven phases. Detailed initiatives at all levels provide guidance and linkage, driving implementation plans. Assign clear responsibility for each item in the implementation plan process. Remember, this is where the real change occurs that aligns everyone in and out of the process. Most processes and projects take multiple resources both internal and external to the actual process. Your team and your project plans should include cross-functional, cross-departmental and cross-process members to ensure the entire realm of possibilities is considered. The team will have extensive discussions within and between departments and ensure process owners and team members are invested, which is vital to the success of implementing improvements that stand the test of time. After these plans have been put into final form as action plans, bowling charts and countermeasures, continually monitor each using your monthly SD review meeting. Any deviations should be highlighted using a standard stop light color pattern on the bowling chart, which also records actions taken based on results. A strategy is completed when the strategic goal is obtained. Our website at *www.g3limited.com* provides free copies of all the SD forms and information on training SD with results-orientated Lean conversions.

The SD process helps an organization learn from both the problems solved and the business successes. This is fundamental to building a Lean learning organization. SD enables an organization to collect and study performance information about itself from both day-to-day and long-term measures. Finally, it helps the organization think about where it is headed and the best way to get there, without having to look in the rear view mirror to find the best way forward.

Key Lessons Learned:

1. Nearly every organization starts with too many metrics.

2. Strategy Deployment is about FOCUS on the critical few, not the trivial many.

3. Strategic Deployment contains the critical few metrics to measure how we are meeting our Annual Improvement Priorities (AIP's).

4. Strategy Deployment makes a distinction between 'Targets' and 'Business Fundamentals.'

5. All other "metrics" that your business prefers to measure would drop to a "Business Fundamentals" listing. We do NOT measure everything in Strategic Deployment.

About the Author

Dave Goodman is a former naval officer commissioned from the University of Michigan, a real-world operations executive and international consultant/Sensei for Fortune 500 companies. He has more than 20 years of experience and has led and been part of world class operations teams that have achieved the *Shingo Prize* for Manufacturing Excellence, *Industry Week Magazine's* America's Ten Best Plants Award, Automotive News PACE awards, and the U.S. Senate Productivity and Quality Award. He was formally trained by Shingijutsu and honed his skills with the Danaher Business System, where SD is used to drive the business and continuous improvements that have made Danaher into an organization that is highly regarded as one of the best in the world.

Chapter Six

Proven Solutions for Success in Health Care: From the Eyes of an Operational Manager

Sheree Lavelle

Overview

This chapter is intended for health care managers, executives and Lean Six Sigma sponsors and project leaders who are interested in learning how to eliminate waste without jeopardizing quality in health care. There is a focus on the human side, often neglected but necessary for making changes that not only last, but show respect for the workers involved. It is time to put the heart back into Lean Six Sigma.

The economy is forcing changes in health care because the system cannot sustain the rise in costs that have occurred in the past. Currently at 16% of GDP, the Congressional Budget Office is predicting this percentage will nearly double over the next 25 years – to 31% of GDP. Despite the prevailing belief that health care in the United States is the best in the world, studies show major quality deficits and startling differences in outcomes.[1] Clearly, this is a wake-up call that health care systems need to eliminate waste while improving quality – a situation that is a perfect fit for Lean Six Sigma methodologies.

We present the practical strategic and methodological framework through two case examples: one in the clinical setting and one in the hospital. These examples are typical in health care, and the improvements were successful and duplicable.

This chapter will help you to:

- Learn basic rules in laying a foundation for improvement in a health care organization.
- Understand how Lean and Six Sigma work best together.
- Realize the people-side of process improvement is as important as the tools.
- Consider projects in your health care organization with ideas from the case studies presented.

Seven Basic Rules to Implement before Starting Lean Six Sigma

1. It's got to start at the top.

Not only does it have to start at the top with buy-in, but senior executives must have ongoing involvement in the process to deliver consistent, repeated, and obvious support for the project, and make it clear to everyone in the organization that the changes are part of the new way forward. This gives the implementers the "air support" from above to make those difficult choices and changes, and it works to change the mindsets of those who don't buy in immediately. Often, consultants will make a presentation that demonstrates how applying Lean and Six Sigma can reduce costs by at least 30% and improve service delivery time by even more. There are many examples of this in the literature from top companies that have started Lean Six Sigma programs: GM, Lockheed-Martin and Stanford University Hospital, to name a few. This might be enough for executives to get on board, but participation and support from the physicians is critical and more challenging. You must be ready and able to demonstrate how improvement projects will benefit both doctors and patients.

2.   Hire consultants that begin by teaching Change Management.

It is impossible to make the changes necessary for lasting improvement when employees are stuck in the mindset of "this is the way we've always done it." Even if you are able to convince them to try a new process, it won't be sustainable. They will think of a thousand ways to impede it without a proper Change Management education component. It's like teaching an adult to swim the breast stroke when all they ever knew was how to dog paddle: In times of crisis, the person will revert to what they know best, even if they know they won't survive long.

3.   Hire consultants with expertise in both Lean and Six Sigma.

Lean is a continuous improvement methodology designed to eliminate waste from a process in order to increase process speed and improve quality. Six Sigma is a continuous improvement methodology using data and statistical analysis tools with a focus on reducing defects and variation. Lean, by itself, cannot bring a process under statistical control. On the other hand, Six Sigma does not provide the tools for analyzing process flow and delay times at each activity in the process. Lean will focus on velocity in the process, separating value-added from non-value-added work while getting to the root causes of non-value-added work.[2] Six Sigma will show how to recognize opportunities and eliminate defects with an emphasis on quality and Voice of the Customer (See Chapter 16 on VOC). Six Sigma has better statistical tools to help data-driven decision making and a framework for effective problem solving. Marrying these two methodologies provides the speed of Lean with the systematic analytical abilities offered by Six Sigma. This produces better solutions. It's a one-two punch strategy for reducing process problems and identifying viable solutions.

4. Hand-pick your first group of employees to train in the process.

Look for those informal leaders in your company. They might not be the directors or managers – although you need them involved too – but look for the people that employees admire and respect most. These are the people that others want to follow; they are the Pied Pipers of the group that will validate your efforts and form the foundation for long-term change throughout the organization. Change is difficult for many people, but if they see a colleague they believe in embracing it, they are far more likely to get on board.

5. Go for the low-hanging fruit first.

You need a few success stories early on in the process to inspire employees and management. Managers and directors have a sense of processes that they know need improvement, either because they have had customers complain, they have lost market share, or other departments have noticed the waste. As the saying goes, success breeds success. When you have early success stories, get those stories out to *everyone* in the organization. Use all of your various communication methods to make sure everyone hears about it.

6. Decide on a process to use for choosing which projects to take on, how many, and in what order.

Your consultant should help with this task. Six Sigma Black Belts can expertly identify and prioritize projects that will maximize value. Ask the consultant to assist with a "readiness scan" of the organization so that you can identify any potential roadblocks that might impede progress and take preventative steps to avoid them.[3] As you put your process into action, be realistic about how many projects you can take on in a single year. Don't hammer away at just one department. Don't burn out your best people. When big changes are made, people will always need some time to adjust and recover before taking on another project.

7. Make the commitment to terminal process improvement.

Some people in the organization may see this process as the latest management craze and assume that if they sit and do nothing, it will go away in a year. Don't let that happen; eliminating waste and improving process functions are not fads. The truth is that any business that wants to *stay in business* for the next decade must continually look at processes, ways to improve those processes, and methods to eliminate waste.

<u>A Typical Story</u>

The real-life case study we will use to demonstrate the application of LSS involves XYZ HealthCare as they implemented several Lean Six Sigma projects. One of the projects in the clinic involved nurses changing to a new standard process. During the trial week, one of the nurses broke down in tears, saying that she could not do it. Each day, she had a different excuse as to why she could not comply with the changes, and the project manager insisted she had to try. Finally, one of her co-workers convinced her to "play along," assuring her that after the team left, they could go back to doing things the old way.

Sound familiar? This is what happens when organizations focus solely on the technical/process-side and not on the people-side of process improvement. This study addresses relationship building and how to work with the people affected by the changes you want to implement.

Case One – Improve Patient Flow in the Clinic

We've all been there: You have a clinic appointment and arrive in the waiting room, check in with the receptionist and sit down to wait. It could be five minutes or it could be 20, you never know. You pick up last year's magazine to pass the time. Finally, your name is called. The nurse takes you back to an examination room, gets your weight, takes your vitals, goes through your history, and asks a few questions. She gives you a gown and leaves. You change and wait. And wait. Enough time passes that you start snooping around the room, opening drawers and doors, wondering if you'll get caught or bored first. The doctor finally arrives and asks the same questions the nurse already asked. Finally, you get the care you came for and you're done, but the total process took an hour and a half.

The question is: why is there so much wait time in health care? For unknown reasons, the healthcare industry has gotten away with treating customers poorly. If customers had to wait like that for any other service, clinics wouldn't stay in business long.

In most cases, the top reason why we have to wait so long (non-value-added for the customer) is that no one in the clinic has taken the time to study the process. However, by applying Lean technology, XYZ HealthCare was able to reduce patient wait time by 25% and add 20% more patient volume. This improved customer satisfaction and increased revenue for the clinic.

Initially, you want to make sure that you have people from the targeted department involved on the team. Start by gathering data: Nothing speaks louder to clinicians and nurses than data. Yogi Berra said, "You can observe a lot just by watching." This step is all about watching and observing. To begin the process, follow and time the patients with a stopwatch. Record how much time patients spend at check in, in the waiting room, with the nurse in the exam room, wait time before the doctor arrives, and how much doctor time is spent with the patient. Record the type of visit – whether it was a well visit, problem visit (and type), or a return visit. Gather enough timing samples that you can identify a pattern. Draw out the <u>value stream map</u> for each type of visit to show each step in the process and write in the average time each step takes (Figure 6-1).

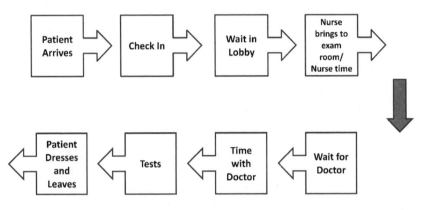

Figure 6-1: Patient Flow Value Stream Map (XYZ HealthCare)

Next, observe all of the workers involved with the process. Start where the patients start – with the receptionists. Look to see if all of the receptionists are following standard work procedures (the same agreed-upon "best practice" process) for the check-in. Did they have the information they needed for each patient at their work station, or if not, where did they have to walk to and how far? Time every step and draw out these steps if they left their desk. Follow the same process with the nurses. Ask all people involved in the process for their ideas to eliminate the wasted time, make the process more efficient, and provide the patient better quality services.

Take a good look at your exam rooms. Are they standard – all arranged the same way? Were they stocked the same and did they have everything they needed in the room? How many times did a nurse or clinician have to leave the room to get something that wasn't there and how long did that take? Talk to the clinicians and ask them what they believe would make them more efficient. Find out if they could agree on standard work for some of the top problems. Look at their schedules and hours to see if they are working the hours specified in their agreements. By involving employees in the problem-solving process, you empower them to be a part of the changes that will ultimately be implemented and give them a sense of ownership over the solutions. This goes a long way toward participant acceptance.

Enter all the data into the statistical tool sets you have chosen. Brainstorm a list of ideas that the team believes would make the greatest improvements and try them for one week. Following is a list of quick-hit ideas we found in one clinic, which made the process flow more smoothly, reduced wait time for patients, and allowed for more appointment slots:

- In looking at clinician schedules, we noted that not all of them were working the agreed-upon hours. By enforcing compliance, several appointment slots were added.

- Clinicians need to stagger their start times so patients don't all arrive at the same time and create a bottleneck in reception.

- Create a template for the clinicians' schedules that has a certain number of slots for long appointments and short appointments each day. Varying this mix creates better flow and less wait times for patients when clinicians get behind.

- Reorganize and standardize the exam rooms so everything is in the same place in each room. Label the drawers and cabinets by contents and standardize the amount of supplies.

- Standardize the check-in process (script it out) and see how it could be made more efficient. Something as simple as adding a fax machine may save valuable time and steps.

- Create standard work for the nursing process and make sure that the information they need to access is conveniently located for retrieval by the doctor.

- Ask for ideas from all of the people involved in the process.

Finally, it is critical that one person on the team who has the best managerial skills is designated to work with the employees who are having a difficult time coping with the changes. There is bound to be at least one person, or possibly more, who resists the new process. The team is busy with the tools, graphs, tables, and numbers and doesn't have the time to deal with "resisters." Unfortunately, time not spent dealing with these people will come back to haunt you later, because they will continue to resist even after the team is gone, and the chances for lasting improvement will be diminished. Ask these employees what, in their perspective, inhibits their compliance with the proposed changes and what they feel would make compliance more acceptable for them. Verbalize your understanding back to them and ask questions until it is clear that you do understand their perspective.

Work your way up from that point the same way, explaining and clarifying the new process and the benefits to the patients, the department and the organization as a whole. Continue this dialogue until everyone agrees that the new process is better than the old one. Finally, ask if there is anything they can think of that would prevent them from doing the new process. Together, come up with a plan to deal with any obstacles.

Once you've erased the "us against them" factor, your entire staff will be on the same side. Although this process does take time, the payback comes not only from having a cohesive team effort, but from greatly increased odds that the new process will stick in the future.

One benefit that is not always obvious is increased morale. When employees feel heard, understood, and see the benefit of process improvement, they will become cheerleaders for those improvements across the organization. The talk that goes on under the radar has far-reaching effects. If employees feel they are forced into changes they don't agree with, the organization will end up wasting valuable time trying to figure out why people are resisting and why the process improvements are not lasting. Lean Six Sigma needs to have heart.

Case 2 – Savings in Surgery

There is a list of tools, instruments and supplies in the surgery department that go on a case-cart for every type of surgery. As new physicians join a group, they usually add their own list of instruments and supplies particular to their needs, so the list grows. Often, after physicians leave the hospital's employment, no one is responsible for taking their items off the case-cart because they don't know who else might be using them. All of these instruments and supplies need to be subjected to a rigorous sterilization process, which takes time and manpower.

For one project, a team chose five different types of surgeries to study. Once again, start by gathering data: How many surgeries are performed and how often? Who performs them? You need to study the items on the case-cart list and take it to the person who fills the case cart. Observe her or him filling the carts for each of these five surgeries on multiple occasions, timing every step with a stop watch.

Create spaghetti charts that map out the steps each person takes to gather their supplies. To create a spaghetti chart, begin by sketching a floor plan of the work area. As the employee walks to each area to obtain supplies, draw a line showing their movement. As the employee continues, the chart will begin to look like spaghetti. This chart is then used to streamline the workflow. (Fig. 5-2)

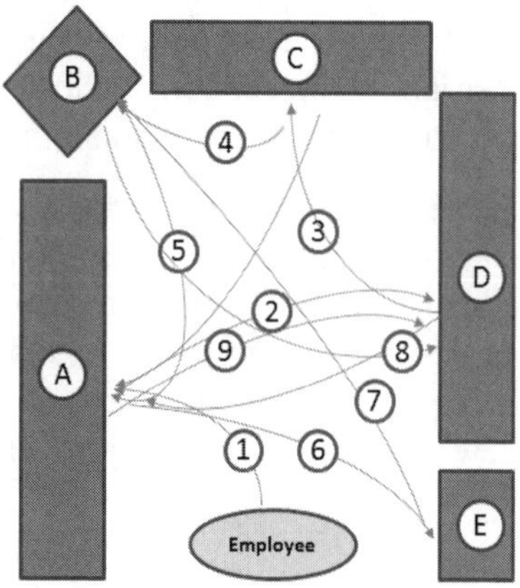

Figure 5-2: Spaghetti Chart

The next step involves actually going into the surgical suites. Dress in surgical scrubs, follow the procedure for observers in the surgical suites and follow the cart into the surgical room. Watch the surgery and write down all the items that were used for each of the surgeries. Observe these surgeries with each of the physicians several times to ensure reliable findings.

In our case study, the team found that each of the five surgeries had an average of 100 items in the case-cart. The amount of items actually used during any of the surgeries observed was less than 20, regardless of which doctor was performing the surgery. The team called a meeting with the doctors performing those surgeries and told them that the case-cart would be reduced to those 20 items. They made a list of the items and informed the physicians that if they wanted to discuss the improved case-cart, they needed to come the meeting. The physicians came. A few items were added to the list, along with some specialty items that would be placed in a "just-in-time" cart. The just-in-time-cart was to be located immediately outside the door and contained items that were rarely used, but if needed, would be needed right away.

The cost and time savings realized were significant. The reductions affected several areas and many people – workers who filled the cart; those who needed to wash, sterilize, and package the instruments; and the people who had to keep track of the supply, the storage space, etc. The team also reorganized the supply room so that items needed for most common surgeries were located in the same bins. This is an excellent example of the benefits of Lean Six Sigma practice and can easily be replicated with any type of surgery.

A control plan should be in place to make sure that these gains stick. Sometimes, after a project like this ends, some physicians will work deals behind the scenes with surgery center nurses to hide instruments they still want to use, despite their verbal agreement to use standard instruments. The control plan needs to be structured and closely monitored to make it difficult for the process to revert back.

Finally, it is always good to take the time to celebrate the close of each project. Coordinate a monthly event showcasing the projects and have the teams responsible present their success stories. Invite all employees to this "story-telling" time and make sure to have someone record the event so the stories can be communicated to all employees who are not able to attend.

Conclusions

Service organizations such as health care are new to implementing processes like Lean Six Sigma. Initially, it can be difficult to figure out how and where to begin to incorporate this process, which was originally designed for manufacturing and assembly lines. The seven basic rules outlined herein will aid in laying the right foundation for process improvement change. The case studies described provide just two ideas for some basic processes you can start with in any clinic or hospital and have been proven to produce positive results. By focusing on relationship building and by paying attention to the people-side of Lean Six Sigma, projects will flow more smoothly and produce lasting changes. You will build mutual respect between all involved. This will result in enthusiasm for improvement among employees, a key factor in successful organizations. For additional ideas on where to start implementing Lean Six Sigma, visit *http://lavelleandassociatesllc.com* for a free White Paper on how to coax Lean non-believers into believers. Other helpful websites are listed below.

Key Lessons Learned

1. Lay the groundwork for a successful foundation by teaching Change Management at the front end.

2. Invest sufficient time to get buy-in from the physicians, managers and informal leaders by showing them the benefit to the patients and to themselves.

3. Make sure the people involved in the process are part of the improvement team. Use their ideas and have them make a solid team commitment to carry the changes forward.

4. Celebrate the close of the project and lock in the gains with a control plan that makes it impossible for the process to revert back.

5. Paying close attention to the people-side of change will not only enhance the odds of success but will do it less painfully for the staff and for the organization.

About the Author

Sheree Lavelle, MS, earned her bachelor's degree in Social Work and her master's in Public & Human Service Administration at Minnesota State University-Moorhead. She is a Six Sigma Black Belt and earned her certification in Lean by successfully completing the Global Production System Japan Gembe Kaizen program in Japan. Sheree has more than 20 years of experience as an Operational Manager in both clinic and hospital settings. Currently, she is president of Lavelle and Associates, LLC, a consulting firm specializing in Lean Six Sigma Process Improvement, where her unique skills in relationship building increase the odds of successful project implementation. For more information or to contact Sheree in person, visit her website at *http://lavelleandassociatesllc.com*.

Acknowledgements

The author acknowledges John Black and his associates for their teaching and guidance with the Lean certification track at Park Nicollet Health Services, Minneapolis, MN, and Ted Wegleitner, VP, for his steadfast support and encouragement of his managers throughout the entire certification process.

---

[1] A. Kabcenell and D. Berwick, "Pursuing Perfection in Healthcare," *Six Sigma Forum Magazine*, 1(3) (2002): 18-22.
[2] H. DeKoning and others, "Lean Six Sigma in Healthcare," *Journal for Healthcare Quality* (March/April 2006).
[3] M. George, *Lean Six Sigma for Service*. (New York: McGraw-Hill, 2003), 185-196.

Methodology

Historical methodology, as I see it, is a product of common sense applied to circumstances.

– Samuel E. Morrison

Chapter Seven

Daily Management: The Foundation for High-Performance Organizations

David Dubinsky

Overview

This chapter is intended for business leaders, managers and anyone else who is serious about driving extraordinary performance in their business. Organizations that are interested in making significant advancement in their journey toward Operational Excellence and Lean will resonate with and find great value in the depth and breadth of these methods proposed. We will outline a comprehensive management and improvement system that is on steroids compared to what other businesses have in place today.

This chapter will help you to:

- Discover the 10 foundational methods of a Daily Management system;
- Evaluate the effectiveness of your current Daily Management System; and
- Create extraordinary passion for and commitment to dramatic improvement via change management.

Introduction: Building a Case for Change

Regardless of the business or occupation you are in, the speed at which we all must change and relentlessly improve is dramatically increasing every year. Simply coping with the increasing pace and complexity of performance demands is simply no longer good enough. A coping strategy will just put you farther behind the competition, and ultimately, in last place with respect to your competitors.

A critical analysis of the highest performing organizations and individuals most often reveals an uncompromising attention to the basics:

- driving to a set of performance goals;
- measuring performance against those goals;
- taking proactive action to resolve issues and make improvements quickly; and
- increasing performance expectations once targets are met.

Most organizations and individuals apply these methods to some degree already, but very few have a comprehensive and integrated system with the level of rigor and aggressiveness needed to drive impactful and sustainable results on a daily basis. It's like comparing someone who works out in the gym a few times per week versus an Olympic athlete who trains rigorously every day with extreme focus, attention to detail and a set of actions specifically designed to improve their daily performance.

A friend of mine started competing in triathlons two years ago. After a year of exercising and training, he entered the Chicago triathlon and placed in the 50th percentile for his age. This was a great accomplishment for anyone competing in their first triathlon. After an additional year of aggressive training and dieting, he placed in the 80th percentile. This year, he plans to do even better. However, when you compare his performance to professional athletes, there is still a huge difference.

In the case of business, if you are in the top 20%, it's not necessarily that bad, but it's not that great either. If you rest on your laurels, it's quite easy to drop back to the middle of the pack, placing your business in jeopardy. Alternatively, if you don't manage your performance aggressively and change what you are doing, you will never compete at the highest levels. Companies that are extremely mature in their Lean or Operational Excellence journey are likely competing at the highest levels in their market. The critical questions you must ask yourself include:

1. How much more competitive do you *need* to be to:

    a. reach and/or compete with the highest performing competitors in your market?

    b. sustain your current position in the market to remain viable?

2. How competitive do you *want* to be?

In most cases, I will reference the application of daily management to an organization. However, daily management is just as easily applied at an individual level.

Daily Management Introduction and Framework

Whether you are a healthcare provider, service organization or manufacturing facility, having a mindset of doing only what is necessary to get by perpetuates a reduction in competitiveness and puts businesses at risk. This approach results in constant firefighting that escalates year after year as competition increases. To achieve truly extraordinary levels of performance, organizations need a strategically aligned and culturally driven daily management and improvement system that quickly identifies and resolves the most critical improvement needs of the business.

Organizations focused on driving Operational Excellence and/or Lean use many of the tools and processes proposed in this chapter that make up a robust Daily Management system. However, most often it's only the highest performing organizations that apply them in as comprehensive, integrated and rigorous a manner as outlined here.

The tools and processes needed to deploy Daily Management (shown on page 90) can be broken down into ten areas.

1. **Business Strategy:** The business strategy defines the critical initiatives required to realize the business' objectives and goals. Many organizations have a business strategy in place, but it is often outdated and fails to incorporate any linkage to actual daily work. The objectives and goals of the business should be clear and aggressive, as well as realistic. A clear, realistic sense of urgency provides a focused call to action and the required backbone for any continuous improvement effort.

2. **Goal Deployment:** A clear vision and strategy enable organizational performance goals and key performance indicators (KPI) to be established. These goals and KPIs are then deployed down through each successive organizational level and then to each individual. This is done to ensure that there is clarity and alignment of performance expectations across the organization.

3. **Daily & Weekly Performance Measurement Dashboards:** Performance dashboards are created for each department. Typically, one or sometimes two of the most critical KPIs per performance category are selected for each department. Below are example performance categories for various industries:

Manufacturing	Safety	Performance	Quality	Delivery	Cost
Healthcare	Safety	Quality	Equipment	Access	Cost
Service	Safety	Service	Quality	Customer	Cost

Each department's daily and weekly dashboards have customized performance charting that is fine-tuned to optimize visual control as well as to ensure the charting is easily updated and maintained. The daily performance board information is updated at least daily and reviewed at least once per day during action planning meetings to drive continuous improvement efforts. The dashboards include effective at-a-glance charting of the performance results for each indicator, a supporting <u>pareto chart</u> to indicate performance losses, and an action plan for improvement. An example of a performance indicator chart is shown in Figure 7-1 for the equipment performance category. In this example, we can see the performance trend is improving. However, individual analysis of each work center may show that one or two work centers cause the greatest reactive downtime.

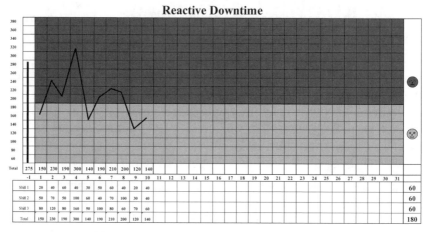

Figure 7-1: Performance Indicator Chart

4. **Daily Action Planning Meetings:** The daily action planning meeting is a short, 5- to 10-minute meeting to quickly uncover performance issues and decide who will take action to prevent recurrence. This is not a finger-pointing meeting or a gripe session. The meeting is all about quickly identifying where the department did not meet performance goals, quickly understanding the apparent or root cause of the issue, and assigning someone to be responsible to identify, eliminate and/or mitigate the effects of the root cause.

5. **Problem Solving & Decision Making:** As part of the daily improvement process and action planning meetings, area teams need to understand and apply, at an appropriate level, critical thinking skills and tools to understand:

- How to separate and distill performance concerns into well-defined actions;
- How to clearly specify problems and identify the most probable causes;

- How to make the best balanced decisions based on clear objectives; and
- How to prevent failure and mitigate negative consequences as a result of taking any particular action.

These skills are the foundation of any high performance organization.

6. **Daily Operational Tours:** Every leader in the organization should perform daily tours or scans of their operations, *i.e.*, Gemba walks. These scans are highly customized for each leader and are substantially different for executives than they are for first-line supervision. The primary focus for executives is to ensure the Daily Management system is implemented correctly and is effective. For front-line supervision, the primary focus is on assessing and taking action in areas that affect the day-to-day performance of their business. However, regardless of the management level, these scans include the people, processes, systems, materials, equipment and environmental conditions that are most critical or problematic for each leader's area of responsibility. The purpose is to ensure that each leader's team is set for success each day, and that they take proactive steps to address the concerns identified during the scan.

7. **Short Interval Performance Boards:** The short interval performance boards (hour-by-hour boards) are a critical part of the daily management system (Figure 7-2). These boards drive personal accountability for performance targets and initiate real-time performance improvement throughout the day when targets or process/performance standards are not met. These boards are highly customized based on the operation being measured. Processes that are more repetitive and transaction-oriented, with numerous transactions per hour, can be measured on an hourly basis. Work that is not repetitive or transactional may be measured in longer blocks of time, *e.g.*, 4 to 8 hours. Regardless of the operation or process, performance standards/expectations can be established and visually tracked to drive greater accountability and shorter improvement cycles.

For example, in a hospital emergency department you could track the number of patients served per hour based on the number of on-duty staff; or in a school, the percentage of daily curriculum covered per class against the plan. To ensure short interval performance is not overemphasized to the detriment of other performance areas, it's necessary to have a balanced set of performance indicators on your performance dashboard.

Short Interval Performance Board			

Process:_____ Date:_____ Shift:_____

Time Range		Performance		Cause and Action
		Target Perf.	Actual Perf.	
7:30	8:30	85	80	Lost 10 min on Set-up....Improve 5S
8:30	9:30	85	90	
9:30	10:30	85	93	
10:30	11:30	85	75	Roller failure lost 15 min...Called technician to fix and analyze root cause
11:30	12:30	85	70	Changed roller and updated PM process...Lost 15 min
12:30	13:30	85	90	
13:30	14:30	85	85	
14:30	15:30	85	80	Received bad material lost 10 min...contacted supervisor
15:30	16:30	85	75	Supervisor resolving material issue upstream
16:30	17:30	85	70	Supervisor resolved material issue upstream...reworked lot...lost 35 min total
17:30	18:30	85	90	
18:30	19:30	85	85	
Total		1020	983	

Figure 7-2: Short Interval/Hour-by-Hour Board

8. **Coaching & Development:** Coaching and development of the leadership is the lynch pin that ensures effective implementation of the system. Executive leaders in the organization typically require guidance on the actions and behaviors needed to demonstrate their commitment to the system and resolve barriers to change. Middle managers, supervisors, and support staff are also coached on the actions and behaviors they must drive to support the area teams in the processes and culture needed to effectively apply daily management. These include: how to provide effective one-on-one coaching; how to design and enforce process standards; how to communicate and build consensus with their teams; and how to effectively instill accountability, motivate their team

members and drive continuous improvement using the system. Through these coaching interventions and specific training sessions, knowledge and skills are developed across the organization to successfully design, implement and execute the daily management system.

9. **Performance Management Architecture:** Performance Management Architecture guides the design of the Daily Management system. This system includes all of the necessary building blocks to ensure that each person's environment, performance requirements, personal capabilities, measurement system, reward system and feedback channels are well designed and function as intended to drive the desired behavior, performance and improvement. The critical elements of this system include the assessment, design and implementation of the following for each person in the organization:

- Environment: Clear performance expectations, capable processes and tools, and a clean, safe work environment

- Individual: Capability of the individual to perform as desired

- Measurement: Measuring and assessing performance achieved

- Rewards: Positive and negative rewards that drive the desired behavior and performance

- Feedback: Appropriateness, timeliness and effectiveness of the feedback to the individual

10. **Guiding Principles:** The guiding principles are customized to the Operational Excellence or Lean culture of the organization. However, common guiding principles include: the relentless elimination of waste; "do it right the first time"; maintain a customer focus; and consistently practice open and honest communication. These guiding principles and others are the foundation of an organization's culture that is focused on driving Operational Excellence throughout the entire business. A well-defined foundation of Operational Excellence guiding principles is essential to drive the organization's behavior to support and sustain an aggressive Daily Management System.

Figure 7-3: Daily Management System Framework

Daily Management Assessment

It's likely that each of the areas described in the Daily Management framework are already established and practiced in your organization to some degree. However, there are several questions you need to answer honestly to gauge their effectiveness.

1. Does everyone at all levels of the organization understand the operating objectives and end-state vision of the business and how they personally contribute to achieving them?

2. Do performance measurement boards support rapid, at-a-glance understanding of daily and weekly performance that relates to the operating objectives?

3. Are your area teams taking ownership of driving real-time improvements to ensure that hourly and daily performance targets are met?

4. Are support staff, supervisors and executive management spending time in work areas throughout the business with hands-on coaching and roll-up-your-sleeves, just-do-it activities?

5. Do your leaders visibly and consistently demonstrate commitment towards driving relentless daily improvement?

6. Does the organization live by a clear set of guiding principles that align the organization to focus on standard work, continuous improvement, capability development and accountability?

7. Do the performance measurement and reward systems drive the desired behaviors and performance results of each and every person in the organization?

8. Does the business routinely resolve problems down to the root cause level via a common and effective approach that results in no recurrence?

If you are unable to give many positive responses to these questions, your organization is probably struggling with how to improve in a coherent fashion to meet urgent customer and business needs.

Creating Passion and Commitment to Improve

The reality is that the regimens of an outstanding athlete or a world-class organization are fairly easy to understand technically, but extremely difficult to put into practice every day. In an organization, the dynamics of people and culture must be aligned and a daunting level of discipline developed to sustain and continually improve performance. These challenges are the soft side of the Daily Management solution.

To successfully implement Daily Management, you must concentrate your efforts on soft solutions as much as or more than the technical solutions. Quite often we see the emphasis placed on the technical parts of a solution because that is the easiest to understand, measure and control. A focus on technical solutions with little emphasis on soft solutions is a mistake many companies make. At best, this results in a Daily Management system that is technically correct, but in reality, the organization is just going through the motions. Results may be achieved, but they will likely be piecemeal and eventually backslide. It means the difference between intermittent compliance versus true passion instilled in every member of the organization. Which would you prefer? Which will deliver the greatest and most sustainable results?

To create rock-solid commitment for driving continuous improvement, your approach should include passion, involvement and a systematic approach to managing change.

Passion: The will, focus and drive to relentlessly improve and differentiate average performers from true operational excellence leaders. A passion to drive not just ordinary – but *extraordinary* – improvement on a continuous basis must be felt and lived by the majority of people in the organization in order to see truly remarkable results. This passion must start at the highest executive levels of the organization. The executive leadership is then responsible for energizing everyone else in the organization with the same level of passion, focus and drive.

Involvement: Team members must be given the opportunity to inject their own DNA into the Daily Management system by reaching consensus on issues and designing solutions to resolve them. Through involvement, team members not only align themselves with the issues, but have a personal ownership over the detailed solutions. Once someone is vested in the solution, they are more likely to work hard to ensure the implementation is successful.

Change Management: There are several critical attributes to managing change that must be addressed throughout the Daily Management implementation. An effective implementation must be supported by actions that address the following factors:

Need: Create a burning need for repeatable, daily excellence that each and every team member feels. The pain of living with the status quo must be greater than the pain of changing. Most people don't like to change, especially when implementing a system like daily management that may be measuring and driving employee/department performance for the first time. Creating a sense of urgency and compelling need to implement daily management is required to convince everyone how important it is to the business' long-term competitiveness, and ultimately, everyone's job security.

Vision: Establish and communicate a future-state vision aligned with the Daily Management system that everyone internalizes and for which they clearly understand their personal contribution. People need to understand what the business wants to achieve. They also need to understand what they must personally do and precisely for what they are accountable. Once achieved, each person can then personally align their heart, mind and actions to what the business is asking them to do.

Means: Provide individuals with the knowledge, skills and abilities (KSA) to successfully execute and implement the Daily Management system. Also, provide the time, resources and money required to get the job done. Understanding and agreeing with the business need and vision is not enough if people feel they don't have the KSAs to do what the business is asking. The organization must give each person an opportunity to develop their KSAs to help them feel that they will be able to do what they are being asked. Without the proper KSAs, people will resist implementing Daily Management. In addition, if people feel that they are not given the time, money or manpower necessary to implement daily management, they also will resist implementation.

Measures and Rewards: Design and implement performance measurement and rewards that drive the Daily Management system. To drive the desired behavior and performance at all levels in the business, these performance measures and rewards need to be aligned from the executive suite all the way down to the individual contributor.

Communication: Reinforce open and honest communication with effective channels that promote bottom-up, top-down and cross-organizational exchange of information on a timely basis.

Leadership: Develop and reinforce high levels of leadership commitment towards Daily Management through visible actions and behaviors.

Risk: Understand and address any risks associated with the Daily Management system and the problem-solving and improvement initiatives that come out of it.

Momentum: Ensure that sufficient momentum is built for the Daily Management system to create early enthusiasm and results that are continuous and sustainable.

Capacity: Assess and address the organization's level of daily work and improvement initiative demand versus the organization's capacity to implement all of the initiatives and normal operating requirements of the business.

Involvement: Determine the level of involvement offered to key stakeholders and process owners during the design and implementation process. Ensure that each person has the opportunity to incorporate their own DNA into the design and implementation efforts.

These soft engineering efforts, combined with effective technical designs and solutions, dramatically improve Daily Management implementation. Within six to nine months, this hybrid approach can deliver sustainable, double-digit improvements regardless of the industry or operation. Below are examples showing the typical results of applying daily management in healthcare and general industry over a 6 to 9 month period.

Healthcare

- 10-20% improvement in productivity and/or patient face time

- 10-25% improvement in equipment uptime and room availability/utilization

- 20-50% reduction in nursing, physician and/or ancillary service errors

- 20-40% reduction in length of stay

- 3-7% reduction in operating costs

Industrial

- 10-20% improvement in total productivity or throughput

- 10-25% improvement in equipment effectiveness

- 20-50% reduction in operator errors

- 20-40% improvement in on-time delivery performance

- 3-7% reduction in operating costs

Conclusions

In your journey to world-class performance, Daily Management can refocus your energies on the technical, operational, managerial and cultural attributes that create a sustainable step-change in performance improvement. The need for this integrated approach increases as the levels of sophistication and competition in your markets increase. Furthermore, organizations that aggressively drive daily management will be better equipped to do more with less and do it more effectively than they ever have before. This new level of performance places organizations in a much stronger and more profitable position to better weather any economic or competitive situation. Few industry leaders can achieve and sustain their leadership position without a high performing Daily Management system. The business environment is just too competitive to take a passive approach to managing daily performance.

For additional information on how to implement Daily Management, visit *www.op-excellence.com*. Op-Excellence can provide a no-cost, no obligation design review of your daily management system to identify the improvement opportunities and impact that exists in your organization to improve your Daily Management system.

Key Lessons Learned

1. The passion and commitment to implement Daily Management must be driven from the top. Effectiveness is commensurate with the level of passion and commitment demonstrated by executive leadership.

2. Daily Management is more of a people solution than a technical solution. Once you gain everyone's commitment and interest to improve, measuring and making improvement becomes much easier and more enjoyable.

3. To maximize value, you must approach your design and implementation of Daily Management much in the same way an Olympic athlete would train to optimize their performance. This requires extraordinary discipline, tenacity and attention to detail every hour of the day.

About the Author

David Dubinsky is the president of Op-Excellence, a management consulting and Lean transformation services firm. David has provided Operations Excellence consulting, coaching and transformation services over the past 20 years in the areas of: Operations Strategy, Lean Manufacturing, Six Sigma, Maintenance Management, Business Process Re-engineering, Change Management and Organizational Development. Each of the transformations David has led focused on delivering high-impact results that meet five distinctive criteria:

- a 20% or greater reduction in conversion cost;

- double-digit improvements in lead time reduction, inventory reduction, quality improvements, overall equipment effectiveness improvements and/or productivity improvements;

- development of an internal operations excellence improvement team;

- creation of a robust continuous improvement culture; and

- at least a 5-10x return on investment.

For more information about the author or Op-Excellence, visit *www.op-excellence.com* or e-mail David at *ddubinsky@op-excellence.com*.

Chapter Eight

Change Management Street Smarts

Jeff Cole

Overview

In these brutal economic times, the rules have changed. What our text books taught us years ago didn't necessarily foresee the extent to which America's workforce has been stretched thin. Hourly fears of job security and layoff survivors being overwhelmed by the work left behind from fallen comrades is the order of the day. Global markets are churning, and the corporate landscape is seismically shifting before our eyes. A key to personal or organizational survival and advancement lies in mastering core fundamentals of organizational change. Some say that's 80% of the battle in DMAIC projects.

This chapter is dedicated to the people in charge of making improvement happen: the CEO, executives, department managers, Six Sigma Belts, Lean facilitators, and the floor supervisor. Each of these people play a role in managing change in the organization, and the tactics and tips presented here are applicable to each and every one of you.

This chapter will help you to:

- Get a clear understanding of why you must attend to the human side of any process change.
- Use the nine strategic and tactical tips to address the human side of change in a Six Sigma effort.
- Learn how to get a group of people who don't report to you to change their behavior and use your process.

Why aren't people using the new process?

Leo was puzzled. Last month's meeting seemed to go very well; he had been invited in to show all the managers the process changes made by his project team. They all seemed friendly enough, smiled and said they understood the new process. By now, everyone should have changed, but the reports showed only a few people were actually following Leo's new process. He was very curious about how things had gone so wrong.

Leo is not alone. The harsh reality is that you or I can come up with the world's finest, most brilliant process, but if the humans who need to use it don't do so, we've wasted our time and money. Unfortunately, there's no button in Excel® or Minitab® we can click to make somebody follow our new process.

Like many before him, Leo had attended dozens of hours of training on the technical side of process improvement and maybe an hour or so on the human side. He was technically very savvy in isolating and fixing root causes and identifying sources of variation and waste. In a methodology like Six Sigma that is jammed to the rafters with cool technical elements like degrees of freedom, residuals, and p-values, it is easy to get absorbed in the technical side of process improvement while the human element gets short-changed. More than a few projects have crashed and burned because of this very problem.

The Need for Street Smarts

Leo thought he had the human side covered – he even read a book on teaming and ran his project team very well. So what went wrong? What Leo lacked in this case was the *street smarts* required to get the dozens or hundreds of people who don't report to him to change their behavior – to stop doing things the old way and start doing them the new way.

The market is rough. It's no longer good enough to say your business follows Lean or pull together a bunch of metrics and processes and lay back on your laurels, feeling confident that process improvement will take care of itself. Special times call for special tactics, and that is where our journey begins. The following tips are not intended to provide you with a soup-to-nuts change management approach (download a free workbook for this chapter at *www.jcolegroup.com/book.htm* for recommendations). These are change management secrets and practices that were born of the hard-earned successes and gut-wrenching failures of many project managers who walked this path before you. Let's get started.

Tip #1: Recognize the need

Change management is the process of helping an organization move its people, processes, strategies, culture, and systems from the current state (status quo) to a new, desired state. If you design a new process or change an existing process, change management likely needs to be addressed. Think of the need for change management as a spectrum ranging from 0% (no need) to 100% (definite need). Any project that impacts human beings has some need for change management. The question, however, becomes, "How much?" As part of your Six Sigma project risk assessment, consider the following questions:

1. *To what extent does your process change potentially impact others?*

If you're conducting a small-scoped Green Belt project on a process you personally own, and you're the only person impacted, you likely don't need the full arsenal of change tools. If, however, your project potentially impacts a number of other people, your need to formally address change increases correspondingly.

2. *How complex is the process change?*

Often, the more complex a project is, the greater the need for formal change management.

3. *To what extent does this change fit with your organization's culture?*

The further away from your culture the process change strays, the more critical managing change becomes.

Tip #2: Start early

One mistake some people make is to assume that change management is an issue to be addressed only in the Control step of DMAIC. (See Chapters 13 and 19). Not true. Start as early as the Define stage by a) understanding who will be impacted by this process change, and b) what their potential issues will be.

There's a world of difference in having something done "to" you versus "with" you. People like to feel they have a say in what they do and how they do it. Starting early allows you to identify those who will be impacted by the change and find ways to engage them throughout the process. This will help build a sense of ownership in their minds and reduce potential resistance during rollout. There are many opportunities where you can bring in ancillary team members for this purpose: process mapping, VOC, FMEA, data collection, DOE, pilots, control plans, etc. By implementing change management techniques early on, you can also start understanding where your target audience's concerns or issues may lay. Consider these questions:

- What are the best ways to communicate with those impacted?

- How can we establish two-way communications?

- What should our messages be and who should those messages come from?

- How often and in what format should we communicate?

- How will we involve those impacted by the project so they feel a sense of ownership?

Tip #3: *Don't make human change a separate to-do item*

Integrate your efforts in managing the human side of change into your plans for managing the technical side. Try to weave change management into the fabric of your DMAIC and DMADV efforts rather than bolting it on. Apply your existing Six Sigma tools to the human side, too. Force field analysis, FMEA, CT trees, and C/E Diagrams all work well for both the technical and human sides. Ensure your Six Sigma tollgate reviews include progress checks on the human side of your process changes.

Tip #4: *Select a method*

When you enter the world of Six Sigma, it's hard to avoid running into methods like DMAIC and DMADV. It's nice to enjoy standard, proven ways of fixing broken processes or building new ones. There are over four hundred books in print on Six Sigma. Pick any dozen at random and chances are there will be significant overlap in the method they describe. When you read the books on change management, however, there is no one industry-standard method. There are *many* methods. One organization had a best practice in which they evaluated several leading change methods and used a Pugh Selection Matrix to build their own hybrid approach. In the 2007 publication, "Best Practices in Change Management," a study by Prosci showed a positive correlation between having an effective change management program and an organization's ability to meet project objectives and stay on schedule.[1] In this study, the 436 participants indicated the use of over 70 different change management methods. Bottom line: Despite what authors tout, the evidence does not indicate there is one best method. You need to research several methods. Pick one. Get good at it.

Tip #5: *Recognize that culture eats process for lunch*

During a discussion of company efforts to improve quality, I once heard a manager say, "You know, culture eats process for lunch." As soon as I heard that, I knew immediately that he had street smarts: He "got it" when it came to managing process change, and his sound bite captured it perfectly. Culture devours massive amounts of well-intended process change throughout corporate America. This leaves some unaware teams scratching their heads as they stare in amazement at the smoking wreckage of what was anticipated to be a simple process improvement. How do we avoid that? It all starts with the basics.

Think of culture as the shared assumptions, beliefs, and behaviors of an organization.[2] It's like a wild river flowing through an organization. If you launch a process change going in the same direction as the culture, that culture will serve to propel your change forward. However, if your change is headed in the opposite direction, you can experience what I call cultural blowback - where a well-meaning change blows back in your face at 200 mph.

Avoiding cultural blowback is conceptually pretty simple. First, you assess the consistency between the current culture and those cultural attributes required for your process change to work. (See the complimentary workbook at *www.jcolegroup.com/book.htm*). If there is a great deal of overlap between the two cultures, you are in good shape. If not, some degree of adjustment will be necessary. Also take into account the strength of the current culture when determining your actions.[3] (See Figure 8-1).

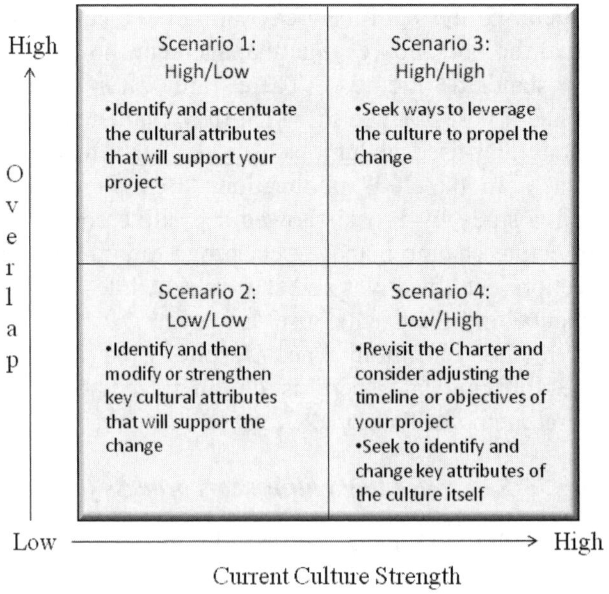

High ↑	Scenario 1: High/Low •Identify and accentuate the cultural attributes that will support your project	Scenario 3: High/High •Seek ways to leverage the culture to propel the change
O v e r l a p	Scenario 2: Low/Low •Identify and then modify or strengthen key cultural attributes that will support the change	Scenario 4: Low/High •Revisit the Charter and consider adjusting the timeline or objectives of your project •Seek to identify and change key attributes of the culture itself
Low	Current Culture Strength	**High**

Figure 8-1: Culture Overlap Matrix

Case Study

In the early 1990's, the Midwestern tech firm I worked for acquired a data warehousing company in southern California. The cultures were polar opposites. The parent company: a suit-and-tie, multinational, conservative, Fortune 100 firm with lots of red tape. The acquired firm: a shorts and sandals, flextime, fast-moving organization that was started in the founder's garage. Many large cultural disconnects existed. While it would have been easy for the parent firm to suck the soul right out of the smaller company, to their credit, they didn't. There were bumps in the road, but the parent firm was smart enough to see that part of the "magic" of the smaller firm lay in the shared beliefs, assumptions, and behaviors of their people. By being sensitive to their culture, they successfully merged, and over time, grew into a new culture together to the point where that division became the parent firm's leading unit.

Sometimes, cultural issues aren't readily apparent. They lie hidden in the corporate landscape. I call these "cultural landmines." One such cultural landmine occurred during a simple process change as part of another merger. The change: everybody in the acquired firm had to exchange their existing ID badges for new ones with the parent firm's name and logo. Click…Kaboom! They stepped squarely on a cultural landmine that took weeks to unravel.

In the acquired firm, name badges for one particular unit were slightly different, and in their culture, that ID badge was really a badge of honor. Reporting to that unit was a big deal and people looked up to them. So, by giving everyone the same generic ID card, the purchasing firm wasn't simply standardizing a process, they were effectively lowering the status of key personnel and erasing their identity. Fortunately, they resolved the matter, albeit in a reactive manner.

Tip #6: Avoid change saturation

When you are met with change, it requires mental, emotional, and sometimes physical or financial resources to process or absorb that change. A person's ability to absorb a change is much like a sponge's ability to absorb water. Once that sponge is completely full, it can no longer absorb any more water. Similarly, when a person is presented with too much change at one time, their "change sponge" gets saturated, and they can no longer process change in a functional way. This is called change saturation. At that point, people tend to escalate through a set of dysfunctional behaviors in a somewhat predictable manner.

Perhaps you have witnessed a relatively minor change trigger a disproportionately volcanic response in someone. That change was simply the "straw that broke the camel's back" for that person. Their change sponge was totally saturated and at that moment, they lacked the resources needed to process that change in a functional manner.

Some changes are like little spills we instantly absorb and deal with. Others are like a spilled bucket: They take quite a lot to absorb. People come equipped with different size change sponges – some people are naturally more resilient and can take in more change than others. To confound matters, each person's change sponge is at a different level of fullness based not only on what is happening at work, but in their personal lives as well.

Say you have just made small changes to the look and feel of the company's internal home page. That is a relatively minor change. Most people may instantly absorb the change or spend a few minutes grumbling about the change before becoming accustomed to it. A handful of people may have a slightly stronger reaction. For example, perhaps they just finished creating an employee handbook with screen shots of the old home page - those "minor" changes cause much more disruption for these people.

In contrast, say you have just reengineered the entire time and expense reporting systems. Each individual is impacted on a greater level. It requires a greater amount of time to load and learn new software, to adjust to different forms and procedures, and it produces a greater mental and emotional burden. This level of change will fill up a lot more of a person's change sponge than the simple revamping of a website. This can be compounded in that most companies have multiple changes happening at once.

Now that we recognize the phenomenon, how can we deal with it?

- Assess the current level of capacity to absorb further change within your organization. (See the free workbook at *http://www.jcolegroup.com/book.htm* for more information).

- Understand how big a "spill" your existing and planned process changes are.

Analyzing the above allows you to see how much available capacity your organization has until its collective change sponge is full. If there is insufficient capacity to absorb an upcoming change, you can look at several tactics to address the situation such as: see what can be removed to free up capacity; alter the timing of a planned change; alter the content of the change to require less personal resources; train the workforce to be more durable to change (*i.e.*, increasing the size of everyone's individual change sponges).

Tip #7: Establish air traffic control

When you are in the midst of a multi-month DMAIC project, it's easy to lose track of the fact that the people impacted by your process change are also likely impacted by other changes at the same time: policy changes, IT changes, reorganizations, and possibly other Six Sigma projects. Every change that gets launched needs a solid landing place. It is important that organizations establish "air traffic control" over all the changes being pumped into its "air space." This is a form of governance, which is a duty owned by the leadership of an organization. You don't want to launch one change and immediately have another land on top of it, effectively undoing the first change you implemented. You also want to guard against generating collateral damage in other processes or departments during the rollout of each Six Sigma project.

Street-smart Six Sigma Champions establish a metaphorical radar screen of all current and upcoming changes. This allows them to properly manage the level of change saturation within an organization to optimize productivity levels. Some projects will show up on the radar as huge neon blips, while others will be minor. As discussed above, these changes require resources to properly implement. Those resources are limited, and air traffic control is an excellent way to manage that change process. This requires a degree of hard work and ongoing leadership diligence to maintain, but it is worth the effort. As warning signals flash across your change radar, you can be proactive by using several tactics:

- Modify the timing and locations of Six Sigma project pilots.

- Ground certain changes to create runway space for other, higher-priority changes.

- Alter the content or scope of a project to avoid contention.

- Combine similar projects to create synergy.

Tip #8: Evaluate your sponsor

The definitions vary slightly according to which author you read, but every Six Sigma project should have a sponsor and a champion. The sponsor is the person who determines if the project exists or not, is usually senior management in the organization, and serves to provide resources, remove roadblocks, and review progress. The <u>champion</u> owns the process that is being developed. Champions provide access, data and resources; help create an environment for success; and will act as the person to ensure the gains are held on your improvements after your team disbands. From a change management perspective, these leadership figures are very important and it is vital they understand their roles and are able and willing to fulfill them.

Usually, the people who must change their behavior don't report directly to you – they more often report to the sponsor or champion. Most Six Sigma training instructs you to have a meeting up front with the sponsor and champion. They have evaluated you and determined that you should be the belt running the project. In turn, you need to evaluate them, from a change perspective, to ensure you get the management horsepower needed to drive change throughout the organization. You can evaluate them on a 1-5 Likert scale against some key sponsorship criteria. Any criteria with a neutral or low rating is a red flag. This should go on your agenda for the first sponsor meeting as you share expectations with one another. You want to proactively apply <u>FMEA</u>-type thinking toward the sponsorship area very early on in a project and have plans in place to address any sponsorship gaps you encounter along the way.

There are many topics you may want to consider in evaluating your sponsor. The free workbook at *www.jcolegroup.com/book.htm* contains tools for your use. A sample of topics to consider includes:

- To what extent do they [the sponsor or champion] personally feel pain with the way the current process works today?

- Do they have and will they commit the necessary resources to this project?

- Will they participate actively in reviews and communication activities, both one-on-one and large group?

- To what extent do they understand the Six Sigma and change management processes?

- If push comes to shove time-wise, resource-wise, and/or priority-wise, will they continue to support this project?

- If roadblocks are encountered, will they intervene appropriately?

- Are they willing to reward early adopters of the change and apply consequences to those that fail to change?

Tip #9: Don't let resistance go underground

Here's one street smart rule you learn quickly: While we may never completely eliminate resistance to a large, major process change, we can manage resistance if we know about it.[4] Sometimes it feels as though humans are genetically hard-wired to resist change. Physics tells us that an object at rest tends to stay at rest. A process at status quo tends to stay at status quo until you improve or alter it. If people are accustomed to the status quo and happy with it, you *will* meet with resistance. If, on the other hand, the current process is causing people a lot of pain, your new process may be viewed as the remedy and resistance will be low.

For our purposes, consider resistance as the thoughts, statements, or actions directed against engaging in the process or policy change you are trying to deploy.[5] These resistance behaviors may range from minor and inconsequential to major show-stopping displays. Resistance may be isolated or widespread. It may even be overt or covert.

Why do people resist?

Multiple causes exist, but many of them boil down to this: People resist for one or both of two reasons – ability or willingness. On the ability side, someone may be very willing to engage in a new process but unable to do so for a variety of reasons: lack of awareness, lack of tools, lack of knowledge, lack of appropriate permissions; the list goes on. On the willingness side, they have everything required to follow the new process but choose not to comply. They might prefer the old process, or it is not a high priority for them. They may not perceive (convincing) consequences for not engaging, or they don't want to spend the time required by the change. Perhaps they simply don't like one or more aspects of the new process, feel the new process is taking something away from them or lack a sense of ownership over the change.

Of the two, ability matters are often easier to resolve through simple communication, training and providing the necessary information, tools, and support. Willingness issues are often tougher to remedy and sometimes harder to uncover. A person may be more likely to tell you to your face they aren't *able* to follow a process than to say they *can* but *won't* follow the new process. Instead, willingness issues manifest through feet dragging, avoidance behavior (*i.e.*, lack of attendance at meetings or training), a stated lack of ability or lack of time, or even via direct or indirect sabotage. There is one case wherein a senior executive, while espousing support of a simple process change, actually tasked a person to falsify data in the process monitoring system to make it appear they were following the process when they weren't. While this is an example of extreme behavior, you should keep your sensors tuned in for some potentially dysfunctional behavior.

Going Underground

Assume you are presenting a new process to key personnel in your organization. Each person will leave the session with all the knowledge, permissions, tools and access to make them fully capable of following your new process. You have even run through various process scenarios, testing their knowledge and capability in following the new process. Consider these two response scenarios:

1. Your audience is polite and friendly and asks few questions. They agree to follow the new process.

2. Your audience is mixed: Some are for the process while others are outspoken, perhaps even angry about the process and push back on using it. After a dialogue, you adjourn with an agreement that all will use the process.

To your dismay, you later find that some people in both scenarios are not engaging in the new process. At this point, you really shouldn't be surprised. While Scenario 1 is more pleasant if you are the presenter, Scenario 2 is more useful if you are taking a street-smart approach to managing resistance.

Resistance in Scenario 1 went *covert* – it went underground. You left with the impression that all was well, and then they silently resisted the process once they were back on their home turf. Resistance in Scenario 2 is *overt* – they did you an enormous favor by explicitly stating their resistance. It may not have been the most pleasant session, but once you know about resistance, you have a chance to manage it. If you allow it to go underground, it becomes a much tougher battle.

Case in point: One Fortune 500 firm spent several millions of dollars and over a year re-engineering their sales process. They rolled out the new tools, trained everyone and checked deployment off their list. Because resistance went underground, however, it took several months to uncover that globally, only about half the managers were following the new process. The change consultants rolled in, and hundreds of thousands of dollars later, they realized they needed a sales governance process to ensure their sales process was actually followed.

To combat resistance, there are a few things you want to know:

- *Where* the resistance exists (which groups, management levels, functions, or people).

- The *size* of the resistance. Is it half the company or just a few people in accounting?

- *How* is resistance being manifested?

- The *reasons* for resistance.

Thinking through and addressing these issues is critical to the success of change implementation. However, it will save you a lot of work and frustration if you approach the idea of resistance proactively; it will keep you from having to sniff out the resistance underground. There are several ways to keep resistance from going underground:

- Don't wait until the end of your project to think about the human side of the equation. Consider it on the front end and throughout.

- Anticipate resistance and find ways to engage potential resistors in the project to give them a sense of ownership, a sense of being in charge of their own future. This can greatly reduce resistance. You can include them in a process mapping exercise, a focus group, walk-about interviews and the like.

- Ensure open channels of communications for people to overtly and/or anonymously provide feedback to your project team. Web sites, an e-mail address for a go-to person, feedback box, or dedicated voicemail are just a few suggestions I have seen work well in the past. This system should passively collect feedback and create an environment where it is safe to give feedback.

- Proactively encourage and collect feedback throughout the project from those who are actually affected by the change and implementation of the new process.

Conclusions

Sadly, many people believe that successfully implementing major process change is as easy as simply announcing the change. Then they have to hose down the area where their change crashed and burned and get interested in how it really works. That's where this chapter comes in: by providing nine Street Smart tips for ensuring successful change.

Put these tips to work on your next Six Sigma project and you'll be well on your way to securing a timely and effective change. If you have a success story or Street Smart tip of your own, we'd love to hear from you. Send an e-mail to *info@jcolegroup.com*. We'll post your ideas on the book's website, and maybe even feature you in a future publication.

Key Lessons Learned:

1. We can have the best process in the world, but if the people who have to follow that process don't do so, we've wasted our time.

2. The shelves of your local bookstore may be filled with Six Sigma books with very valuable statistical and engineering topics. However, ensuring the success of major organizational changes in the "real combat conditions" of today's fast-paced life involves employing tactics well beyond the scope of your Six Sigma technical toolbox.

3. You can vastly improve your chances for success by supplementing the technical side toolbox with a human side. A great way to begin that journey is by implementing the nine proven Street Smart tips we've outlined here, starting today.

About the Author

Jeff Cole is Owner & Principal, JCG Management Consulting. Mr. Cole is a former quality executive with over 20 years of industry experience, and has trained and coached over 4000 individuals in Six Sigma across a variety of industries. Jeff is a Lean Six Sigma Master Black Belt, holds the ASQ CSSBB and CMQ/OE certifications and is certified in Change Management. He has served two terms as a national examiner for the Malcolm Baldrige National Quality Award and sat on the Board of Directors for the Ohio Award for Excellence. In addition to being a frequent speaker at conferences, he is the author of the monthly column "Street Smarts for Change Management," at *www.sixsigmaiq.com*. For more information, contact Jeff at *jeff@jcolegroup.com*.

---

[1] Prosci Research, *Best Practices in Change Management*. Prosci Change Management Series (Loveland, CO: 2007): 9.
[2] D. R. Conner, *Managing at the Speed of Change* (New York: Villard Books, 1992): 164.
[3] H. Harrington, D. Conner and N. Horney, *Project Change Management* (New York: McGraw-Hill, 2000): 119-121.
[4] Conner, p. 128.
[5] Harrington, p. 12.

Chapter Nine

Driving Value through Project Selection

Steve Pfeiffer

Overview

This chapter is designed to help business owners, department heads and project sponsors gain insight into Lean/Six Sigma/process improvement project selection and prioritization. Selecting the right projects is critical to the ongoing success of any improvement program. Without a solid selection of projects, all the momentum you experience from early project success will die off quickly as resources are spent working on projects that do not drive real results.

But what do you do to keep things moving in the right direction after the initial excitement has worn off?

This chapter is about maintaining that initial enthusiasm and momentum by picking the right projects to attack in your organization. We will provide a framework of critical elements that enables a solid selection process and provides some concrete examples of utilizing the tools and frameworks described in the chapter to demonstrate their use and value.

This chapter will help you to:

- Find good, actionable projects to maximize resources.

- Learn how to do an initial benefits estimate.

- Identify projects that significantly contribute to your company's bottom line.

- Prioritize projects appropriately.

Why Project Selection Matters

Developing a process to select improvement projects is one of the most critical tasks facing business owners and others responsible for driving improvement in the organization. If you take on the wrong projects, it is likely the results will not meet leadership expectations, and as a result, everyone in the organization may question the value of the improvement effort as a whole. Worse still, the people that are most effective at driving the improvements, those directly involved in the processes, will no longer be willing to be part of a program that does not drive real, tangible improvements they can personally see and feel. The organization will sour quickly on the program, and your initial improvements will not be sustainable.

Beyond cultural reasons, there are two more bottom line reasons to focus on the right projects: limited resources and the time value of money.

Limited Resources

Every organization deals with issues associated with limited resources. After years of cost cutting and general downsizing throughout American businesses, workers are now stretched thin to complete the myriad of tasks assigned to them. Nowhere is this more evident than in the deployment of an operational excellence program, which at least at the onset, is simply one more task for an already busy person to complete. In many cases, these projects are done on a part-time basis in addition to the day-to-day responsibilities of the team members.

With this in mind, we, as leaders of these programs, need to be certain that the time we ask our project leaders and team members to devote to these efforts deliver value – not only for the organization but also for the people involved in these processes. Without real results, our efforts will do nothing but result in "busy work" for the people assigned to carry them out.

Time Value of Money

The time value of money concept describes the idea that money held today is worth more than in the future because you can invest it and earn interest. This concept is also used to evaluate different investment alternatives: Should we buy the car wash or the laundromat? Should we spend the money to install a solar power system for our electrical needs or save it? In the same manner, this time value of money concept can be used to help evaluate and select projects based on expected benefits.

In project selection, we need to consider our alternative projects as investments. People will invest their time on these projects expecting to see benefits upon the successful conclusion of the project. Therefore, to maximize the value generated by our improvement efforts, we need to select those projects that will give us the largest benefits first. To do this effectively, we will need to develop a method for estimating benefits in the initial stages of project identification (which will be covered later in this chapter, as well as Chapter 20).

Of course, expected benefits are not the *only* criteria upon which we should base the selection decision. Other factors include: required effort, complexity, probability of success and the availability of the right resources. These and other factors will play a role in our decision. But at the core, the combination of the time value of money and expected benefits are two of the most important elements affecting our decision.

Key Elements to a Successful Project Selection Process

There are several critical pieces that need to be put in place within the project selection process in order to create and sustain a successful improvement program:

- Developing a pipeline of projects
- Connecting to the annual planning process
- Initial Benefits Estimation
- Project prioritization

If any of these elements is missing or not implemented properly, it is likely your improvement efforts will stall.

Developing a Pipeline

Developing the list or 'pipeline' of potential projects to be completed will require project leaders and others responsible for business performance to be on the lookout for improvements within their respective departments. Further, it will require that everyone in the organization is willing to view his or her own processes on a regular basis with an honest and critical eye towards improvement.

The leader of the operational excellence program will also need to develop relationships with the various internal business leaders, which will enable him or her to have an open, ongoing dialogue regarding performance issues. Ultimately, through regular interaction with these leaders in the course of monthly and as-needed performance reporting, the leader of the improvement program will become a trusted internal advisor for evaluating and developing solutions to improve performance.

Connection to Annual Planning Process

Practically speaking, pipeline development needs to stem from the ongoing planning and evaluation of the business as a whole that occurs through the financial and operating planning process. Every company goes through an ongoing cycle of planning, operating and evaluating results during a fiscal year. Budgets are created, materials purchased, parts made or staff hired to provide services, and demand is thereby satisfied.

During this planning process, areas with gaps between current performance and desired performance will be identified. These gaps in efficiency, costs, quality or other similar factors, are prime areas of investigation for potential improvement projects.

At any given time, your business leaders may identify dozens of potential improvement initiatives to tackle. Identifying which of these projects is a good fit for your current resources begins with the annual planning process (Fig. 9-1).

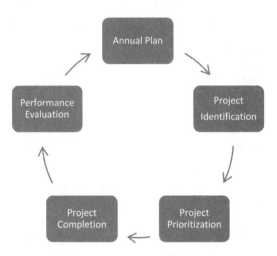

Figure 9-1: Project Identification Cycle

The company as a whole creates an annual plan with financial goals, operating targets and gaps in desired performance identified. Potential projects are then identified based on the targets and gaps outlined in the annual plan. Projects are prioritized based on several factors, including a benefits estimation. Projects selected through these methods are then completed. Both the overall business performance *and* project performance are evaluated, and the resulting performance becomes an input to the next planning cycle.

Initial Benefits Estimation

Developing an initial estimate of benefits is a critical element and a good predictor of project success. If project leaders and sponsors cannot develop a reasonable estimate of the potential benefits of completing a project under consideration, what is the likelihood of the project being successfully completed? How likely is senior management, concerned as they are with the bottom line, to support *this project* over other efforts and initiatives competing for the same resources (time and money)?

In essence, the challenge to estimate benefits early in the process is an screening tool to determine how thoroughly defined the project is in its current state. To develop a solid estimate for the project benefits, the project sponsor and the leader need to answer three critical questions:

1. What performance measures and financial levers will be improved by completing this project?

2. How much do we expect the project to improve things? This actually requires knowing the current performance level to some degree of accuracy as well as the projection of improvement.

3. How much is this improvement project worth? Once measures are identified and projected improvements agreed upon, these improvements need to be translated into financial impact.

One note of caution is worth mentioning: Projects aimed at improving cycle times or improving the delivery of products or services to customers are notoriously difficult to estimate and much care needs to be given in the benefits estimation process. (See Chapter 20 for a discussion of Financial Impact Analysis).

Project Prioritization

Once the benefits have been estimated, an overall portfolio of projects can be analyzed and the various options prioritized. This prioritization process needs to incorporate several key requirements:

- **Be repeatable** so that projects with equivalent evaluation inputs will drive the same prioritization scores.

- **Have standardized and published inputs** for evaluation so project sponsors and leaders can easily prepare projects for the prioritization process in a repeatable manner.

- **Be understandable** to all the various stakeholders so they do not question the integrity of the system.

- **Incorporate, at a minimum, the initial assessments of benefits, projected timing, and relative difficulty of implementing/sustaining the gains**.

Case Studies - Introduction

The real-life case studies presented here are taken from work at two very different businesses in health care supplies. The first case is from work done during the initial launch of Lean Six Sigma at a leading laboratory and hospital supply company. During this period, the company learned how to charter projects and develop solid benefits estimates. The second case is from a leading medical device maker. Their situation was dramatically different. They had been actively involved with Lean and Six Sigma and process excellence in various forms for many years, but struggled to drive significant results that could be seen in the financial bottom line of the company at year-end.

These two cases describe very different situations; yet, each clearly demonstrates how the application of at least one of the principles presented can help an organization move forward implementing Lean Six Sigma in a profitable manner.

Case Study - Estimating Benefits Early in the Chartering Process

Scrap! The production of pipette tips had always been riddled with scrap. Pipette tips are the disposable, sterile tips you see the CSI investigators use to distribute small, precise amounts of liquid into vials for chemical or biological analysis. These pipette tips are made specifically for the individual model of the instrument used to collect and distribute samples, and they have very high profit margins built into their pricing.

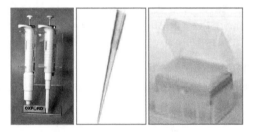

Figure 9-2 – Pictures of a pipettes

Unfortunately, that profit margin was being eaten away by scrap problems present in the injection molding production process. Over the years, people had become accustomed to the scrap. These tips were made by the millions and cost only pennies to produce. Some people had a "gut feel" that this was a problem worthy of attention, yet it never truly was systematically fixed. When the Lean Six Sigma program was initiated, this scrap problem was identified as a potential project and was put into the pipeline for evaluation.

The quality engineer assigned to lead this project was chomping at the bit. He had been working in this company for three years and he was amazed how the scrap problem just would not go away. He knew there were potential solutions even before starting the project. They would require some engineering time to implement and perhaps some minor outlays of capital, but they were all very straightforward. We focused the quality engineer on developing a project that addressed a single family of pipette tips that were in high demand and run frequently. This focus made the benefits analysis and execution of the project much easier.

Before we started any of the various projects scheduled to begin simultaneously across the whole company, we challenged each of these newly minted Black Belts to develop well-constructed estimates of the benefits for their projects. This would allow senior management to track their progress against expectations and provide resources and support to those projects with the greatest potential value to the company as a whole.

Estimating the scrap rate for this project was relatively easy. Millions of tips were produced for a particular product family each week. Through the production scheduling and quality tracking systems already in place, we knew how many tips were produced versus how many were ultimately packed as finished goods. It was not surprising to this outsider when we found they were running consistently at 50%! No wonder the floor was littered in hundreds of little plastic tips.

Once we knew the scrap rates, a series of discussions with the controller provided good, accurate cost data for each of our products. We calculated the scrap rate for the five products in the single product family and found it was running at over $44,000 each week. This number was shocking to some people within the company, especially those who had gotten used to seeing all those scrap tips laying on the floor.

A summary sheet showing the details for the preliminary scrap analysis is shown in Table 9-1 below.

Estimating the improvement we could expect from the project was the next step. The quality engineer leading this project already had some ideas that could potentially be put in place quickly. So, we were confident that a big improvement was possible in a very short time. Eliminating all of the scrap was both unlikely and unrealistic. We finally agreed that an appropriate target for the project was to reduce the scrap rate from 50% down to 20% during our first attempt at process improvement. Based on the estimates, costs attributable to scrap would be reduced by over $26,000 each week for this product family. On an annual basis, this project would be worth roughly $1.3 million to the company's bottom line. Once these numbers were developed and published throughout the company, support for this project was overwhelming. Everyone began looking at these tips lying around in a new light. Ideas for improvement that had been held in check for years began pouring into the team.

	Cost per 1000 units	Cost each	Weekly Production	Current Scrap %	Current Scrap Cost per week	Projected Scrap %	Projected Scrap Cost per week	Projected Improvement (each week)
Product A	$33.130	$0.033	1,000,000	50%	$16,565	20%	$6,626	$9,939
Product B	$27.490	$0.027	1,000,000	50%	$13,745	20%	$5,498	$8,247
Product C	$9.900	$0.010	1,000,000	50%	$4,950	20%	$1,980	$2,970
Product D	$8.320	$0.008	1,000,000	50%	$4,160	20%	$1,664	$2,496
Product E	$9.990	$0.010	1,000,000	50%	$4,995	20%	$1,998	$2,997
						Weekly Total		$26,649
						Working Weeks		50
						Annual Total		$1,332,450

Table 9-1: Initial scrap project benefit estimate based on cost

As good as the story is at this point, it isn't over yet. These tips were highly demanded, and at times, customer orders went unfulfilled or went to backorder because of the low process quality. When a similar analysis was performed based on profit-per-tip, the estimated project benefits jumped to over $3 million per year.

The project concluded in quick fashion, with a significant impact to the bottom line, just as the sales manager predicted. Even better, the solutions developed to reduce scrap in this specific product family were easily applied to the production of many other tip families throughout the company. Consequently, profit margins in the tip business increased substantially over the next year.

Case Study - Getting More with Less

Unlike the previous example, the company highlighted here was an early adopter of Lean and Six Sigma. Their program was fully deployed throughout the organization with an excellent set of company-wide performance metrics that connected nicely to their overall company vision and strategic goals. Black Belts and Master Black Belts were in place to guide projects in every aspect of the company's business.

At first glance, the program seemed to be working very well. There were projects ongoing in operations, finance, engineering, and distribution. Performance discussions were data driven, with determining the root cause and developing solutions the focus of working sessions. However, the most senior management of this medical device maker knew their program could deliver better results.

During a detailed review of their program, we found there were *too many* projects going on and not enough getting done. Projects had been chartered without a clear business reason for completion. Departments were graded and rewarded based on the number of trained Green Belts and the number of projects underway and completed. The result was predictable: There was a lot of action but little in the way of results. This situation was well summarized by a well-regarded senior manager: "We've been doing Lean for a few years, but we really haven't seen it hit our bottom line much." As a result, enthusiasm for Lean in the company was declining.

The approach we took to improve this situation was to: a) evaluate all of the projects in their pipeline for their connection to overall company-wide strategic goals and estimated benefits, and then b) implement a simple and easily understood prioritization process for evaluating current and potential projects. Any existing projects without a clear and well-defined benefits case that aligned to company strategic goals was put under the microscope, and most of these were cancelled or put on hold. This freed up project leaders and other resources to drive the remaining projects to completion quicker, often with better than anticipated results.

This exercise was met with a great deal of resistance initially. There were a number of personal projects that had been put into the list and many of these simply would not make the cut. The prioritization process focused on evaluating the characteristics of each project and assigning a score based on the following criteria:

- Benefits case definition (graded Low to High, based on completeness)

- Annual Benefits (score based on predefined ranges)

- Alignment to key strategic goals (graded Low to High, based on explanation provided in project charter)

- Complexity/Difficulty to implement (grading based on project description and scope provided in project charter)

- Difficulty/Effort to sustain results (grading based on project description and scope provided in project charter)

- Technology requirements to implement/sustain project (grading based on project description and scope provided in project charter)

The scores for the project in each category were totaled in raw form and with predetermined weightings for each category. For example, the annual benefits, benefits definition and alignment with strategic goals were each heavily weighted and the others had smaller relative weights, reflecting the importance of projects with a clearly defined, large benefit impact on the company. A sample review and scoring of a project to improve the production of a one item is summarized in Table 9-2, below.

The effort to prioritize all of the currently running and potential projects that were already in the pipeline was significant. There were close to 100 projects already running and over 700 waiting to start. The team assigned to review these projects was made up of highly respected managers and high potential individual contributors from operations, supply chain and product engineering. Input from the information systems and technology group and finance was sought whenever needed, as well. It took several days to review all of these projects and finalize the prioritization scores.

Criteria	Criteria Weight	Assessment	Raw Score (1-10, 10=Best)	Weighted Score
Benefits case definition	25	Excellent	10	250
Annual Benefits	25	$250,000.00	6	150
Alignment to key strategic goals	20	Aligned to COGS	10	200
Complexity/Difficulty	15	Medium	5	75
Difficulty/Effort to sustain results	10	Medium	5	50
Technology requirements	5	Low	8	40
		Project Totals	44	765

Table 9-2: Summary scoring for a potential cost-focused project

The results of the evaluations were surprising. Over one-third of the projects already underway were poorly defined and were put on hold, and several hundred in the pipeline were cancelled until a benefit case or clear alignment to a strategic goal could be developed.

Once these misaligned projects were put on hold, many of the key resources tied to a number of projects were freed up to dedicate to those projects that survived scrutiny. LSS resources were immediately put to better use moving the remaining projects along more quickly. Improvements in cost, cycle times and delivery performance in particular were realized, as alignment to strategic goals moved along projects that had languished previously.

Conclusions

Applying rigorous and standard approaches to project benefit estimation and evaluation early in the project life cycle has been shown to accelerate the realization of benefits from implementing Lean and Six Sigma. The case studies presented show how the application of these principles drove bottom-line improvements in two very different situations. Requiring the early development of the benefits estimates forces the project leaders and champions to think critically about the scope of the project and how potential benefits will be generated, which leads to better planned and executed projects. Performing the detailed evaluation and prioritization of projects ensures that the organization's limited resources are used in the most effective manner. These techniques, applied along with a solid list of potential projects, will lay the groundwork for a lasting and successful improvement program.

Key Lessons Learned

1. Project identification and selection is critical to the initial and ongoing success of an OPEX/LSS programs.

2. Show significant results early – it is easy to lose momentum otherwise.

3. Proper project selection requires a team effort.

4. Don't discount the effects of seemingly small-ticket items. They may impact your bottom line more than you think.

About the Author

Steven Pfeiffer is an independent consultant for his firm, Melior Partners, LLC. Prior to forming Melior Partners, Steve was Executive Director – Lean Manufacturing and Six Sigma, for a leading life sciences company, where he led the global rollout of Lean Six Sigma, which generated over $6M in benefits during the first year. Steve spent several years as a Senior Manager at Deloitte Consulting where he earned his Master Black Belt in Enterprise Lean & Six Sigma and served as a regional leader.

With over 20 years of experience in industry and consulting, Steve specializes in operations improvement, supply chain strategy and supply chain management. He has significant expertise in business transformation and has served global and multinational Fortune 500 companies, as well as smaller companies across the automotive, consumer products, life-sciences, high-tech, financial services, process and diversified manufacturing industries. His particular areas of expertise include:

- Operations Excellence
- Lean Manufacturing/Lean Enterprise
- Cost Reductions
- Inventory and Demand Management
- Quality Systems
- Process Improvement
- Profitability Improvement

Chapter Ten

Managerial Accounting for the Lean Enterprise

Ron Chandler

Overview

This chapter is intended for Lean Champions, senior executives, Lean Six Sigma sponsors and project leaders who seek to ensure the financial success of their organizations' Lean initiatives. A great deal has been published regarding the inadequacy of standard cost systems as decision-making tools for managing your business. The idea that it is ill-suited for today's competitive environment has become mainstream, but the understanding of a clear and effective alternative continues to be elusive.

There seems to be unending debate over the use of <u>Activity-Based Costing</u> and other approaches for allocating costs. We are no further along today than we were 20 years ago on this issue. For those tasked with using Lean initiatives to improve the financial performance of their company, this results in a high degree of frustration and the feeling that daily decision making is based on faulty assumptions.

This chapter aims to provide some direction. It is not intended as an alternative to the standard cost accounting system, but rather as an alternative decision-making system to the one spawned by any allocation-based approach. By tracing the history of the standard cost approach, we see a clear divergence from the system as an accounting method to its use as a decision-making tool. Our goal is to answer the question: What is an appropriate model for today's competitive markets?

This chapter will help you to:

- Learn how to build a Lean accounting model to identify opportunities for improvement and prioritize and track success.
- Use Lean accounting to rationalize your product base.
- Create a quote system that is consistent with Lean principles.

Dude, where's my profit?

> *"And as a result of this lean event, we have saved the company $250,000 annually!"*

The words were coming from the company's Lean Champion. We were in the middle of one of their manufacturing plants; I stood in the small crowd next to the president, who smiled with approval. He had invited me to attend the final day of their latest "Lean Event" to show me how advanced they were in implementing a "Lean Strategy." I waited for the final request for questions and raised my hand:

"I'm confused about the gains you've stated. May I ask a couple of questions?" I asked.

"Sure," said the unwitting Lean Champion.

"How many direct labor heads were eliminated?"

"Two."

"Who are they?" I asked, pointing to two people standing off to the side.

"They're *water spiders*."

"What do they do?"

"They keep materials flowing to the assembly cell."

"Where did they come from?" I asked, trying to drill down to the core of the matter.

"They came from the cell after we did the event."

"So they are still working in the cell?"

"No they're working *for* the cell," he clarified.

"Do they work *for* any other cell?" I asked.

"No."

"Was there any reduction in the cost of materials?"

"No," he replied.

"Are you going to have an increase in sales from this cell?"

"No." I think he was starting to get the hint by this point.

"After the reduction in direct labor, where is the rest of the cost reduction?"

"Plant square footage. We reduced the amount of square footage that this cell uses."

"Do you pay rent based on floor utilization?" I asked.

"I don't think so."

"Then how is this a cost savings?"

"We calculated the plant overhead cost to be $[XX] per square foot; multiply that by 100 square feet and there you go!" He really was proud of himself at this point.

By this time, I could see both the president and the CFO fidgeting nervously, so I thanked the Lean Champion and we returned to the president's office. As soon as the door shut, I offered to bet my first month's invoice that they would never realize that $250,000 in their income statement. There were no takers.

Clearly, having a measurement system for making decisions and evaluating performance is a powerful tool that management wields in driving the day-to-day activities of the business. The ability to map out a strategy, set priorities and to focus resources is all contained within this tool. Unfortunately, most organizations develop a hodge-podge approach to measurement and decision making using disconnected internal metrics with foundations still steeped in the faulty logic of a standard cost system.

Too often I have worked with owners, presidents, plant managers and Lean champions laboring under measurement systems that are not aligned with operational realities. This misalignment is found in operating methods and organizational structure as well. The approach I have embraced involves developing a set of metrics that are consistent with one another *and* the external market environment.

My experience with the incompatibility of standard cost systems and Lean first came around 1990 at my own company where we manufactured automotive components. We had all read *The Machine That Changed The World*[1] and were eager to begin transforming our operations to make more money and grab a competitive advantage in selling to the Japanese transplants that were popping up in the US.

Like most companies in our niche, we ran our business using a mass production mentality; our operations were geared toward running the highest unit volume at the lowest possible unit cost. The standard cost system we had in place served us well with this business model. Standard cost models were developed to measure unit costs in a mass production environment. While engineers developed standards for the discreet activities within the production processes, accountants worked in parallel to create standard costs for the use of direct labor and materials within those tasks. Our indirect costs or "burden" were allocated evenly across production units as a function of labor. In our plastics facility where our shop floor was lined with injection molding machines of varying sizes, our accountants calculated a "machine rate" where indirect costs were a function of the size of the machine.

All of our performance metrics were also derived through the application of the standard cost system. Most readers, especially those with manufacturing backgrounds, will recognize terms like unit cost, earned hours, labor efficiency, unit margin and utilization that were all based on standard cost system formulas. These metrics were used to guide and evaluate our manufacturing operations because we believed they were the direct link between our manufacturing activities and our company's financial performance. For years, those metrics told us that any investment in labor-saving technologies was a good one and that adding indirect labor didn't matter because it would be amortized over each unit built and that building more product was a way to utilize excess capacity. The logic we employed was that if an operator is not producing product, or if an injection molding machine was not constantly spitting out parts, then we were losing money. At least it *seemed* logical at the time.

But something happened when we started learning and applying the Toyota Production System (TPS) to our business. As we began to implement a pull system of scheduling production, all of our performance metrics began to turn negative. As we shut down production lines and equipment after we had enough parts to meet our latest pull signal, efficiency and utilization went in the tank. Worse yet, as we took our inventory down from 30 days to one week, our financial performance took a hit. Think about this: We were producing fewer parts per run; we had eliminated all overtime, and in fact, we had laid off several direct labor personnel because we found we had way too many people in the plants for the amount of parts we needed to make; we were still selling parts at the same rate we were before the changes; and our accounting was telling us that we were losing money at an alarming rate!

We were actually having a go-around whether or not to abandon Lean because it suddenly seemed to be killing our profits. While we logically argued that with less payroll, less overtime and an elimination of premium freight, we *had* to be making more money somewhere, our CFO stubbornly defended his numbers as accurate. And they were – we were executing the wrong system with 100% precision and accuracy.

It was around this time I started reading a book entitled *The Goal* by Eliyahu Goldratt and Jeff Cox.[2] The book described very closely what we had discovered as we sought to bring down inventory. More importantly, it described a different way to look at our cost structure, described as Throughput Accounting. While the book never gave a solid foundation for creating the system, it did describe the concept enough for us to build a model and compare it to what we were seeing in our operation through the dark glass of cost accounting.

Throughput Accounting – A New Perspective on Cost Allocation

The basic argument of Throughput Accounting[3] was that we were wrong to allocate our costs to the products that we made. The problem with any allocation method, including both standard cost systems and Activity-Based Cost (ABC) methods, is that they are all based on the premise that all costs are variable in relation to some activity. This simply is not the case in the real world, and as production and service processes have improved over the years, the amount of truly variable costs associated with the sale of a product or service has continued to shrink as a percentage of the total cost of the business. The majority of expenses allocated, in whatever allocation system you choose, do not truly vary with volume of production or service and/or mix, or with any other variable. Hence, the allocation only serves to confuse our business model and causes us to make irrational decisions.

According to Goldratt and Cox, "Before we can deal with the improvement of any section of a system, we must first define the system's global goal; and the measurements that will enable us to judge the impact of any subsystem and any local decision, on this global goal."[4] If we all agree that your company's goal is to make money now and into the future, we will need measurements that are purely financial in order to determine if we are moving closer to our goal. To judge whether or not your company is moving toward its goal, you will have to answer three questions:

1. How much money is generated by your company?

2. How much money is captured by your company?

3. How much money do we have to spend to operate our company?

Goldratt turned these questions into formal definitions:[5]

Throughput (T): the rate at which the system generates money through sales

Inventory (I): all the money the system invests in purchasing items the system intends to sell

Operating Expense (OE): all the money the system spends in turning investment into throughput

Let's expand on these definitions and see how they apply to different types of businesses.

Throughput – the rate at which the system generates money

Note that I have left off the last two words from the original definition – "through sales." If the system generates money through dividends and interest, *e.g.*, a brokerage account, it is still throughput. The only purpose for the last two words is to deal with the paradigm of your average business manager. Most executives believe that if you produce something, it is throughput; however, throughput cannot be associated with the shuffling of money internally, such as when the molding department produces a piece of plastic for the assembly department. Throughput is the result of *new money* coming in to the company from the outside, thus the use of the term "through sales."

We can thus modify the definition of throughput to mean 'all money that comes in to the company, minus what is paid to the vendors.'

The formula used to calculate throughput is as follows:

$$Tu = P - TVC$$

Where: Tu = throughput per unit of product or service

P = price per unit, and;

TVC = Totally Variable Cost, (the amount of cost that actually does vary with the fluctuation in the amount of sales of the product or service)

Then, Total Throughput per product is defined as:

$$TTp = Tu * q$$

Where: q = quantity sold in the period

The company's Total Throughput = Σ TTp

As you can see from the equation, there are two components to throughput: a revenue component, Selling Price, and a cost component, Totally Variable Cost (TVC). The terms *variable* and *cost* can be confusing as they are used in standard cost systems as well. The key differentiator is the term 'Totally' – *Totally* Variable is in relation to the quantity of product sold. A TVC is an amount incurred when one more unit is sold. The most obvious example of total variability is raw materials or a component. For each additional unit produced, the company incurs a cost equal to the raw material or component required to make the product. Simply put, if the cost is directly proportional to the variation in production volume, then it is a TVC and should be subtracted from the product's selling price to calculate the throughput.

Later on, many practitioners began to use the term *contribution margin* (CM) in place of throughput in order to make it have a more 'accounting sounding' name; but the concept is still the same. The contribution margin is the selling price of the product or service minus any totally variable costs. From this point, I will use the term 'contribution margin,' as it has been the term that I have found most acceptable when introducing the concept to my clients.

Inventory (I) - all the money the system invests in purchasing items it intends to sell, which includes raw materials, purchased components, work in process and finished goods inventory.

Inventory is the second term introduced by Goldratt and it is still a key measure that I use for managing an operation, whether you are making automotive components or hamburgers for a major franchise. This definition of inventory differs from traditional cost accounting systems. First, this definition does not add any value to materials or components as they are processed through the system. The traditional view is that inventory "absorbs" labor and overhead as it is transformed into the final product; so under a traditional approach, the value of inventory would increase through each step of the manufacturing or assembly process.

The assumption that "value" increases as material flows through the production system is misleading. In reality, not only is no value gained, but in fact, "value" actually may be lost, as the materials and components will lose their flexibility as they are processed. For example, raw plastic is received in the plant in an unmolded, uncolored form. Once it is mixed with a colorant and injected into a mold, it cannot be used for any other product. Therefore, if I were to use up my materials to make blue plastic bowls when there is no demand for them, not only was no value created (as no one wants to buy them), but I will have to replace the material to make a different product when an order comes in.

Many times, I have walked through a warehouse and found parts that have been sitting on the shelf for over a year waiting to be sold. Ask yourself, if you were acquiring that business, would you want to have those parts included in the purchase price?

In order to avoid such distortions, we need to value all inventory at the original value or cost that was paid when it was acquired. Secondly, we only count as inventory those materials we intend to sell. Any expendable tools or materials used in processing are accounted for in the last category to be defined – Operating Expense – since the company does not intend to transform these items and sell them to make money.

Operating Expense – the money spent by the company to convert Inventory into Contribution Margin

Operating Expense includes all the money spent by the system, with the exception of the money spent to purchase inventory (or alternatively, the Totally Variable Costs).

$$OE = \text{actual spending to turn I into CM}$$

There are two critical differences between this definition and the traditional cost accounting systems. First, there is no distinction made between direct and indirect labor. Both of these costs are used in the conversion of inventory into a final product, and the flow of that product to the customers. All personnel-related expenses are included in OE.

Second, operating expense only includes *actual* expenses. It counts real money or checks written as opposed to items such as variances. Under a traditional accounting system, if a worker is able to perform his or her activity at a faster rate than the engineering standard, that operator is generating a positive variance and the cost of his work per piece will be lower, even if the parts are backing up at the next operation. In a lean accounting system, there would be no change in CM, no change in I and no change in OE (since the operator's wages are unchanged).

To illustrate the concept of CM, OE and I, let's look at a small burger franchise. There are only three items on the menu: burger, fries and soft drink; the materials and components are standard in size and quantity for each, and the Contribution Margin for each item is as follows:

Item	Selling Price	Material Cost	CM
Burger	$1.00	$.65	$.35
Fries	$1.00	$.45	$.55
Soft Drink	$1.00	$.35	$.65

So, regardless of the mix of items, the total Contribution Margin for any period can be calculated by adding the Contribution Margins of each component by the quantity sold during that period.

To find the inventory in the system, we need to find the purchase value of all the food components in the franchise location. This would include the hamburger patties, the buns, pickles, mustard and ketchup; it also includes and special wrappers or bags for the fries as well as the syrup, carbonated water, cups and straws for the soft drinks. This inventory would *not* include the oil for cooking the fries, nor would it include other supplies like those used for cleaning the kitchen area, office supplies or special signage.

Operating Expense includes all the costs incurred to open up the franchise at 11:00 AM and serve food until 7:00 PM each day.

Monthly Operating Expenses

Category	Amount
Salaries, Benefits and payroll taxes	$13,000
Rent	$1000
Utilities	$300
Supplies	$200
Payment on Equipment Purchased	$2,000
Interest on Borrowed Funds	$400
Other Miscellaneous Items	$100
Total Operating Expenses	**$17,000**

In order for the franchise to turn a monthly profit, they must generate a Contribution Margin greater than $17,000 per month. If an average meal is determined to be one of each item, then:

Contribution Margin per Burger = $.35

Contribution Margin per Fries = $.55

Contribution Margin per Soft Drink = $.65

And:

Contribution Margin per meal = $1.55

Therefore:

OE/Contribution Margin = Total Quantity Needed to Breakeven

Dividing $17,000 by $1.55 gives us roughly 11,000 meals that we have to sell every month in order for our business to turn a small profit.

The first question we have to ask is whether or not we have enough capacity to meet that target. If we plan to be open Monday through Saturday, we have roughly 26 days to make those sales. Therefore, we need the capacity to produce 424 meals per day. If we buy all of our hamburger patties pre-made, we can determine a cook time as well as determine the number of patties we can place on the griddle at one time to calculate the maximum number of burgers that can be made per hour. We can do the same for the fries. If we assume that 50% of demand will occur between of 11:30 – 1:00 and 4:30 – 6:00, we can quickly figure out if we have the capacity to meet that demand.

If we find our capacity lacking, we then have to determine how an increase in capacity would impact our OE and then recalculate the number of meals we would have to sell in order to break even. Another alternative would be to consider pricing: Could we sell any of the items at a higher price to produce greater Contribution Margin at the same volume of business? Finally, we can look at our Totally Variable Costs to see if we can purchase the patties, potatoes or soft drink components at a lower cost to increase our Contribution Margin at the same price levels.

Hopefully it is now intuitively clear that for this business to make money, we have to have enough Contribution Margin to cover our Operating Expenses, and that our OE has to be based on the level of capacity required to generate the volume of product to meet the demand. All business improvement activity should be focused on three areas: generating more sales, spending less on the conversion of inventory into product, and reducing the amount of money tied up in inventory.

Going back to our story at the beginning of this chapter, it should be clear now that our Lean Champion had spent a lot of time and effort fixing an area that would have no impact on the profit of the operation. In order for a Lean Initiative to be effective, one of three things has to occur: an increase in sales, a reduction in material/outside service costs, or a reduction in operating expenses (including direct and indirect labor).

In the case of our manufacturing customer, while they had opened up floor space, they had no additional business to fill the space. Since overall labor remained the same and there was no change in the cost of purchased materials or services, it was easy to see why this Lean Event would not result in any positive bottom-line impact. Floor space was not a business constraint impacting their profits. Their efforts had been wasted. Usually when we hear how "that Lean stuff doesn't work for us," we find it was actually a lack of prioritization and proper performance metrics that were at the core of the failure to produce the desired results.

Many companies rely on accounting ratios to identify opportunities for improvement. While we do look at *sales per employee* and *sales per square foot* in benchmarking (comparing similar sized companies in similar industries), it is dangerous and misleading to use metrics based on the arbitrary allocation of overhead expenses to labor rates, floor space or products.

A Performance Improvement Professional should begin any engagement by building a cost model that is based only on costs that can be accurately traced through the business. This cost model becomes the basis for identifying and prioritizing constraints affecting the company's profitability through the use of "what if" analysis. It is also the basis for verifying that the results of each initiative meet expectations after implementation. Following this process of modeling, prioritizing, implementing and verifying results, a company can ensure that all Lean initiatives deliver their intended purpose: adding to the bottom line.

A Final Word about Inventory

Since the level of inventory does not directly affect net profit, many believe that the reduction of inventory is not as important as increasing Contribution Margin or reducing Operating Expense. The argument I have heard over and over is that the cost to carry an extra few days of inventory is insignificant compared to other costs of the business. While this is true, a reduction in the cost to carry is *not* the driver of inventory reduction.

In many of the operations I have seen, the biggest impact inventory has on the business is the reduction of productive floor space – that area needed to make product. In 2002, we were engaged by a small machining company to apply Lean principles to make them more profitable. Without doing anything other than fixing their schedule to take them from 30 days of inventory down to five, we were able to free up enough space in their main plant to allow them to stop renting offsite warehouse space where they were storing excess inventory. Along with the savings from the space rental, they were also able to cut the rental of a fork lift and eliminate the forklift operator who was stationed part-time at the offsite location. By reducing inventory, we had an immediate impact on net profit by reducing operating expenses.

Piece Cost and Quoting

The final objection I get when recommending a Lean accounting system is that the standard cost system is required to identify piece costs for make or buy decisions and to quote new business. As outsourcing is still a controversial area, especially overseas, let's start with product rationalization.

I once had a client who made mixing machines for the auto collision repair industry. The president wanted to outsource a few components to a supplier in China, basing his analysis on the cost of the product using the summation of materials, labor and burden – a typical standard cost formula. The owner was not comfortable with the analysis and asked us to look at it. We began by building a Lean accounting model based on Contribution Margin and Operating Expense for the entire company. Once we had the model built and verified, we simply replaced the Totally Variable Cost of each part with the new purchase price from China and then went line by line down the OE model and asked whether or not the item cost would go down or stay the same if they no longer made the part in-house.

We used the following equation for calculating the benefit in outsourcing the work:

$$\text{Net Benefit} = \text{Change in CM} + \text{Change in OE}$$

If you've already been through this, you already know the real benefits were not as high as predicted by the standard cost model. Of all the line items in OE, the only one that went down was plant labor – by merely two head count. This savings was offset by an increase in warehousing costs, as the long lead time to get the parts from China required more inventory to be held in the pipeline, which meant renting space offsite to keep extra parts.

When the president asked to see a part-by-part comparison, we simply took the change in OE and divided it by the quantity of parts shipped during the time period: Piece Cost = Totally Variable Cost per piece + Change in OE/Quantity Shipped.

In the end, the company did outsource the work, as the president was determined to do so, but at least the CEO was able to have a clear understanding of what was going to happen and to have it ready at review time when the promise of cheaper parts from China did not deliver as expected.

This discussion leads us nicely into the quote process for Lean accounting. Most businesses I deal with now are faced with pricing decisions based on aggressive purchasing tactics by their customers. When quoting, here are the steps you should take:

1. Determine whether or not you have the capacity to take on this work.

2. If not, calculate the cost of increasing capacity.

3. If yes, calculate any changes in OE required to produce this product or provide this service.

4. Calculate the Totally Variable Cost (TVC) involved with the product or service: Piece Cost = TVC + Change in OE

If you have the tools and equipment needed to produce a part and the capacity to do so, the opportunity is likely a good one, as long as the selling price is above the TVC, as this will yield an increase in Contribution Margin without increasing OE. If, on the other hand, you need to make an investment in order to have the capacity to produce a part, you need to calculate the Return on Investment by dividing the investment amount by the CM, minus the Change in OE.

By using this Lean accounting model and focusing on the true, measurable changes on the system of adding new products or outsourcing components, the predictability of the expected results will be substantially improved.

Conclusions

The performance measurement and evaluation systems inherent in standard cost models have contributed significantly to inappropriate actions, poor decisions and dysfunctional behaviors in both manufacturing firms and service providers. Such systems routinely focus on localized performance without regard to the impact that performance has on the overall system.

The adoption of a Lean accounting system using Contribution Margin, Inventory and Operating Expense can help managers and owners develop a more global perspective for decisions impacting their operations. Focusing on these measures will help the company evaluate the impact of specific actions and decisions on overall business performance. This, in turn, will enhance the quality of decisions made throughout the organization and improve the competitive position and profitability of the firm. For additional ideas on how to implement Lean accounting models, contact me at *rchandler@chandlerwilesgroup.com*, or through LinkedIn at *http://www.linkedin.com/in/ronchandler* and inquire about free articles.

Key Lessons Learned

1. Standard cost accounting and activity-based methodologies misrepresent the true cost of producing goods and services.

2. A Lean accounting system will help you avoid misallocating resources to projects that have no real ROI.

3. Lean accounting principles have the ability to show you which Lean projects will have a real impact on your bottom line.

About the Author

Ron Chandler has over 29 years experience in serving in an executive capacity in Sales, Engineering, Program Management, Product Development and Operations. Since 1988, Ron has been a student and practitioner of Lean Enterprise Principles, first in his own businesses and then as a consultant. He has applied Lean Methodologies to implement financial and operational turnarounds since 1994.

Ron has a Bachelors Degree in Chemical Engineering from the University of Michigan and has an MBA from the University of Detroit. He is Certified in Lean Manufacturing and Six Sigma Methodology – Black and Green Belt by the University of Michigan-College of Engineering.

Acknowledgements

I would like to acknowledge my partner, Stu Wiles, for his steadfast commitment to Lean and for always making my crazy ideas work under many difficult circumstances. Also, Rick Noell, who walked with me on the Lean journey and whose knowledge and wisdom carried us through many obstacles.

References

[1] J. Womack, D. Jones, D. Roos, & D. Carpenter, *The Machine That Changed The World* New York: Free Press, 1990.
[2] 2004. North River Press.
[3] T. Corbett, *Throughput Accounting, TOC's Management Accounting System* (Great Barrington, MA: North River Press, 1998).
[4] E. Goldratt, *What is This Thing Called The Theory of Constraints?* (Great Barrington, MA: New River Press, 1999).
[5] E. Goldratt, *The Haystack Syndrome: Sifting Information Out of the Data Ocean* (Croton-on-Hudson: North River Press, 1990): p. 19.

Chapter Eleven

QPE: A LSS Approach to Process Management & Sustainability

Matt Stewart

Overview

Most, if not all, of my colleagues in the consulting world would agree: when you ask the majority of companies, whether management or the workers, most know *what* must be done to fix their woes. Knowing how to get it done and implemented in the "Express Line, 10-items-or-less" method, however, is the issue that seems to stop everyone in their tracks. Many companies have tried the shotgun approach to Lean Six Sigma (LSS), firing away with kaizen events or Six Sigma projects, with no solid methodology, plan or purpose behind their attempts. This ultimately leads to failure, followed by scrapping the whole thing. As a result, Lean Six Sigma has left yet another company with a bad taste in their mouth. True Lean Six Sigma companies approach their methodology with sound program management principles using a defined approach to select the projects on which to work.

The foundation of a successful business is having the process pillars (Financial, Operations/Supply Chain, Quality, and Launch/Change) in place with robust processes supporting each one. When one pillar contains a weak process or a new requirement is introduced with no supporting processes, the pillar can become unstable, producing detrimental effects on other process pillars, compounding the issue. No matter how severe the damage or how deep the hole you may be in, there is a LSS methodology that can help: QPE – Quantify, Prioritize and Eliminate. QPE is an institutionalized process for the continuous elimination of constraints throughout the entire value chain.

This chapter will help you to:

- Create a defined, process-based approach to QPE.
- Discover which situations call for QPE.
- Identify the main players in QPE.

QPE within the Four Process Pillars of Every Operation

QPE is the LSS methodology of making improvements and/or repairs to business processes through the DMAIC approach: establishing relevant metrics, disciplined collection and quantification of data, prioritizing the work to match capacity, and eliminating constraints through proven tools and methodologies. This is the shortest and most cost effective way to ensure ongoing, sustainable success in any business environment. (See Chapters 12 and 19 for details about DMAIC).

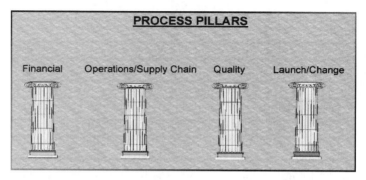

Figure 11-1: Organizational Process Pillars

Allow me to use story told by my good friend and colleague, Ron Chandler of the Chandler Wiles Group LLC, on how QPE could even work for your golf game:

> *Anyone who knows me knows that I'm a very consistent golfer – consistently bad that is. Over the course of any season, I will consistently shoot between 95 and 105 on any given course any given day.*
>
> *While someone in my position may be inclined to follow the advice from the latest advertisement in Golf magazine and buy the new Cobra Titanium-Ceramic Mega-Hit golf clubs for $5000 and hope that the latest and greatest flavor of the month club improves my game. Or I can seek the advice of a professional who has lived through clients like me before.*
>
> *Let's say I contact a professional. His first step would be to conduct an assessment of my game, perhaps by playing a round with me and evaluating all aspects of my game.*
>
> *During the assessment, I make sure I mention that my clubs were bought at K-Mart for $100 and show him the ad for the Cobra Mega-Hit clubs, pointing out the statement that they will lower my handicap after only 4 rounds. However, after the assessment, he sits me down and tells me things that I really don't want to hear: the clubs are not the immediate problem.*
>
> *The pro explains that we need to first fix my putting; by doing so, I will be able to improve my game by 15 strokes in 90 days. So, I*

engage him in the implementation of a better putting method and my score range moves to 80-90 in about 90 days.

So, I'm now ready for the Cobra's? Nope. Next he explains that by improving my short yardage game, I can improve my score by 10 strokes in 60 days. So, we implement the next phase, and in 60 days, my score range has improved to 70-80. Finally I can make a real improvement by purchasing the Cobra's! Well, not yet.

The data indicates that I can take an additional five strokes off my score by improving my course management, making good decisions and immediately fixing mistakes before they become disasters. So I implement his methodology and within 30 days, I am consistently scoring 65-75 per round. At $100 per lesson, I have spent $400 and improved my game to the point where I can compete with just about anyone. So, I'm done, right?

Wrong. In the interest of ongoing improvement, the pro suggests an incremental investment in new clubs: not spending all $5000 all at once, but instead replacing one club at a time, starting with the club I use the most (guess what, it's the putter!), and making additional purchases after I see whether or not the previous club made an improvement. In some cases, I find out that I use a club so rarely, I can take it out of my bag instead of spending the money to replace it.

So, the pro started with an assessment of the client's current game, identified all opportunities to improve any area of the game, and then implemented the best, most specific improvements based on the their impact on the client's overall performance. This is QPE, and it is still the most effective way we have found to achieve the greatest performance gains at the lowest relative cost.

As we move through the details of QPE in the next few sections, the case study we will use is from the manufacturing sector, within the process pillar of quality, but suggestions will also be made as how to use the methodology in additional industries and throughout the other process pillars.

QUANTIFY – Defining and Measuring the Process

When we review the definition of QPE, a couple of key elements stick out. QPE is an *institutionalized* process for the continuous elimination of constraints throughout the entire value chain. Constraints can be any problem or limitation on the free flow of the process; for example, defects, process steps, transactions, scans, moves, transfers, sign-offs, launch gates, inspection checkpoints, etc. Elimination or limitation of these constraints allows the process to move to completion much quicker because there are fewer steps, less stop/starts and less red tape. Or, to sum it up – less waste. Setting up the methodology of defining and measuring each waste is important because of the need to have consensus between all team members, as well as to be detailed enough to allow the measurement to produce clearly defined targets for elimination.

Within the quantify stage, the basics of data collection are implemented, both in procedure and action. This can be at a work cell, product line or department level, depending on the necessity of a swift impact, with the eventual intention of implementing QPE company wide. During a QPE implementation, a team establishes performance metrics, then establishes the processes for data collection and compiles the first initial data.

The important questions to ask within the team at this stage include: What is the process for data collection? When is the data collected? When is the data distributed? Who collects the data? Who reviews and distributes the data? Who gets the data? Who is accountable? Who is responsible? The acquisition of reliable data is extremely important during this stage and will likely include the negotiation of defect terms/types with the customer.

The trick here is to be tenacious concerning customer buy-in to the correctness and validity of the defects found. A daily review with the customer and all inspectors of the questionable defects will, in most cases, resolve any differences of opinion. Another best practice is to make sure all of the data recording sheets use the same terminology. This removes the "we said/they said" aspect of the QPE process.

To complete this stage of QPE, confirm the data is flowing throughout the value chain, from customer defects all the way to supplier defects. Be sure not to focus solely on your internal operations, *i.e.*, don't let the collection of data stop at either the receiving or shipping docks, as this will become highly important during the next phase.

PRIORITIZE – Analyze the Process

As we begin the Prioritize stage, we must keep in mind that QPE is an *institutionalized process* for the *continuous* elimination of constraints throughout the *entire* value chain. This phase is where data is given significance and containment changes are made. The team reviews and prioritizes the data, implements immediate containment activities between the different areas of inspection, and implements the initial corrective actions.

This phase needs to be implemented in an orderly fashion so you are not working on all of the cures for the all of the defects at the same time. By prioritizing defects into a Top 10 and Top 3 <u>pareto chart</u>, you will bring the visual aspect of the QPE process to bear and make the direction you are heading readily understandable to anyone who cares to view the system. By attacking just the top three defects, you will most likely have an effect on close to 50% of your total system defects.

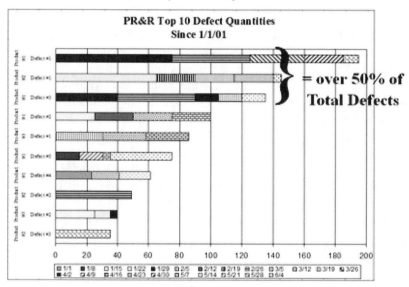

Figure 11-2: Top 10 Pareto of Customer Defects

Prioritization for the elimination of the defects generally should be as follows:

1. Customer

2. Contain Controlled Shipping Issues

3. Intermediaries

4. Controlled shipping

5. Internal

6. Process

7. Supplier Quality Engineering   (drive to zero)

Now that your containment initiatives are moving in the right direction, it is time to move on to the Elimination stage, which includes the institutionalizing, or permanent cultural change, of QPE.

ELIMINATE – Improve and Control the Process

This phase includes implementation of permanent corrective actions, confirmation of the elimination through data, communication to all employees and proper timing to move to the next initiative. As you conducted the prioritization stage, you no doubt found easy fixes or stop-gap measures for some of the Top 3 defects and quickly moved to implement corrective action.

Does your data reflect the elimination of these defects? In other words, have those defects been eliminated from reaching the customer through a corrective action that does not include inspecting them? If not, the potential for defects to reach the customer still exists. A good indicator of a *permanent* elimination of a specific defect is not finding the defect at any intermediary, final or in-process inspection locations. Not finding them anywhere in your process? Pat yourself on the back, and if necessary, request removal from the controlled shipping inspection process. Back up your request with the data. Remember: Additional inspection points and retraining operators *are not* permanent corrective actions, nor are they sustainable intermediate corrective actions. Make the changes to your *process* so the issue/defect/waste never comes back.

Just a few examples of corrective process changes include: initiating standardized work and process scrolling, witness marking, reducing the off-line rework (*i.e.*, do it on the line, in-process), push-click-pull or tactile confirmations, the rollout of a sustainable SQA Program, addition of a production resource, initiating quality review of all rework, an electronic error-proofing system (including Andon), changing an assembly sequence, applying power to an assembly, revising the design to include poke-yoke fixes or improvements, and the addition of protective coverings on both A and/or B surfaces. With the implementation of these process changes, are your defects eliminated? Confirm it with data and communicate it to the customer and your employees by celebrating your success and commitment to QPE.

Create Buy-in through Communication

There are many employee communication methodologies that may be used with the ultimate goal of getting all employees involved in the QPE process. Here are a few ideas to get you started:

Communication Board

A strategically placed communication board can provide up-to-date data from all locations (including QPE priorities), daily production data and supplier data – a must in the world of employee involvement.

Post Business Metrics

Posting your business metrics gives customers, suppliers and employees a complete understanding of how you run your business. Post both your business metrics and your customer metrics. For example, if your QPE project has had a visible, significant impact on product profit margin, what better way to inspire employees to continue to eliminate waste?

Hold Communication/Reward Meetings

Your employees have great power to either help you or hurt you in the movement toward your QPE goals. Having bi-weekly, or at least monthly, meetings with the employees to communicate direction gives everyone a chance to pause and take a collective look at where you are going. Make this mandatory for all employees. It provides you a chance to pass on rewards to those who have given implemented suggestions or to those who have a demonstrated knowledge of the status of the current business measures and QPE/defect priorities. This can be a lot of fun and bring whole shifts together, just for the cost of a few gift certificates to McDonalds or Wal-Mart.

Have Multiple Gate Reviews

If you want to kick-start the defect identification and elimination process, hold multiple <u>gate reviews</u> on each shift. A gate review is the review of all end-of-line defects at the point where the next step is getting the product or service to the customer. By having full staff participation in these events, the assignment of defect hunting goes to the proper executive, eliminating roadblocks and potential opportunities for reprioritization. Conducting these 5- to 10-minute reviews also has the cursory benefit of showing employees that you and your staff are truly dedication to the elimination of defects.

Implement Operator Line Stops

Another way to eliminate defects from reaching the end of the line (and making your gate review board) is to employ line stops. In this process, the operator stops the line and a SWAT team consisting of the supervisor/team leader and other indirect personnel immediately swarms to the defect location. They then determine the cause of the defect and implement corrective actions or process adjustments, including inspection of each prior process to determine that the in-process is clear of defects. A short report is completed and forwarded to management so the implemented change can become institutionalized across the company.

Visual Business Management (VBM)

A Visual Business Management system is a process for communication at all levels of your company. It creates a work environment that is self-explanatory, self-ordering, self-regulating and self-improving. It empowers your employees to take control and manage their own processes. The premise behind this methodology is, "What else can you tell them?" Are you communicating everything you possibility can to your employees, the customer and your suppliers? Do you know what you need to know? Do you know what you want to share and with whom? This system utilizes slogans, posters, photos/storyboards, newsletters, charts and graphs to promote involvement and knowledge.

Checks and Balances

The QPE process is very common sense in nature. But have you thought about how are you going to check and balance the process so that it becomes institutionalized across the organization? Using process auditors to confirm the operational sequence, re-instructing operators by conducting complete, full-floor reviews twice per shift, and having the data sheet that is collected reviewed by the executive staff fulfills part of the checks and balances system. Conducting executive audits with full management also supports the system of standardized work.

The important concept here is that you are auditing the process, not the people. The Standardized Audit Procedure is designed to review work area safety and then operator safety, including:

- All materials needed – present and of good quality
- All tools/machines needed – present and operational
- Operation/manufacturing process is conducted in proper sequence
- Operation/manufacturing process is done within scrolled or posted process time
- All quality alerts are conducted properly
- Quality of final product is within specifications

The most effective executive audit programs require all salaried positions to audit two work stations per shift on all shifts, and audit participation by individuals and groups is tied to performance bonuses. Remember, the company does not make money by having salaried personnel; money is only made *through* the operators who are directly tied to the process.

Case in Point

QPE was initially developed in a desperate situation: I had just become plant manager of an operation that had just become the number one worst supplier on a major OEM's worst supplier list and was carrying over 14 days inventory. The operation was new and a joint venture. The workforce was relatively inexperienced in manufacturing, quality and LSS techniques, which worked both to our advantage and against it.

Within six months of implementing QPE, the operation had moved off the OEM's radar. Direct labor had been reduced by 27%, inventory levels were reduced to 48 hours and we were exceeding product industry standards for defects per million.

Celebrate Your Success

Typical QPE implementation projects range from 32 to 78 weeks in length before reaching the closing step. While the process is not yet complete, the last step in the QPE process is contained within the process itself. You will be able to validate your QPE efforts through charts, graphs and data showing customer defects have been eliminated, internal defects have been reduced, process variations are reduced, your supplier quality has improved and employee participation has increased. Throughout the QPE process, many goals and successes will be achieved. Celebrate these successes and then apply the QPE process to other areas of your business.

Once you have your internal QPE system in place and operational, perhaps it is time to implement steps to improve your supply base to allow defect-free shipments to arrive at your door. The best practice to convey your expectations is through the establishment of a Supplier Quality System. Through this system, your expectations are passed on to your vendors so they will know where they stand with you, the customer.

Conclusions

This chapter has provided some easy steps to move quickly into the express lane of Lean Six Sigma techniques for the elimination of constraints throughout the entire value chain. By quantifying, prioritizing and then eliminating constraints in your processes, your quality will increase as your costs go down, and customer satisfaction will skyrocket. Furthermore, communicating these successes throughout your organization will drive employee satisfaction and further improvement in your value chains.

Key Lessons Learned

1. QPE is a systematic approach that has multiple process applications.

2. This system is simple and applies to most every situation.

3. Proper communication creates buy-in throughout the organization.

4. QPE provides a good place for small and medium sized business to start their journey in becoming Lean organizations.

About the Author

Matt Stewart is the President, Chief Lean Transformation Implementation Specialist, and Operations/Quality Turnaround Expert for GBWS Limited. Having trained and championed over 140 Lean/Six Sigma events, Matt has led projects in many different industries ranging from implementation of quality improvement systems to Lean manufacturing conversions of plant-wide operations. The industries Matt has worked in include automotive, steel, resin technology, paper, heavy truck, machining, injection molding, assembly, fitness centers, and many others. Matt received a Bachelor of Science Degree in Chemical Engineering from Michigan Technological University. He has received Certification in Lean Manufacturing and Six Sigma Methodology – Black and Green Belt from University of Michigan College of Engineering. The best way to contact Matt for further information, additional resources and discussion is through e-mail at *GBWSLimited@comcast.net*.

Chapter Twelve

Operational Excellence in Non-Profits

Ira Weissman

Overview

FY 2009 proved to be an extremely trying year for non-profits. With major philanthropists cutting back on their giving, and states and foundations cutting back on their grants, non-profits are having a difficult time continuing to provide services. This is especially telling as state and federal social service programs are being cut, adding more burden onto non-profits to pick up the slack and help those in need.

Adding to these problems is the demand for meaningful metrics in non-profit organizations. Prior to four or five years ago, the main metric for non-profits was the ratio of program-to-administrative costs. However, funders began to demand metrics tied to accomplishments. New types of metrics were required to satisfy funding agencies and a new generation of philanthropists. This is especially daunting to the small and medium non-profits who provided social services and are not used to thinking in terms of measureable accomplishment.

This chapter will help the reader to:

- Identify non-profit processes and metrics that will help the non-profit organization to succeed and satisfy its major funding sources.
- Learn how use a SIPOC chart to become more effective.
- Tie your vision to your processes and the metrics to show whether or not the organization is working towards its vision in the most effective manner.
- Identify opportunities for improvements.

Vision Statements and Customers

The first step in applying operational excellence tools is to understand an organization's overriding vision. Most for-profits and non-profits alike have a vision and vision statement that help guide their activities. In the for-profit world, a vision eventually leads back to the profit/survival motive, irrespective of the product or service being sold. This in turn leads to the customer, who buys the product based on desires and needs. The for-profit then builds its activities around those desires and needs.

The vision of the non-profit typically defines a state of society where a client's condition is improved by the service the organization provides. Because of the broad span of activities that non-profits cover, it becomes very difficult to define who is the "customer." The person or group paying for the services is not always the individual or group receiving the benefits of those services. Should the non-profit focus on the needs and wants of the people receiving the services, or the demands of the people/groups paying for the services?

A local community orchestra's vision or mission typically involves expanding the local community's appreciation of orchestral music while providing an opportunity for musicians of all levels to play, learn and perform music with and for others. Who are the orchestra's customers? Is it the people who buy the tickets to attend the performances, individual donors who give annual or ongoing gifts to the orchestra, a foundation who gives a grant to support ongoing activities or special programs, or even the orchestra members themselves?

Next, consider a parole board whose mission is to enhance public safety by making carefully considered parole decisions and successfully transitioning offenders back into the community as law-abiding citizens. Additionally, the parole board's mission may also include partnering with governmental, non-profit and private agencies to connect ex-prisoners with vocational, mental health and other services to break the cycle of crime. Who are the customers of the parole board? Is it the parolee, the prison system, the public, the partnering agencies, or the crime victims and their families?

It quickly becomes evident that each non-profit has at least two main customers: the people and groups who donate to the organization (donors), and the clients who utilize the non-profit's services. Further, it may be necessary to separate the donors into institutional and individual donors. It is important to make these distinctions because each one of these groups may have different needs and priorities, which may not fully align with one another. Thus, it becomes even more important to have a strong vision statement so that both the donors and clients understand what the organization is trying to accomplish and how it is going to achieve its goals.

Identifying the Needs of the Customers (Donors and Clients)

Once the customers have been defined, each group of customers' needs must be identified. Too often, the needs are described in such general terms that the non-profit is unable to focus its efforts to meet the expectations of its donors and clients. This can lead to the belief that the non-profit is not being effective in its activities. To translate a need into a more quantifiable goal, a <u>Critical to Quality (CTQ) Tree</u> is ideal.

A CTQ Tree seeks to move from the general to the specific by uncovering the drivers of the need. For example, a client of a credit counseling program may seek financial freedom. How does one convert that into something tangible? In the case of a client, it may be a case of asking where does it hurt the most (*i.e.*, what things cause the individual the most problems). Examples might include harassing bill collectors, poor credit rating and lack of available money. These in turn need to be framed in positive statements and broken down one more time to get to activities that are quantifiable. Below is an example of a CTQ tree showing how the broad desire of financial health can be broken down into specific, measurable characteristics.

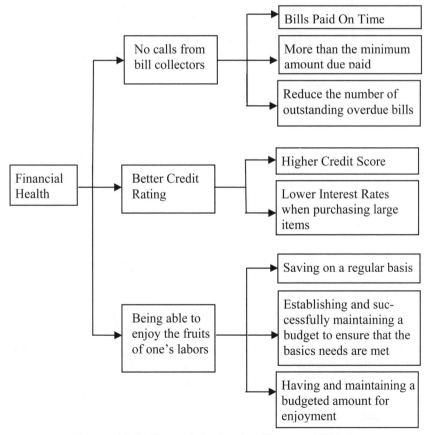

Figure 12-1: Critical To Quality Factors (CTQs)

A similar CTQ tree can be created for grant providers by looking at the criteria for receiving grants. For individual donors, it will be more difficult to predict what their needs and wants are, and it may require getting together a focus group of donors to obtain their input.

A second example to consider is a grief counseling group. How can a CTQ tree be used to convert the wants of the customer into tangible results and metrics?

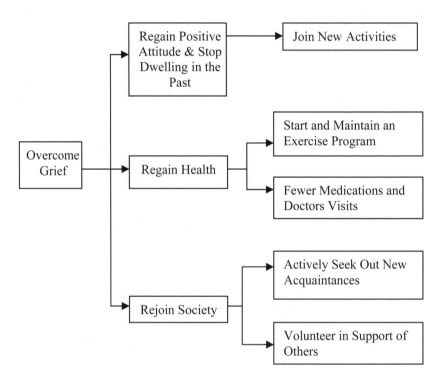

Figure 12-2: Grief Counseling CTQ Tree

It isn't just enough to go through the exercise of determining the CTQ factors. These factors must also be validated by going back to the client and/or donor to find out if they are accurate. Getting feedback on the accuracy of the CTQ factors can be done through one-on-one interviews, surveys, focus groups and the like. Once the CTQ factors are established, they will point the way to the appropriate metrics to be used for judging the effectiveness of the program's processes and the overall success of the program as a whole.

Organizational Processes

Once a non-profit organization has its vision and knows what its clients and donors are seeking, the organization then needs to look at the processes by which it satisfies those needs. Processes can be broken into three basic categories: value added, non-value added and enabling.

Value-added processes contribute to accomplishing the organization's vision. They are also those activities that: 1) the customer would be willing to pay for, 2) cause some type of change, and 3) are done right the first time. Non-value added processes do not contribute toward accomplishing the organization's goals. Non-value added processes actually *detract* from organization's ability to succeed by drawing away resources that are needed elsewhere to support the non-profit's vision.

Enabling processes are those activities that *need* to be done by the organization but do not directly contribute to achieving its vision or goals. An example of an enabling process might be filing the new IRS form 990-N for non-profits with an income of less than \$25,000/yr. While these processes/activities do not help the organization reach its vision, they are necessary to comply with the laws of the land.

Common complaints typically voiced by non-profits when the topic of processes is raised include:

1. We don't have processes because we deal with individuals, which makes everything we do unique;

2. Processes would just stifle our ability to meet the needs of our clients;

3. So much that we do depends on our ability to sense the situation and use our gut feelings;

4. Trying to develop processes is just an extra burden we don't have the time or resources to do; and

5. Non-profits are typically made up of social workers, artists or other non-technical types who are not comfortable with or inclined towards the rigorous analysis requirements of operational excellence.

These responses focus on the typical view of step-by-step compliance requirements of a bureaucratic organization. Many people do not recognize that by identifying an organization's processes and the key steps involved, it gives the organization an opportunity to set some broad guidelines to help its staff and volunteers assure that services provided to its clients meet a minimum level of care. It also uncovers those activities that don't support the organization's vision, which are then discontinued. This frees up people and funds to help support those activities that are most important to the organization. Some processes common to most non-profits are organizational management, service delivery, development, marketing, volunteer management and support services.

Usually when we think of processes, we think of detailed flow charts showing each step in a little box on a sheet of paper covering an entire office wall. A much simpler way to think of process charting is in the form of Suppliers, Inputs, Process, Outputs, and Customers (SIPOC):

1. Who are the suppliers to the process?

2. What are the inputs to the process?

3. What change(s) do we want to occur?

4. What are the outputs or outcomes of the process?

5. Who is the recipient of the outputs of the process?

In answering each question, you need to be aware of not only the physical, but the informational items needed to achieve the desired results. Take for example the recruiting of new volunteers, which is essential to most non-profit organizations. What does it take to bring a new volunteer into an organization and make them a successful contributor to the organization? First, we need to begin with the customer in mind, which in this case constitutes all the departments within the organization who are looking for volunteer help.

Usually when someone thinks of customers, they tend to think of someone outside of the organization. What most people don't realize is that it is also possible to have internal customers within an organization, where one group in the organization provides information, resources, or some activity to another group within organization.

Besides the group requesting volunteers, could there be any other parties who might be beneficiaries of the recruitment process? Could the volunteers themselves also have specific needs they want to have met as part of volunteering process?

The first question we need to answer is: What are the needs of the requesting organization and those of the volunteers? For the requesting group, are there particular skill sets needed, number of people required, physical attributes particular to a specific volunteer function? A few examples of special requirements might include a valid driver's license, being compassionate, being available twice a week, being multilingual, or perhaps being female or male.

For the volunteer, do they want to apply their skills and knowledge to a worthy cause, do they want to learn new skills, do they want to do something they cannot in their normal job, or perhaps just meet new people? Once the needs of the requesting department are understood, the recruiting process can begin; but in order to gain a volunteer who will stay with the organization and be happy volunteering, we have to address the volunteer's needs as well.

The next step in the recruitment process is to seek out those organizations that can either supply volunteers directly or support the acquisition of the volunteers (*i.e.*, suppliers). In order to help the recruitment department attract the right volunteers, the suppliers (e.g., Retired and Senior Volunteer Program, Corporate Community Affairs Departments) must be made aware of the organization's need and the requirements expected of the volunteers who are being sought.

If it is necessary to recruit people directly, the question becomes: How do we reach the people? The traditional answer is through newspaper ads or articles, radio ads and word of mouth. The new way of reaching out to people, especially young people, is through online social networking sites. These are our modern suppliers, and we have to make sure we provide them with sufficient and correct information so the right volunteers are attracted to the organization's cause.

Once a candidate has stepped forward, what has to be done to make the individual a useful volunteer? Are there forms to fill out, training to be given, a uniform or other apparel to be provided? These resources and individuals also can be considered inputs into the process, not just as customers. It is important the inputs to the process are identified. Think about how much time and effort is lost when just one item is forgotten in a process. Having to redo something is considered a non-value added activity and is a form of waste.

We can then engage in the actual process by which the inputs are changed into an output. This process could be anything from filing out a form to training someone how to greet a client, or even emptying a bed pan. The output does not need to be something physical. The point is that during the process stage, something occurs that takes us towards the end result we want to achieve. In the case of the new volunteer, the process will include filling out forms, signing required paperwork, being given an introduction to the organization and its cultural mores, a tour of the facility, receiving training on the specific tasks to be performed, being assigned a place to work and being provided with the appropriate materials.

The outputs are those outcomes desired by the customers: a client able to cope with grief, an effective volunteer, a person whose self-worth is improved, a river where trash has been removed, a cure for a disease or a host of other possibilities. The list of potential outputs is as varied as the non-profit organizations out there. It is even possible the output of one process will be the input to another process.

By using the Supplier, Input, Process, Output, Customer (SIPOC) method, you can gain a high-level view of the organization's processes and what is needed for the organization to be successful.

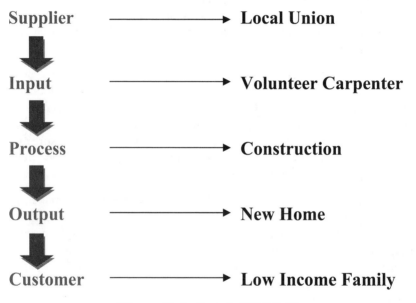

Figure 12-3: Sample SIPOC Chart

Looking For Ways to Improve

Once an organization's processes have been identified, we want to look for ways to improve those processes. The primary reason behind process improvement is to make more resources available to address the urgent needs of the organization. Processes can be improved in many ways: eliminating processes entirely, simplifying steps, reorganizing work areas, adding resources and eliminating sources of mistakes.

The first step is to look at which processes are <u>value added</u>, <u>non-value added</u> or <u>enabling processes</u>. Non-value added processes are easiest to address: they should be eliminated first. For processes that are value-added or enabling processes, the question is: Where are the areas that can be improved?

Those processes most in need of improvement are usually well known within the organization but are not openly discussed – the elephant in the room that nobody talks about. They are typically those processes that take the longest time, consume the most resources, are always backlogged, have the most difficulties, must be repeated due to errors, cause problems between departments, etc. Using a cross-functional team to identify problem areas will allow not only individual departments' problems to be identified, but will also help to point out those problems that occur between departments, *i.e.*, where one department supplies another department with information, materials, reports or other value-added activities.

In fact, good teams will identify more issues than the organization's management will be comfortable with accepting. This is a moment of truth for the organization, and especially for senior management. Most of the organization will know about the cross-functional team and its mission, even though it may not be publicized. If management chooses to do nothing or merely gives token support to the team, it sends a very strong message to the organization as a whole that management does not really care about improving the organization. On the other hand, if management publicizes, encourages and celebrates the actions of the team, it will find the organization itself will be more likely to get behind the improvement efforts.

The processes selected for improvement should be those that have a significant impact without demanding a large amount of resources or effort. Usually, the cross-functional team will be encouraged to look for waste in the process – those items that can be eliminated without having any meaningful negative impact on the process itself. It cannot be said enough: The importance of eliminating waste is that it frees up (scarce) resources that can be used elsewhere more effectively. Additionally, eliminating waste speeds service delivery. (See Chapter 9 for an in-depth treatment of project selection.)

Typical examples of waste are mistakes and rework, waiting, excess movement, excess processing, unnecessary transport of items and performing tasks before necessary. Waste could also include overcapacity that is not being used appropriately.

Mistakes and waiting are self-evident waste, but what makes movement or transportation a waste? In the case of movement, it may mean that someone has to continuously get out a chair to use a piece of equipment or to see if someone has entered an office. How often does the office secretary have to pick up the phone when a headset could be made available? These are examples of motion waste.

A transportation waste occurs when there is too much handling of an object or too great a distance traveled. Could a form be sent and signed electronically rather than couriered between sites? Or could the need for the signature be eliminated entirely? A lot of transportation waste occurs with bringing in out of town employees for meetings. Can you save time and money by using a commercially available web conferencing site?

An additional waste is the non-utilization of peoples' capabilities, especially volunteers. Too frequently volunteer usage follows the historical stereotype of greeters and stuffing and addressing envelopes. This does not take into consideration that the volunteer may be an accountant, marketing manager, CEO or other professional. Even when a volunteer does step forward to offer a suggestion, the idea is often turned down because it comes from someone who may not be a staff member or because the basis of the idea comes from the for-profit world (and thus seems inappropriate to a non-profit situation). Consider how much was lost when an IT professional offered to develop a free software package to look for fraudulent expenditures in a financially struggling school system and was turned down. Too often the answer to why something is done a particular way is, "It has always been done that way." Many times, the real reason is that it was done originally because of a grant or agency requirement that no longer applies.

One waste that affects every process is waiting. Waiting can be caused by a limitless number of factors: delivery schedules, a poorly designed process that funnels all activities through a single (choke) point, software that is not user friendly, an overburdened individual or piece of equipment, lack of training, not having information readily available, or an overly complicated form. Identifying the reason why delays are occurring will involve studying both informational and material inputs, how the work is done, and how the outputs are passed on to whoever is to receive them.

The cause of the delays could occur at any point in the process. The simplest way to determine where the delays are occurring is to actually observe the work being performed and then trace the delays as far back as possible to assure that all the reasons for the delays can be identified.

A simple data sheet is all that is needed. If desired, a video tape can be made of the work flow. Both will allow the process to be studied by an individual or group to determine the causes for the delays and the best way to address the identified causes of the delays.

Activity	Start Time	End Time	Activity	Actual Working Time	Non-Working Time	Reason for Delay
1						
2						
3						
4						

Table 12-1: A Simple Chart for Identifying the Causes of Delays

The chart can be modified to suit each organization's needs, but the key point is to identify the non-productive times in the process. The exercise forces people to look in detail at how the work occurs and how to eliminate those things that prevent work from flowing.

If the cause of delays is due to a bottleneck or constraint, the typical response is to throw more resources at it (more people, fancier and faster computers and/or software programs, etc.). However, to eliminate a constraint, the process associated with the constraint first must be understood. Too often people look at where work is piling up without looking for the true source of the problem. Once the constraint is identified, you must do three things:

1. Make sure the individual or resource is dedicated to the critical task and ceases all non-critical activities (*e.g.*, having social workers doing record input versus a clerical person, or providing the social workers with electronic forms or a database).

2. Redesign the rest of the processes to allow the constrained individual/resource to focus on the critical tasks of the job and to feed work to that point at a rate the constraint can handle.

3. Expand the capacity of the constraint by adding additional equivalent resources (*e.g.*, more personnel or more equipment).

Once one constraint is addressed, another constraint will typically appear somewhere else in the process. This does not mean the efforts to remove the constraint were unsuccessful; rather, it is the nature of processes that once a constraint is successfully addressed, other limitations will become visible.

Finally, there is also waste associated with errors and having to correct those errors that have occurred. What is often not clearly recognized is that by taking the time to do any task properly, even if it appears to take longer than desired, doing the task correctly the first time still takes less time overall than performing the task incorrectly and then having redo the task a second or even a third time until the task is done correctly.

Finding the Problem

When trying to correct a problem, the place to start is to define exactly what the problem is. The problem statement should be as descriptive as possible including the issue, its impact, the length of time it has existed and what is the desired result. Additionally, the problem should be written in such a way as to not imply what the solution might be.

> *XYZ Charities has, over the past year, failed to gain any of the five available federal and state grants to continue its highly acclaimed homeless program, which will mean that funding for the program will run out in six months.*

Once the problem statement has been created and agreed to by all parties involved in trying to solve the problem, information needs to be gathered as to why XYZ Charities did not receive the grants. If the information has not already been provided by the government agencies or foundations who were offering the grants, then XYZ Charities may want to ask the government agencies or foundations why they were not successful in winning the grants. If the government agencies or foundations are unable or unwilling to answer the question, then XYZ Charities might try contacting one of the agencies who did receive the grant to see that agency's grant proposal to determine what differences might exist between the two. The key point is that before any solution is imagined or attempted, there needs to be some research and facts upon which to base any corrective action.

When looking for the causes of errors or problems, the natural response is to point the finger of blame at an individual. However, the *root* cause is seldom the individual. If deadlines are missed, we need to ask whether the individual is overloaded. Perhaps the individual would benefit from a refresher course in grant proposal writing. The bottom line is to keep digging past the blame and root out the real causes for process failure.

One way to drill down to determine the source of a problem is to ask the question: Why did this happen? And you must ask yourself this at least five times. Each time this question is asked, you will dig a little deeper into determining the true cause of the problem. Using the failed grant application as an example, the 5 Why methodology might go as follows:

1. Why was the grant application rejected?

   a. The grant application was received after the cut-off date.

2. Why was the grant application received after the cut-off date?

   a. The grant application was mailed the day before the application was due.

3. Why was the grant application mailed the day before the application was due?

   a. The application was not ready for signature until the day before it was due.

4. Why wasn't the grant proposal ready for signature until the day before the grant application was due?

   a. The grant writer did not become aware of the grant until the week before the application was due.

5. Why did the grant writer only become aware of the grant a week before the grant application was due.

   a. The agency only heard about the grant from another agency.

In this case, the final cause might be that XYZ Charities has no definitive means of finding out when new grants become available. This is an information problem, not a people problem.

Another means of analyzing the problem would be to try to imagine all the possible causes and to group them into basic categories. One visual tool for grouping the problem causes is a fishbone diagram where each fish bone represents a different basic problem area. Typically, the problem areas are grouped into the following basic categories:

1. Machine or Equipment related problems

2. Materials related problems

3. Methods related problems

4. Measurement related problems

5. Mother Nature or Environment related problems

6. Man/Woman (People) related problems

The fishbone diagram is a visual tool that helps find common threads. Once the common threads are identified, a decision can be made as to where to dig deeper and which problems to address. (See Chapter 13 on the 6 M's).

For example, a fishbone diagram might be used to determine why a fundraising event lost both credibility and funding for a non-profit.

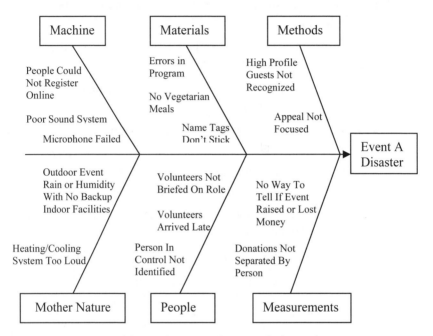

Figure 12-4: Fishbone Diagram for a Failed Fund Raising Event

Once the reason for the failure is known, an appropriate solution can be devised to prevent a reoccurrence of the problem in the future. In the case of late grant applications, the solution might be to sign up for a service that sends out notices of new grants of interest to the agency or having a staff member visit key foundations and government websites on a regular basis looking for information on new grants.

Another point to consider is any potential weak points of the solution. For example, if an individual is assigned to scan key foundations and government websites and that individual is out for a period of time or is not diligent in their work, XYZ Charities may find itself back in the same situation.

This leads to the last part of our problem-solution methodology, which is to build the solution into the agency's day-to-day operations and to revisit the solution on a regular basis to determine whether the solution is working as expected. If the solution is working as expected, XYZ Charities is submitting its grant applications on time and receiving the grants it needs to keep its programs running; XYZ Charities then should look for ways to further improve its processes. If XYZ Charities is still not winning grants, they need to go back to the root cause identification stage to see if there is something it missed and again analyze the information to assure it has addressed *all* the problems preventing it from winning the grants it needs. Many problems we see as consultants have more than one root cause.

Organizations have many opportunities to improve. Studies show that between 20% to 80% of an organization's activities are *not* value added. When trying to improve, organizations must attack those problems that a) have the most impact, and b) have a solution that requires the least amount of resources. The first step in finding areas of improvement is the willingness to recognize that things can be improved and to look at the organization in an honest light. A number of different wastes have been described in this section. Using these as a guide will allow your organization to reassess how well it is doing and find ways of improving without having to invest large amounts of time or resources. Once areas of improvements are recognized, the methodologies in this section can then be applied to reduce waste and free up resources for areas where they are most needed.

Conclusions

Too often when attempts are made to apply operational excellence methodologies to non-profits, the attempts are met by the feeling that it is just another burden, or they aren't applicable to the activities of the non-profit. This is a disservice to all of those involved in the attempt. What is frequently forgotten is that building a culture of organizational excellence doesn't have to be done all at once, rather, it can be done one step at a time. Each step the organization takes in the direction of operational excellence is another step towards helping the organization survive and prosper.

This chapter has sought to provide some questions that will help the non-profit enterprise use the tools provided in this chapter to focus and streamline its activities in such a way as to maximize the organization's efforts and increasingly scarce resources. Success will come to those who are willing to learn from each attempt and to build on those lessons learned.

Key Lessons Learned

1. Lean and Operational Excellence tools *can* be applied to the activities of non-profits to eliminate waste and institute process improvements.

2. Increasingly scarce resources and higher demand for non-profit services require organizations to apply Lean Thinking principles, metrics and tools if they want to continue to provide services.

3. Non-profits have the unique need to identify a host of different customers: donors, clients, suppliers, all of whom have different needs and desires the organization must satisfy.

About the Author

Ira Weissman is a certified Lean Six Sigma Black Belt. He has spent over 30 years in the commercial nuclear power industry where he was involved in quality, project and program management; training; and computers. Mr. Weissman also brings with him a passion for non-profit work, where he has spent over 15 years in high-level volunteer positions and experience working for a non-profit coordinating agency.

For more information about applying Lean and Operational Excellence tools to non-profits, contact Ira at *idea.innovations@live.com*.

Universal Tools

A determined soul will do more with a rusty monkey
wrench than a loafer will accomplish with all the tools in a
machine shop.

– Robert Hughes

Chapter Thirteen

DMAIC: A Common Sense Approach to Healthcare

Karen Young

Overview

Newly trained Lean Six Sigma practitioners, middle managers and project team members in the healthcare industry will benefit from this simple explanation of the Lean Six Sigma DMAIC approach to solving quality problems. Unlike some tools in the Lean Six Sigma tool box, DMAIC is a universally applicable tool that can carry over into any industry. Healthcare is different than manufacturing, high tech or other service industries, as healthcare quality issues are unique: failure to identify, fix and control issues can mean the difference between life and death. If the proper procedures and processes are not in place, and if we don't follow the process carefully, the costs are much higher than an analysis of the financials.

In this chapter, we will look at a common sense approach to applying the five phases of DMAIC to healthcare improvement initiatives. Some of the essential tools and tollgates will be discussed in a way that hopefully removes the "scary mask" that frightens many people about Lean Six Sigma and its emphasis on statistics.

This chapter will help you to:

- Learn how to select the right tools to improve healthcare.
- Follow specific healthcare examples demonstrating the correct use of the essential tools, common to most projects.
- See the logic behind some of the "not so intuitive" concepts.

Common Sense is a Universal Tool

A 45-year-old-man was brought into the emergency department in an ambulance. He had been in a serious car accident that rendered him unconscious with possible extensive internal injuries. The trauma team was faced with two decisions. First, they needed to assess the current condition in order to stabilize the patient; second, determine the correct course of action to repair any injuries. Both decisions needed to be made quickly and correctly under extreme pressure. Clinicians have several diagnostic tools available to aid them in making a diagnosis. Some tools quantify the problem, some provide images of the problem, some provide pathways to identify the causes of the problem and others prescribe solutions to the problem. The key is to know the purpose and functionality of each tool so the user can choose the right tools for the job. These choices are not made arbitrarily. There is a common sense approach to this process. Clinicians follow a structured set of guidelines, algorithms, and visual clues to help make decisions that lead to improving patient outcomes.

Within the healthcare industry, there are numerous inefficient or ineffective processes that lead to waste and mistakes. Identifying them requires the efforts of specialized teams using specialized guidelines and tools to improve outcomes. Lean Six Sigma provides that structured approach using process information to solve many of the quality problems faced by clinicians. It is coordinated around a five phase process – Define, Measure, Analyze, Improve, and Control (DMAIC). Each phase involves specific objectives and tollgates designed to guide teams to improve overall effectiveness and capability, strengthen competitiveness and improve key metrics for the organization. This philosophy focuses on the delivery of continually improving value to its customers and stakeholders. Philosophy? Yes, philosophy: a shared belief in attaining excellence through the elimination of waste and the reduction of process variation. But getting there requires a culture transformation with buy-in from every level within the organization.

The Define phase is the discovery period where we identify the problem from the customer's perspective. Critical to Quality characteristics (CTQ's) are determined and validated against customer requirements. Initial performance standards are then set as a basis for measurement.

In the Measure phase, we study the voice of the process and the voice of the customer. Current state process capability is assessed and performance objectives are finalized. It is important to validate the measurement system at the beginning of this phase and again at the end of the Analyze phase. This criterion is often overlooked, resulting in bad data that leads to bad decisions.

The Analyze phase is where we encounter the "scary mask" of statistics. Here we have the opportunity to identify and understand the sources of variation in the problem process. Potential causes identified in the measure phase are analyzed in an effort to get to the root of the problem. From that, hypothesis tests are performed to determine if the data support the organization's claims about current performance. The outcomes provide insight on potential solutions that feed into the Improve phase.

The Improve phase gives us a look into the relationships between process variables. Here we test, confirm and validate the solutions slated for implementation. Finally, in the Control phase, process capabilities are redefine based on the new current state and a process control plan is implemented to monitor sustainability.

DEFINE – Get the Picture

Tollgates provide an excellent opportunity for the project champion to review work done to date and to give guidance. Tollgates represent a minimum set of tangible deliverables that must be present before the team can move forward. Key tollgates in this phase are the project charter, SIPOC, and tools that evaluate the voice of the customer. The project charter is essential in making our case for selecting a project. However, many teams work without one to the detriment of the project. There are key elements that must be included in every good charter. (See Chapter 19 for a simple sample charter). It must have a compelling business case, a specific problem statement, a succinct project scope, clearly defined goals and objectives, realistic milestones, constraints and assumptions, and clearly defined roles and responsibilities for the team. As you finish each section, go back and ask yourself, "Is it in there?"

Support for the project starts with the business case. Here you are trying to connect the project, the problem process and the customer requirements to the organization's goals and strategic objectives. Explain the issues you are addressing and why this project is important. What are the consequences if a project is not initiated now to fix this problem? Be brief, specific and create a sense of urgency.

Business Case *Is it in there?*	The ordering practices of managers vary across the health system. Some managers order monthly as needed, while others order three to six months worth of supplies at one time. Too often, supplies get thrown away because they expire before being used, resulting in huge cost overruns.

Problems result in customers or stakeholders not getting what they need from your organization. A well-written problem statement paints the finer picture. It must be quantifiable and measurable, identify the specifics of what is causing the problem and describe any gaps in performance. In other words, where are we compared to what is desired? Most importantly, the problem statement must identify the pain or the severity of the impact that this problem is having on either the organization or its customers. Be sure to use facts and not assumptions when writing the problem statement.

Problem Statement *Is it in there?*	Within the last 12 months, one company found 31% of the glucose strips ordered for the diabetic clinic were discarded due to expiration. Since this type of error is at least 95% preventable, the cost of poor quality was estimated at approximately $150,000.00. Based on the current failure rate, the process was performing at ~ 2.0 sigma.

The <u>goal statement</u> specifies what the project will deliver. Identify the metrics you plan to improve and a reasonable timeframe to expect results. You may find it convenient to incorporate the milestones section of the charter into this section.

Goal Statement *Is It In There?*	This project will reduce the number of glucose strips discarded due to expiration by 95%. Project work will begin immediately upon approval of this charter and will deliver results in six months. Major milestones will be set at two months, four months and six months with expected deliverables of 30%, 45%, and 20% reductions, respectively.
Scope Statement *Is It In There?*	The ordering and usage tracking protocols for glucose strips in the diabetic clinic will be the focus of the investigation. Only the activities from receipt of shipment to inventory count prior to the next order placed will be addressed. Other products or clinic processes will not be included at this time.

Next, you must define the <u>project scope</u> statement. Most people erroneously believe this is the part of the project plan that outlines the actions the team will take to fix the problem. Instead, the project scope statement establishes the boundaries of the problem process in an attempt to prevent <u>scope creep</u>. Start by identifying the process that is producing the problem. Give it a name. Then, state where this problem process begins and ends. Too often project leaders confuse this with the project schedule. The scope must be specific and realistic. Know your team's limitations. Many project failures can be traced back to teams biting off more than they can chew.

The rest of the charter elements are fairly simple to write and are shown in Chapter 19 of this book.

A companion to the charter is the SIPOC map. (See also Chapters 12). As a general rule, use simple language to list in sequential order five to seven major activities critical to the process (vertical flow). Align the first and last steps of this map with the project scope (Table 13-1). Horizontal flow runs across the map. Take each process step and identify the predominant things that come out of that step. I emphasize *things* because people are not outputs. Outputs are the result of the process step transforming an input into something of value to a customer. Customers can be people, places or things; internal or external, depending on the process.

	Horizontal Flow				
	Suppliers	**Inputs**	**Process**	**Outputs**	**Customer**
V e r t i c a l	Patient	Patient info Insurance info	Admissions/ Intake	Patient face sheet Initial acuity level	Nurse Billing Dept.
	Patient/ Triage Nurse	Face sheet Reason for visit	Triage	Initial care plan Vital signs	Nurse Physician
	Nurse / Mid-level providers	Care plan Acuity level assessment	Diagnosis/ Treatment	Preliminary diagnosis Tests/meds orders	Lab Pharmacy Physician
F l o w	Physician/ Ancillary providers	Labs Meds Assessments	Ancillary services	Tests results Prescriptions Treatment plan	Physician Nurse Patient
	Physician	Final diagnosis Treatment plan	Discharge/ Admit	Discharge teaching Admission process	Patient, Hospital receiving staff

Table 13-1: SIPOC Process Map

Inputs are the things that are transformed by the process step to become outputs. The first column of the horizontal flow identifies the predominant suppliers of the inputs. Suppliers can be people, places or things, customers from a previous process step or an upstream process. This simple chart illustrates the key elements involved in delivering the necessary care to our car accident victim in the opening story.

Lean Six Sigma projects are customer focused, so identifying the right customer is the first step towards success. The next step is to get to know and understand the voice of that customer. Is there a difference between customer requirements and customer needs? A need is something essential that is missing while a requirement is some specification that fulfills a need. There are several ways to capture the voice of the customer: Interviews, market research, surveys and customer complaints are the more popular tools. Unfortunately, most organizations use customer complaints as the primary source of data. Once you collect the customer's voice, what will you do with it? Feed the information into one of several prioritization matrices. Use a CTQ tree to identify the need, the drivers of that need and the measurable outcomes of the drivers. A Kano Model helps to sort customer requirements. This diagram divides requirements into four groups:

> **Satisfiers**: the things that the customer must have;
>
> **Dissatisfiers**: things the customer must have but are not getting;
>
> **Delighters**: things that the customer did not expect but is excited when they get them; and
>
> **Nice to haves**: things that the customer may want but can live without.

Whichever model you use, it will give you an advantage into accurately defining your problems.

MEASURE – How Are We Doing?

Why do we take measurements? To help us make decisions about our process. Each measure we take must have a purpose. With that in mind, we need to ask a few questions. Why do we need this data? What role will it play in the decision-making process? How will the data help us see the connection between the problem and the organization's goals? What relevant CTQ does the data quantify?

Your ability to see the magnitude of the problem will depend on the type and amount of data you collect and the size of the unit of measure. There are formulas for calculating minimum sample size. Generally, minimum is okay, as long as you understand the risks. Selecting the type of data is much simpler: The accepted rule of thumb is to collect one process measure, two input measures, and three output measures.

Use the preliminary data to quantify the current state of the process. Establishing baselines is the first step to answering the question, "How are we doing?" Six sigma teams use <u>sigma levels</u> to quantify the health of processes. Suppose you were presenting a project proposal to the senior leadership team about a problem with wait times in the outpatient pharmacy. Customers were getting frustrated, canceling their orders and taking their prescriptions to commercial pharmacies. Preliminary data showed a baseline sigma of 2.5 and cost of poor quality at $250,000.00 for the previous fiscal year. Someone on the selection committee asked, "How did you get this baseline sigma?"

The basic calculation starts with defects per unit, moves to defects per opportunities, then to defects per million opportunities (DPMO). Use a conversion chart or statistical software to convert DPMO to sigma. If the process generates attribute data, then there is only one opportunity for failure. Attribute data is two-state: The characteristic being considered is either present or absent. Processes that generate continuous data can have several opportunities for failure. However, you want to select only the critical few that have a significant impact on the product or service.

ANALYZE –Guessing and Testing

At this point, we have a pretty good understanding of what is happening in the process. Our next step is to identify the root causes and test our assumptions. This will require the use of some special tools. An <u>affinity diagram</u> is an "idea generator" that can be used to generate the master list of potential causes. Brainstorm with the team and process owners to uncover as many causes as possible. I call this process "mining for causes." It is not uncommon for teams to generate as many as 100 or more ideas. Organize ideas that share a common theme into groups.

A cause and effect, or <u>fishbone diagram,</u> along with the <u>Five Why's</u> drill down, allows us to see what we are doing wrong. Write a micro or <u>granular statement</u> of the problem in the head of the fish. Use the <u>6 M's</u>[1] as the category headers for the spines. Narrow the list from the affinity diagram to only the most likely causes and place them under the appropriate category heading.

Wrong-patient errors are a growing concern for hospital-based clinical laboratories. The National Patient Safety Goals performance guideline states that two patient identifiers are to be used when collecting blood samples and other specimens for clinical testing. Identity verification failures cause delays in diagnosis and treatment with the potential to negatively impact patient outcomes. Delays can also translate into rework or increased length of stay, both of which are costly.

Let's revisit our patient in the emergency room. The physician ordered some diagnostic tests; however, an hour later, the doctor discovered the blood had not been drawn. Phlebotomy services in this case are provided by the laboratory. The reason given in the computer for the delay was "unable to collect – patient I.D. uncertain." These occurrences are currently at 12% in this hospital - higher than the national average. How might a cross-functional team investigate the causes and propose solutions to reduce this defect rate?

The team would start by brainstorming with the people who work the process to get ideas for the "idea generator." Ideas are sorted into the fishbone 6M categories. Then, create a micro problem statement from the macro problem statement found in your project charter. This will go in the head of the fish.

Take each category and ask a series of 5 Why's. The first why comes directly from the fish's spine: "Why was there a mismatch?" Answer the question with a "because" statement: "Because the patient assigned to the bed did not match the name on the lab request." The second "why" is formed from the previous because statement: "Why did the lab request show a different patient for that bed assignment?" Answer with another "because" statement. Continue this process until you have drilled down to five why levels.

Root causes that come from this process must be validated before recommendations for solutions can be implemented. At this point, all recommendations are merely assumptions. Your claim is no more than your best guess about the impact of the proposed solutions on future process performance. The good news is, inferential statistics enable you to make decisions about your claim based on the process data and not gut feelings.

The Analyze phase is treated in-depth in Chapter 19, and we need not re-present the material here. Specific analytical tools are presented with examples in that chapter, along with how to read the results. However, the following basic steps are common to all hypothesis tests.

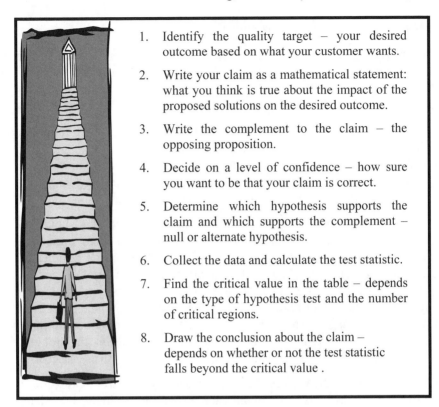

1. Identify the quality target – your desired outcome based on what your customer wants.

2. Write your claim as a mathematical statement: what you think is true about the impact of the proposed solutions on the desired outcome.

3. Write the complement to the claim – the opposing proposition.

4. Decide on a level of confidence – how sure you want to be that your claim is correct.

5. Determine which hypothesis supports the claim and which supports the complement – null or alternate hypothesis.

6. Collect the data and calculate the test statistic.

7. Find the critical value in the table – depends on the type of hypothesis test and the number of critical regions.

8. Draw the conclusion about the claim – depends on whether or not the test statistic falls beyond the critical value .

Figure 13-1: Analyze Phase

If the **null hypothesis** supports the claim and the data shows the claim to be:

True: We fail to reject the null. There is not enough evidence at the % confidence to disprove the claim or to say the alternate is true.
False: We reject the null and accept the alternative. There is enough evidence at the % confidence to disprove the claim and say the null is false.

If the **alternate hypothesis** supports the claim and the data shows the claim to be:

True: We reject the null and accept the alternative. There is enough evidence at the % confidence to prove the claim and say the null is false.
False: We fail to reject the null. There is not enough evidence at the % confidence to prove the claim or say the alternate is true.

IMPROVE – The Future Depends On It

Sometimes we come out of the Analyze phase with a pretty long list of solutions. However, before implementing any of them, it is wise to study these factors to see which ones will truly make a significant change in the process.

Most healthcare professionals are scientists familiar and comfortable with the scientific method. Early scientists were limited to trial and error methods that were expensive and time consuming. Today, we have <u>Design of Experiments</u> (DOE). The more common types are very cost effective and allow us to test several factors simultaneously.

Successful experiments require careful planning. A good plan should be in writing and supported by everyone involved. It should include a statement of the objectives, a list of key input factors, the number of trials and a timeframe for conducting the experiment. A brief discussion of how the results will be analyzed is also helpful. Properly defining the objectives is the most critical of all the planning steps. Vague objectives lead to measuring the wrong things and drawing the wrong conclusions. A good objective statement includes: *what* the goal is, *where* the problem is, *why* the goal is important, and *how* you plan to accomplish that goal.

Ineffective communication is the most frequently cited root cause for a sentinel event. Effective communication is timely, accurate, complete, unambiguous and understood by the recipient. How might a project team phrase an objectives statement for a DOE designed to study factors that will reduce errors and improve patient safety? The objective of this DOE is to reduce the number of errors due to ineffective communication [*what*] in all clinical areas [*where*] in order to improve patient safety [*why*] by implementing standard protocols for giving and receiving orders and test results [*how*]. Did they miss anything?

The DOE process follows the IPO (input-process-output) model. <u>Input factors</u> are manipulated at different levels to determine their effects on the outputs. These factors are generally associated with the proposed solutions from the Analyze phase.

Let's look at this from the context of a cycle time issue a cancer treatment center was experiencing in getting lab test results. Delays in result reporting were causing delays in administering chemotherapy. Treatment delays translated into extended lengths of stay for patients and overtime costs for the center. A five-factor, two-level design was selected to determine which solutions might yield a significant reduction in the cycle time.

		LEVELS	
		LOW	**HIGH**
F **A** **C** **T** **O** **R** **S**	**A**-Result reporting	Tech calls the results to the nurse	Results automatically print at the nurse's station
	B-Print labels	Print in collection site	Print at nurses station
	C-Specimen transport	Batch	Each
	D-Test order entry	Requests triggered at registration	Requests manually ordered by the nurse
	E-Blood drawn	By phlebotomists	By nurses

Table 13-2: Two-level DOE Design

Assigning levels should be done sensibly. A two-level design is the simplest and sufficient for most experiments. Levels exponentially increase the number of trials. Each trial has an associated cost, so, keep it simple. If cost is an issue, and it will be, then you will need a design matrix to help you select the appropriate design (Figure 13-2).

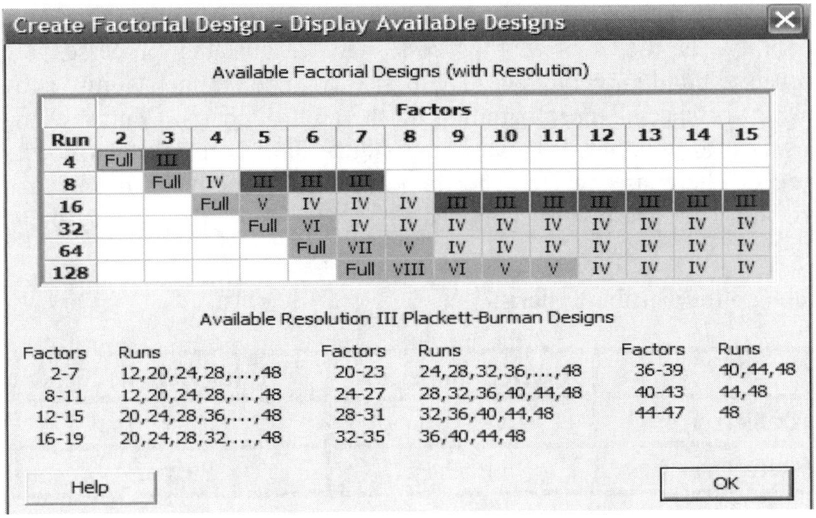

Figure 13-2: Minitab Screenshot for Factorial Design

Ideally, we would like to test all the factor combinations – 32 trials in this case. However, the Executive Director only allocated enough funds to perform eight trials. What are our options? According to the design matrix, the red designs are good, the yellow are better, and the green are the best. Based on our budget, we have two viable options: We can go with five factors and screen the main factors using the "good" configuration, or we can drop one factor and choose the "better" configuration. The challenge, of course, is deciding which factor to drop.

Once we have made our decision and run the eight trials, we need to analyze the results. The desired outcome is finding the right combination of factors and level settings to yield the shortest cycle time. We determined in the cancer treatment center case that our best course of action was to drop factor A. An analysis of the remaining factors indicated that if we set factors B, D and E at their low setting and set factor C at its high setting, we could reduce process cycle time by 60%. Analyzing the results of any design is best done with statistical software.

CONTROL – Hold On For Dear Life

Here we are at the final phase of DMAIC, ready to close out one project and move on to the next. But before we do, process capability must be redefined and a process control plan must be put in place to sustain the gains. These are the tollgates in the Control phase.

There is a basic assumption to consider before calculating process capability. Is the improved process stable? Unstable processes are inconsistent and unpredictable. The best way to determine stability is by looking for special cause variation on the control charts. Control charts allow us to monitor, evaluate, investigate, and control the process outputs. There are two categories of control charts – attribute and variable. The chart you choose depends on the type of data being collected.

There are four attribute charts:

	Fixed Sample Size	Varying Sample Sizes
Defects use	C Chart	U Chart
Defectives use	NP Chart	P Chart

There are several variable charts; the more commonly used are:

Xbar – R	Use when data is easily obtained
Run Charts	Use for single-point data
X - mR	Use when data is limited
Xbar – S	Use when sigma is readily available

In the 1920's, Dr. Walter A. Shewhart created a set of rules to predict future quality within certain limits based on the amount of observed variation generated by the process. Any points that fell beyond those limits were considered "out of control" and should be investigated for special causes that might explain the occurrences. This model is known as SPC – Statistical Process Control, and is widely used as the guideline for interpreting control charts. Selecting an appropriate set of guidelines depends on the process owner's knowledge and understanding of the day-to-day functions of the process. These guidelines are not absolute; do not assume that one size or set fits all. Chapter 19 contains a graphical representation of a control plan for a supply chain process.

Control plans come in all shapes and sizes. A good control plan has four components:

- The *communication plan* outlines how project knowledge will be transferred to the process owners.

- The *measurement plan* is the same format as the one in the Measure phase.

- The *monitoring plan* sets the schedule for checking process performance.

- A *mistake prevention/corrective action plan* outlines how future defect occurrences will be handled.

Make sure your control plan is flexible, easy to understand and easy to implement. Don't hesitate to make adjustments when necessary. Successfully sustaining project gains requires a balance of inspection and prevention approaches.

Conclusions

The DMAIC process is a wonderful tool you can apply universally across industries and business units. It engages you in a systematic method of problem solving to recognize problems in your organization's processes. Understanding when and where to use the tools of Six Sigma will present one of the biggest challenges you will face, especially if you are in an organization that has little understanding of the LSS philosophy or mindset. Often, the first challenge in implementing LSS is in getting buy-in from those with the power to support change, and then garnering support from those who are affected by the change.[2]

Becoming a successful practitioner of Lean Six Sigma tools and techniques will enable you to effect real change throughout your organization. Applying Lean Six Sigma tools appropriately produces significant cost savings and creates a positive result in the bottom line..

Knowing where to get started and applying these tools to real-world situations can require the use of a professional LSS expert to put the process in motion. Healthcare is an industry where waste and problems proliferate and beginning the problem-solving process can be daunting. For a free one-hour consultation on any one of the 12 process items in the Malcolm Baldrige Award criteria booklet, contact me via e-mail[3] and include the book title in the subject line. I will provide written feedback on the strengths and opportunity for improvement in your selected item's content area. For more information on how Lean works in the healthcare setting, visit *http://strategicsolutionsthatwork.com/index.html*.

About the Author

Karen Young is president of Strategic Solutions and Associates, LLC, a consulting group specializing in operational excellence assessments. She has a Masters' Degree in project management, a Master's Certificate in Six Sigma from Villanova University and 33 years experience in healthcare. She is an inspector for the College of American Pathologist (CAP) and a member of the Georgia Oglethorpe Award Board of Examiners, a state-level quality award program based on the Malcolm Baldrige Award criteria. Karen is an adjunct professor for Villanova University On-Line Professional Education, teaching the Lean Six Sigma Green Belt and Black Belt courses.

---

[1] See Chapter 14 for an in-depth treatment of the 6M's.
[2] See Chapters 7 and 8 for a guide to approaching change management issues.
[3] *kyoung@strategicsolutionsthatwork.com*

Chapter Fourteen

Are You Seeing All the Waste?

Gary Wickett

Overview

This chapter is for everyone and anyone responsible for eliminating process waste to improve bottom line results in their organization: from the senior executive all the way down to the line operator. It presents a structured approach to ensuring those involved with waste elimination projects are not overlooking many of the hidden wastes and the possible causes often ignored in today's businesses. This method can be applied to any industry or business, including manufacturing, service, healthcare, back office and IT.

In today's economy, stagnant wages and concerns over high unemployment have contributed to lower overall consumer spending – a heavy blow to every corporate bottom line. To remain competitive, companies are being forced to seek out ways to lower costs and provide higher quality and improved customer service. To do so, they must take an honest look at their processes and strip out all the waste. This chapter outlines an analytical approach that roots out the existence of all possible wastes and their likely causes to help you Lean out your processes.

This chapter will help you to:

- Understand types of waste that exist in your process
- Identify possible causes that contribute to waste
- Learn to drill down to the true root cause of the waste
- Provide a methodology to review types of waste and likely causes

A Review of the Eight Wastes

Since the dawn of Lean, there have been thousands of <u>value stream mapping</u> exercises and <u>waste walks</u> performed in all types of industries geared toward indentifying process waste. Are all the wastes during these activities being seen and captured? I can't tell you the number of times I have returned with a team from a waste walk, value stream mapping exercise or a <u>kaizen</u> event and heard, "I missed that waste – nice catch."

<u>Waste</u>, or the Japanese word *muda*, means: *any activity that does not add value to the customer and is not needed to meet the customer's requirements*. The customer can be the external end user of the product or service, or an internal downstream recipient. Often, waste will be right

in front of us and yet go undetected. We may not be familiar with the process and may interpret a particular waste as an integral part of the procedure, or we may be so familiar with it that waste is overlooked, ignored or assumed to be a normal part of the process. Many people observe and record only the obvious wastes in a process, such as those resulting in wait time, defects or inventory problems, and those more subtle wastes live on like parasites in our processes.

Toyota listed seven types of waste that can be present in any process.[1] These are: Over-production, Waiting, Transportation, Processing itself (extra processing), Stocks (inventories), Motion (of people), and Defects. I have developed an eighth waste category from my own observations and experience: Neglected Resources (see below). The acronym DOWNTIME outlines these eight wastes.

Defects – creating product or information that does not meet customer expectations. It can manifest as a damaged or improperly functioning product, missing or inaccurate paperwork, poor quality, late deliveries, cost overruns, or rework.

Overproduction – converting material or information before it is needed by the end user or downstream customer. It applies to work-in-process and finished goods.

Waiting – person or machine that is idle due to lack of information or material required to continue operation.

Neglected Resources – omitting, neglecting, ignoring or misusing the best resources available for the application at the time. This includes not using the best talent, equipment, machines or software available.

Transportation – unnecessary movement of product or information that does not add value to meet the customer's requirements.

Inventory – raw material or initial information in a process queue. Inventory also applies to the initial job request or information source.

Motion – unnecessary movement by people that does not add value to meet the customer's requirements. This includes reaching, bending, walking or any other unnecessary movements.

Extra Processing – producing and providing more features, information or work than what is required to meet the customer requirements and includes a poor or sloppy process design.

Seven Causes of Waste

Let's take a look at where these wastes come from and what may be the corresponding causes. Traditionally, six causal categories are identified with respect to waste: Men/Women, Methods, Machines, Materials, Measurements and Mother Nature. These are often referred to as the "6M's" and are described below.

Men/Women – These are the manual and mental skills used by a person to execute an assignment. People can create waste if they lack adequate training or standardized work to do the job correctly. Poor job design can create boredom and inattention, which may contribute to waste. A common mistake is to blame *people* when the problem may be with the *process* itself.

Methods – These are the sequences and steps necessary to create the conversion of materials or information into a product or service. A poorly defined set of procedures or lack of standard work with inconsistent applications will create waste.

Machines – These are mechanical, electrical or electronically operated devices used to perform a task. Using the wrong machine for the wrong task or using a machine to perform tasks it wasn't meant for can be a difficult waste to identify. One question you should ask yourself: Is there a better machine out there for this particular task?

Materials – Material is information or physical matter that can be converted or acted on to create another form with added value.

Measurements – An action using a physical device to record a characteristic and compare it to a standard or expected outcome. Use this category only if the waste cause is the instrument itself. If the person taking the measurement causes the error, categorize the waste as either Men/Women or Methods.

Mother Nature – In this application, Mother Nature refers to the environment and the immediate surroundings of the task or process. It can include such factors as weather, humidity, moisture, temperature, wind, noise, dust, odors, lighting, and vibration

There is one other cause of waste that deserves high-level attention and is often one of the top contributors to process wastes. The seventh M – Mindset – is a fixed mental attitude about a situation, event or belief. It may be derived from a culture, value system, experience or management directives. It is characterized by inflexibility and does not allow for change or new ideas. It is the attitude and culture of people in a company and their resistance to change that is often the greatest barrier to successful Lean and Six Sigma implementations.

Drilling Down to the Root Cause of Your Waste

Make sure you get to the root cause of the waste. Taiichi Ohno would recommend asking "why" five times as a way to drill down to the source of the problem so effective corrective actions can be put in place.[2] For example, a machine may be producing defects; however, the root cause may be inferior material being fed to the machine. Figure 14-1 shows the "5 Whys" tool for determining root causes.

Figure 14-1: The 5 Whys Applied

Often, the causes of waste overlap. For example, a new person may be causing errors using a computer system upgrade. Is it the person (training) or the data entry steps (methods)? Or both? The important issue is that the waste is captured and acted on to get to the root cause.

Figure 14-2 is a snapshot of a worksheet tool I used while at a company performing value stream mapping and <u>kaizen</u> events to evaluate a process, review possible wastes and causes, and thoroughly understand the true root cause of the waste I identified. This tool can be used with any type of business or industry.

Are You Seeing All the Waste Checklist

Operaton:_____Analyst:_____Date:_____

DEFECTS

Mindset. Is the culture, mindset or management of the organization causing defects?
No____ Yes____ Explain _____

Man/Woman. Is the lack of job training or poor job design causing defects?
No____ Yes____ Explain _____

Methods. Are poor process methods or lack of standard operating procedures causing defects?
No____ Yes____ Explain _____

Machines. Are the machines or equipment causing defects?
No____ Yes____ Explain _____

Materials. Are the materials causing defects?
No____ Yes____ Explain _____

Measurement. Are the measuring devices causing defects?
No____ Yes____ Explain _____

Mother Nature. Are the environment and surrounding conditions causing defects?
No____ Yes____ Explain _____

Figure 14-2: Are You Seeing All the Waste Checklist

The 7M Analysis in Detail

Let's take an in-depth look at how the seven causes contribute to the eight categories of waste using our snapshot worksheet in Figure 14-2. Oftentimes a waste may be present and one or more of the contributors may not be immediately apparent, or some other cause may be blamed erroneously. The process outlined below for use on your waste walk or kaizen event will help you correctly identify root causes. This is not a problem solving tool but a means to identify and list wastes and sort through all the possible causes using Ishikawa diagram logic. Below is a description of each waste and each possible cause with a few examples of each.

Defects

Mindset. Is the culture, mindset or management of your organization causing defects? How many times have you heard, "We've always done it that way" or "Don't you think that's good enough?" For ways to address the mindset challenge, see Chapters 7 and 8.

Men/Women. Is the lack of job training or poor job design causing defects? Was a loan application returned because the loan officer was not trained to ask for critical information? Is the task mundane and should job rotation and cross-training be considered? Look for better tools to give your employees. Ask the employees themselves what they need to get the job done. Don't be too quick to point the finger at the people when it may be a poor or inconsistent process causing the problem.

Methods. Are poor process methods or the lack of standard operating procedures causing defects? Is an assembly line allowed to continue with a missing part? Does the length of time to process a credit card application cause the customer to go elsewhere? Method defects are one of the top causes of waste and can often be hard to see. Look closely at your methods and ask the employees who employ these methods what can be done to eliminate these types of defects.

Machines. Are machines or equipment causing defects? Was regularly scheduled preventative maintenance ignored? Is the machine wearing out or simply outdated? Perhaps there is a better, more efficient model with fewer defects and issues to better handle your projects.

Materials. Are materials causing defects? Is the correct material being used for the process? Has cheaper/inferior material been introduced? Does the material conform to your internal requirements and your customer's specifications?

Measurement. Are measuring devices causing defects? Are the gauges properly calibrated? Is the correct measurement instrument being used? Do identical instruments yield the same results? Empower your employees to ensure the devices are current with calibration standards.

Mother Nature. Are environmental and surrounding conditions causing defects? Are humidity and moisture causing rust or degradation of the product? Can your product withstand sunlight, heat, or vibration? Many environmental defects are easily identifiable and curable. Don't overlook the little things. A secretary with cold fingers in the winter is less productive than one in a temperate environment.

Overproduction

Mindset. Is the culture or mindset of the organization or management causing overproduction? Do you operate on the philosophy of 'Just-in-Case' and not Just-in-Time? Are all possible product configurations carried in finished goods without regard to demand? Sometimes large batch sizes are produced because management believes setup takes too long, and this leads to overproduction and high inventory costs. Analyze your policies and the veracity of the underlying assumptions that created them.

Men/Women. Is the lack of proper training or poor job design causing overproduction? Are the employees trained in the principles of Lean? Examine your employee schedules to see if you are appropriately staffed. Cross-training and job rotation can eliminate waste in one area while providing needed support in another. Don't let employees overproduce through make-work to fill up their time: Give them real work and training to keep them busy at tasks that add value.

Methods. Are poor process methods or the lack of SOPs causing overproduction? Are Lean tools such as kanban and the pull system used to restrict overproduction? There are many tools available for eliminating method waste. Looking at your HR department, how many layers does a potential job applicant have to go through before he or she is selected for a particular job? If you have a three- or four-level hiring process that takes four months, chances are this is an area where you can find ways to eliminate waste. Standardize the process for as many jobs as possible and set and enforce decision deadlines for candidates at each step in the process.

Machines. Are machines or equipment causing overproduction? Is an unreliable machine running and producing until it fails? Should an older machine be replaced with a newer one? These are questions that can have significant budgetary considerations. The mindset of the top executives in your organization can overlap these considerations and present roadblocks in addressing the issues.

Materials. Are materials causing overproduction? Are excess products being made because material lot sizes are greater than what is needed? Look at your vendor requirements and see if there are cost-effective alternatives to the one's you have in place well prior to contract end dates (if applicable). If your vendors employ Lean principles in their own facilities, you should be able to negotiate flexible MOQ's. (See Chapter 19 on Lean Supply Chains for more discussion of the MOQ problem).

Measurement. Are measuring devices causing overproduction? Are they creating inconsistent readings and causing overproduction to ensure customer orders are met? Are there sufficient instruments to keep the process flowing? Sometimes, it's easier to build acceptance of measurement overproduction into the production process than it is to replace (possibly expensive) inadequate or antiquated measurement devices. Again, this can be an area complicated by mindset.

Mother Nature. Are environmental conditions causing overproduction? Is extra product delivered to storage to compensate for spoilage in areas of high humidity and temperature? Check the environmental conditions of your storage area for potential environmental problems. Don't overlook the layout: A storage area that is too small can lead to damaged product from forklift operators. Do a maintenance check of the roof and foundation looking for leaks and inlets for destructive animals.

Waiting

Mindset. Is the culture or mindset of the organization causing people or machines to be idle? Are several unnecessary signatures required to process an insurance claim or vendor contract? Does a worker have to run down a supervisor for approval before proceeding with the next step? Identify wasteful policies that increase wait time. Being overly cautious in policy making can be a source of waste. Sufficient training can address any trust issues you have with your employees.

Men/Women. Is the lack of training or poor job design causing waiting in the process? Is the employee unsure of the next step when using a new computer system? The answer is to train, train, and train all of your employees. Lack of adequate training is a significant source of all types of waste. Make sure the training involves a continuous component so that knowledge and skills do not go stale.

Methods. Are poor process methods or the lack of SOPs causing increased wait time? Is a poor line balance causing work stations to wait? Does batch processing of hospital records cause other departments to wait for critical information? Method failures are often easy to identify because we can visibly see where downtime is located.

Machines. Is your equipment the cause of the problem? Is the lack of a good Total Productive Maintenance program causing machine failures that stop the process? Make sure there is enough equipment to keep the processes moving. Ensure that machine repair and maintenance is a top priority.

Materials. Are materials causing people or machines to be idle? Is inferior material causing the production process to stop? Are the medical supplies needed not available? Make sure the quality of your material matches the specifications required by your machines, your external customers and your downline customers.

Measurement. Are measuring devices causing people or machines to wait? Does the process stop for calibrated gauges to return? Are there newer devices available that more quickly and accurately measure the product or process? Ensure there are enough shared measuring devices available for your line. Check to see if calibration time is a factor in line delays.

Mother Nature. Are surrounding conditions causing a wait? If you are in an area subject to frequent brown- or blackouts, look into the possibility of installing a generator system that will allow production to continue even under inhospitable weather conditions.

Neglected Resources

Mindset. Is culture or mindset causing the best available resources not to be used? Does the company hire outside consultants when the talent is available in-house? Does management balk at using newer software or upgrades? Having a technologically friendly mindset is critical in knowing how to fully and efficiently employ the resources you have under your own roof. Look for talented people with the right mindset to promote and to train others.

Men/Women. Is the lack of training or poor job design causing people not to use the best resources available? Are job rotation and cross-training programs being ignored? Make sure your training processes are keeping pace with your technology and policies. Simply announcing a new policy does not ensure implementation. Office situations are prime candidates for waste in this area. If you are using new software, make sure you provide the training necessary for your people to use it.

Methods. Are poor process methods causing you to neglect the best use of available resources? Stay on top of technology. Find out if there is a better software application for a specific job. Don't let a newer and more efficient method be rejected in favor of an older one.

Machines. Are machines causing the best available resources to go to waste? Evaluate whether a time-consuming process can be automated. A top-line printer attached to a 10-year-old computer can lead to waste and lost time due to compatibility glitches. Make sure the workstations are able to run the latest software and that equipment is standardized throughout, unless there is a good reason for the exception. Conversely, don't simply assume automation is the best replacement for human innovation, knowledge and decision making.

Materials. Are materials causing the best available resources to go to waste? Don't assign inferior material to older or less productive equipment. Make sure the format of the information received allows you to use your best software and personnel.

Measurement. Are measuring devices the root cause? Are you letting new gauges lay idle in storage? Don't let good tools go unused.

Mother Nature. Are environmental conditions responsible for the neglect factor? Is a dusty environment preventing the use of a more productive piece of equipment or causing great equipment to fail?

Transportation

Mindset. Is mindset causing unnecessary transportation/movement of product or information? Does management policy require all work-in-process be moved to a central staging area? Are documents needing signatures required to be hand-carried to each signee? Again, review policies and their underlying assumptions to identify areas of waste.

Men/Women. Is the lack of proper training or poor job design causing unnecessary movement? Are parts being carried by hand because people are not properly trained to use material handling equipment? Are office employees trained in electronic communication and document mark-up programs that eliminate the need to transport documents manually? Work stations and desks need to be adequately supplied or located near supply rooms. If you are working in a large area, strategically locate supply areas to reduce unnecessary traffic on the floor.

Methods. Are poor process methods or the lack of SOPs causing unnecessary transportation? Is the method to move material, goods or information not part of your SOPs? Are in-process jobs moved to a central location when each stage of production is completed?

Machines. Is your equipment causing unnecessary transportation? Are the machines properly aligned in the production sequence? Does a centrally located "super machine" cause excessive material movement? Does each health unit have enough vitals equipment to avoid wheeling the machines from one room to another? Analyze your supply needs and make sure you have enough equipment available to do the job.

Materials. Are materials causing unnecessary transportation? Is the material subject to spoilage or obsolescence requiring a controlled environment? Is the volume of material being delivered causing unnecessary sorting and staging? Are materials too bulky to be kept on site in your current storage area? One area that is often missed or neglected is information transportation. Can a weekly newsletter replace the transmission of 100 different e-mails? Look for more efficient ways to transmit material information. If electronic documents can replace hand-carried hard copies, take advantage of the technology.

Measurement. Are measuring devices causing unnecessary transportation? Is the material moved by pallet jack to a central calibration lab to be measured? Can gauges be fixed onsite when they breakdown, or do they need to be removed to somewhere else?

Mother Nature. Are environmental conditions causing unnecessary transportation? Does the warehouse leak when it rains and the material needs to be moved to a dry location to prevent damage? If you live in an area subject to frequent episodes of damaging weather, make sure you have an efficient disaster plan in place that keeps equipment safe with the least amount of movement.

Inventory

Mindset. Is culture or mindset causing excessive inventory? Is "Just-in-Case" overriding "Just-in-Time" inventory control thinking? These are common problems throughout many organizations. Conversely, make sure that those in charge of inventory are adequately educated for accurate and flexible forecasting to prevent shortages.

Men/Women. Is the lack of proper training or poor job design creating excessive inventory? Ensure your employees have adequate Lean training to control the amount of inventory allowed in the system.

Methods. Are poor process methods or the lack of SOPs causing excessive inventory? Are the inventory control policies documented and followed? Is a kanban system used to communicate inventory demand with suppliers? Are vendor-managed inventory programs in place with the suppliers? Analyze your methods to ensure they comply with proper inventory control procedures, and that you have adequate tools in place.

Machines. Are machines or equipment causing excessive inventory? Is the machine being amortized to produce as many parts as possible in the shortest time period, requiring excessive inventory? Do you use machines that break down frequently and damage parts, requiring extra inventory stock to be maintained?

Materials. Are materials causing excessive inventory? Is poor quality or inferior material being compensated by ordering much more than what is needed? Is the MOQ much larger than what is required at the time? Copy paper is a prime office example. The product is bulky and often inconvenient to store.

Measurement. Are measuring devices causing excessive inventory? Are inaccurate or non-calibrated measuring devices causing questionable rejects resulting in more inventory to be carried in the process?

Mother Nature. Are environmental conditions causing excessive inventory? Are unprotected materials getting damaged resulting in the need for replacement inventories?

Motion

Mindset. Is mindset causing unnecessary motion by people? Are employees required to search for a supervisor to sign-off on a job before proceeding to the next step? Does management require employees to attend unnecessary meetings that could be managed through a newsletter or memo? Is mindset preventing the implementation of ergonomic practices?

Men/Women. Is the lack of training or poor job design causing unnecessary motion? Are employees trained to perform the job with minimal reaching, bending and searching? Involve your employees in the design of the workplace.

Methods. Are poor process methods or the lack of SOPs causing wasted motion? Are all tools and material within the ergonomic reach window of the operator? Check for ergonomic design at desks and workstations, on lines and in surgical suites.

Machines. Are machines causing unneeded motions? Can power tools be used to reduce the use of hand tools? Are power on/off and emergency off switches located within operator reach? Does a PC keep rebooting, causing the user to repeat work? Are printers handy to their users?

Materials. Are materials causing wasted motion? Does material need to be unwrapped or worked on before it is used in the process? When delivering material to the next process, orient it for convenient presentation for the next operator.

Measurement. Are measuring devices causing wasted motion? Does the measuring device require stooping, bending or awkward positioning? Are there enough measuring devices to share? Use shadow boards to reduce searching for common gauges.

Mother Nature. Are environmental conditions causing unnecessary motion? Is a windy or drafty environment causing documents to be scattered?

Extra Processing

Mindset. Is culture or mindset causing unneeded or poor processes to be used? Is the product shipped with extra cosmetic packaging that is discarded by the customer? Is the product or service inspected by someone other than the operator? Implement inspection at the source to eliminate the need for downstream final inspection.

Men/Women. Is the lack of training or poor job design causing more processing than needed? Are employees duplicating a previous process step caused by a lack of training or communication?

Methods. Are poor process methods or lack of SOPs causing extra processing? Is the absence of standard operating procedures causing the operator to perform an unnecessary polishing step? Take a close look at your packaging and question if it is required by the customer.

Machines. Are machines causing extra processing? Are the machining tolerances more than what the customer requires? Does your software allow you to edit documents, or do you have to go through a print-white out-copy-rescan procedure?

Materials. Are the materials causing unnecessary or poor processing? Does inferior material require extra preparation before it can be used? Do documents contain more information than what is required to complete a task? Medical forms often ask for the same basic information of patients.

Measurement. Are measuring devices causing unnecessary processing? Are inconsistent measuring devices causing additional work or unnecessary operations on the product? Is the wrong measuring device causing unnecessary steps in the process or checking more frequently?

Mother Nature. Are environmental conditions causing unneeded processing? Does manufacturing or assembly in a dusty environment require the product to be wiped down before shipment?

Case Study Example – Applied Waste Detection

Following is a sample of data collected from one person in an Orlando metropolitan law firm. It serves to show an employee view of process waste and the numerous areas available for improvement in any setting.

Not everything is in its proper place; however, the example shows the flexibility and applicability of the 7M waste analysis.

	Mindset	Man/Woman	Methods	Machine
Defects	Documents can be changed at the last minute: causes missed deadlines/ sloppy writing.	Incomplete training on available software.	Attorneys not maintaining accurate time logs cause under billing	Misfeeds cause defective scan files.
Over-production	The more copies the better.	Not using duplex on copier for drafts.	Lack of organization causes reprints.	No PC fax capabilities – must print to fax then throw away
Wait	No document can be sent out without attorney-owner review.	Boss not always available.	Having to obtain signature from boss at home.	Only one copier has scanning capability.
Neglected Resources	Training on new software costs money, so a great case management program sits idle.	Boss not computer literate. Employees can't use IT resources to full advantage.	Paralegals must act as secretaries, leaving less time for higher function duties.	Some outdated equipment incompatible with newer technology
Transportation	Last –minute changes means documents must be hand-delivered to meet deadlines.	Boss requires hard documents delivered to his home office.	Boss works from home causing employees to leave office to deliver material	Semi-frequent breakdowns require transport to external printer
Inventory	Supply budget too low – difficult to find the right supplies when needed.	Supply orderer not trained in proper supply management.	Insistence on hard-copy review requires higher paper inventory	Desktop printers not standard; requires multiple toners in inventory.
Motion	Coffee pot all the way at the back of the office.	Disorganizatio n causes needless searching	Hand delivery versus electronic delivery	Lack of headsets for phone usage
Extra Process	Last minute irrelevant document changes require repeated proofreading.	More copies needed because boss works from home.	Dictate e-mail; fax for review; revise; re-review; send	Constant misfeeds cause need to review scan files for completeness.

	Materials	Measurements	Mother Nature
Defects	Cheaper paper contributes to misfeeds.	No accounting code devices on PC workstation printers means under billing for copies/prints.	N/A
Over-production	N/A	N/A	N/A
Wait	Not ordering proper (more expensive) materials means we have to "make up" things from scratch instead of using pre-made materials.	No accounting code capability on fax means billing is delayed for someone to add up the month's totals by hand.	Frequent brown- and black-outs in summer cause down time. Hurricanes cause serious downtime, but rarely.
Neglected Resources	N/A	N/A	N/A
Transportation	Not enough copies of up-to-date Rule Books require sharing and tracking down legal resource materials.	N/A	Brown- outs and black outs can cause the need for hand-delivery of materials.
Inventory	Certain MOQs require higher inventory	No measurement devices/forms available for maintaining accurate inventory or order levels.	Large inventory of bottled water needed.
Motion	Misfeeds caused by cheap paper requires finding and fixing constant paper jams.	Lack of account code availability on certain equipment requires hand-recording and tallying.	Brown/blackouts cause changeover to some non-electric devices requiring more motion.
Extra Process	Must reprocess portions of jobs caused by cheap paper misfeeds.	Lack of account code availability requires hand-recording and tallying.	Brown/blackouts cause reprocessing of documents lost due to PC failure.

Table 14-1: 7M Waste Analysis Chart

Conclusion

Are you now starting to see all the waste? On your next value stream mapping, kaizen or waste walk event, spend time reviewing possible waste causes in your surroundings. This step-by-step procedure not only points out the obvious waste and causes, but many that are often overlooked or not apparent. It is equally important to practice waste prevention using the same methodology. Look to see if there is potential for a waste to happen and put an appropriate preventive action and control plan in place. The full summary checklist that lists the wastes and causes described in this chapter can be downloaded by visiting *www.gwlean.com/checklist*.

Key Lessons Learned

1. Make sure the managers involved with waste elimination projects train the people to look for and uncover all possible wastes and causes.

2. Understand there are many wastes in the process surroundings that may not be readily apparent to the observer.

3. Ensue the true root cause of a waste is understood to put an action plan in place.

About the Author

Gary Wickett, BSIE, MBA, is a Certified Lean Master, Certified Supply Chain Analyst, Six Sigma Green Belt and 5S Certified. Gary is a manufacturing, engineering, and supply chain management professional with extensive experience leading Lean transformations. He directed the Lean Integration Office for StorageTek and Sun Microsystems and was one of the original developers for the online Lean Six Sigma program for Villanova University, where he serves as an adjunct professor. He served on the Industrial Engineering Advisory Board for Colorado State University and instructs the Certified Supply Chain Analyst program for APICS Northern Colorado. His article, "Lean Now!" is available in *ASQ IEEE Reliability Society Transactions*, Vol. 58, June 2009.

[1] S. Shingo, *Study of 'Toyota' Production System* (Tokyo: Japan Management Association, 1983): 287.
[2] J. P. Womack and D. T. Jones, *Lean Thinking* (New York: Free Press, 2003): 348.

Chapter Fifteen

The Continuous Improvement Routine: Your Key to Achieving Operational Excellence

Mike Bresko

Overview

Do you know that two-thirds of Operational Excellence initiatives (*i.e.*, Lean, Six Sigma, TPM, TQM, and others) fail to meet expectations, and only 3% report great results? [1, 2, 3, 4] That poor track record occurs despite spending significant time and money on these initiatives and the competitive and economic pressures that organizations face. What is causing this poor performance, and what can you do to help your organization be successful? How do we reach a tipping point where the momentum for the change exceeds the natural tendency to revert to long-standing habits?

When polled, 82% of business leaders say that significant culture change remains their top challenge.[5] If the cause of failed initiatives is an inability to change culture, then you need to drill deeper to identify countermeasures. The main causes of these challenges are a) the failure to change the behaviors of supervisors and managers, and b) the failure to engage a sufficient percentage of the organization's workforce.

This chapter will help you to:

- Understand why most organizations must transform their culture
- Define the Transformation Tipping Point and discover the five primary causes for failing to reach it.
- Understand the approaches to Daily Management and implement the Continuous Improvement Routine.
- Apply eight steps to transform your organization and implement Daily Management to achieve the Transformation Tipping Point.

The Transformation Imperative

No organization is safe from economic pressures and hungry competitors, including those that are currently performing well. As Will Rogers said, "Even if you are on the right track, you'll get run over if you just sit there."

In response, many companies have deployed some type of Operational Excellence initiative. However, even when an initiative appears to be successful, a deeper look reveals that employees often short cut standard work, supervisors lack the skills to reinforce standard routines, and managers seem to prefer to move on to the next initiative. The result is continued service and product snafus, excessive waste, and employees that work more hours and become increasingly frustrated.

Furthermore, processes are becoming more complex and prone to failure. Steven Spear concludes that it is the little things that go wrong all the time that can combine in just the right way to wreak havoc.[6] Major disasters like Three Mile Island, the losses of the space shuttles, and now the BP oil spill in the Gulf of Mexico, all occurred despite indications of vulnerability. In these situations, as in most organizations, people develop workarounds and firefighting techniques, and they fail to address the causes of frequent glitches that cause significant waste and can lead to major disasters. Failure to act on glitches denies typical organizations of the opportunity to learn and improve.

Organizations can no longer be content to improve just a few processes through their Operational Excellence initiative. Certainly, successful kaizen events and completed Six Sigma projects create benefits. However, they simply cannot create a culture where everyone is addressing the root causes of glitches, learning from them, and ensuring that every process is executed flawlessly. As Rother says in *Toyota Kata*, "Let's agree on a definition of continuous improvement: it means that you are improving all processes every day."[7] Such a culture has two major competitive benefits. First, it creates a high rate of improvement – a key to long-term competitive success. Second, it creates a dynamic, enjoyable and satisfying work environment – a key to attracting and retaining competent talent. To achieve this level of excellence, most organizations must accomplish nothing short of a cultural transformation – the Transformation Imperative.

The Transformation Tipping Point

Malcolm Gladwell describes a tipping point as the moment of critical mass, the threshold, the boiling point.[8] Walsh defines a tipping point as "the level at which momentum for change becomes unstoppable."[9] Elaborating on Walsh's definition, I define the Transformation Tipping Point as the time when the momentum for operational excellence exceeds the natural tendency to revert to long-standing habits.

Typical initiatives fail to achieve the Transformation Tipping Point due to five fatal failure modes:

- Failure to unequivocally declare that nothing short of a cultural transformation is acceptable.

- Failure to articulate the cultural True North and build ownership.

- Failure to engage a critical mass.

- Failure to change behaviors of leaders at all levels.

- Failure to follow best practices for transforming culture.

Typical initiatives include appeals like "Operational Excellence – our path forward," or "We will create clear blue water between us and our competition." However, these statements fall short of clearly saying that culture change is necessary. These initiatives either don't describe the desired culture at all, describe it vaguely, or don't build ownership in the desired culture. How many organizations have articulated, communicated and reinforced the unambiguous characteristics of the new culture? For example, an operationally excellent culture has the following characteristics:

- Exhibits accountability for crisp follow-through and execution.

- Promotes a rapid rate of process improvement.

- Attacks process glitches and learns from them.

- Develops the skills and capabilities of the organization to improve.

- Engages the entire workforce.

Typical initiatives focus on the tools for process improvement. They have structured training, projects and certifications for process improvement specialists. People are taught 5S, standard work, and a host of other tools. However, putting the tools and methods into daily practice and sustaining the change is the real challenge for organizations, and that is where typical initiatives fall short. The tools of change contribute to both improved productivity and culture change; however, they are insufficient for transforming most company cultures. What is needed is an increased focus on how leaders lead – their beliefs, the management systems they follow, and their skills in coaching and leading problem solving.

Typical initiatives involve a small percentage of the organization's workforce and actively engage an even smaller percentage. Figure 15-1 represents an organization that has achieved the rule-of-thumb target for Six Sigma deployments, where 5% of the workforce is certified as either Green or Black Belts. Assuming that the entire 5% is actively engaged (which is unlikely), notice how 5% fails to change the "color" of the organization. Even if the organization has provided awareness training and communications to a large percentage of the workforce, there simply are not enough people actively engaged to achieve a tipping point. Organization #2 illustrates an organization that meets guidelines for culture change where about six times the number of people are actively engaged, and 75% of managers are convinced that the status quo is unacceptable. Unfortunately, most organizations fail even to achieve the level of engagement illustrated by organization #1, when they need to surpass the level shown by organization #2.

Failure to Engage a Critical Mass

Two 2000-person organizations (each block=20 people)

Organization #1
Insufficient Engagement

Organization #2
At the Transformation Tipping Point

Typical initiatives target 5% or fewer (<100 people) for serious engagement (e.g., Six Sigma Green & Black Belts)

Critical mass, at least:
• 30% (600 people) actively implementing the change
• 75% of managers convinced that business as usual is unacceptable

Figure 15-1: Tipping Point Critical Mass

In a surprisingly large number of initiatives, too little effort is placed on applying best practices of change management. John P. Kotter defined eight steps to transform your organization.[10] While these steps are straightforward, few organizations have taken the effort to translate those steps to their specific situation and to measure progress along the way.

Management Systems

There are three primary management systems: Goal Deployment, Value Stream Management, and Daily Management. Goal Deployment, also known as *hoshin kanri* or Policy Deployment, is focused on achieving breakthrough improvements on a few strategic imperatives. It engages most managers and those few assigned to the breakthrough projects. Value Stream Management breaks down functional silos that inhibit efficient performance. It primarily engages those who manage the value stream, although the roles of others might change as they shift toward support of the value steam. (See Chapter 17).

Daily Management Elements		
Dubinsky's 10 Foundational Methods	Mann's 8 Lean Management Assessment Criteria	Spear's Capabilities
1. Guiding principles		
2. Business strategy		
3. Goal deployment		
4. Coaching and development 5. Daily operational tours	1. Leader standard work	Leading by developing capabilities #1, 2 and 3
6. Daily action planning meetings	2. Daily accountability process	
7. Daily and weekly performance measurement dashboards 8. Short-interval performance boards	3. Visual controls for production 4. Visual controls for production support	
	5. Process definition	1. Specifying design to capture existing knowledge and building in tests to reveal problems
	6. Disciplined adherence to process (audits)	
9. Problem solving and decision making	7. Root cause problem solving	2. Swarming and solving problems to build new knowledge
	8. Process improvement	3. Sharing new knowledge throughout the organization
10. Performance management architecture		

Table 15-1: Elements of Daily Management Strategies

Daily Management, also known as Daily Involvement System, ensures that every process is meeting safety, quality, delivery, output, and morale requirements. Daily Management engages everyone in the organization. Each management system contributes to achieving an operationally excellent culture; however, Daily Management involves the most people and therefore has the most leverage in transforming culture.

What is Daily Management? Dubinsky describes ten foundational methods of a Daily Management System.[11] Mann describes four principles of a Lean Management System – leader standard work, daily accountability process, visual controls and discipline – and provides a Lean Management assessment consisting of eight categories.[12] Spear describes "high-velocity organizations" as those few organizations that respond to small problems as indications of what needs to be better understood, where improvement is needed, and what must be learned. These organizations want to understand problems, not put up with them. Spear identifies four capabilities in these organizations.[13] Table 15-1 compares these three views.

Dubinsky's list of methods includes some higher-level elements such as business strategy; Mann's list focuses on day-to-day operations; Spear's is more generic. However, they all agree on the core elements of Daily Management. Lists like these help to clarify the desired end state, but where do you begin? Although the answer to that question is unique for every organization, there are key elements of Daily Management that address the fatal failures and provide an excellent starting point.

The Continuous Improvement Routine

Figure 15-2 illustrates the Continuous Improvement Routine (CI Routine), the core of the Daily Management System. It provides a straightforward, frontline-focused method to engage everyone in the behaviors that characterize an operationally excellent culture. It develops the skills of leaders, engages the front line, ensures quality output, and fosters continuous improvement. It is built upon methods from Training Within Industry, Lean and Total Quality Management. The CI Routine follows Deming's Plan-Do-Study-Act cycle and system for profound knowledge.[14] It is a key enabler for achieving the Cultural Transformation Tipping Point.

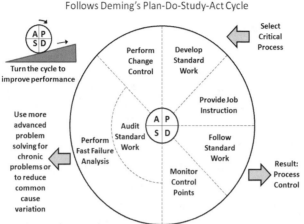

The Continuous Improvement Routine
Follows Deming's Plan-Do-Study-Act Cycle

Figure 15-2: Continuous Improvement Routine

The CI Routine follows seven steps, outlined below.

Step 1: Develop Standard Work

The team leader (*i.e.*, supervisor) leads development or refinement of standard work with support from the front-line workforce and technical experts. The team leader applies the <u>Job Methods</u> approach from <u>Training Within Industry</u> to break down the job's steps then to determine if steps can be combined, eliminated or streamlined.[15] The team leader then facilitates the testing and refinement of the standard and ensures buy-in from the front-line and higher level mangers.

Step 2: Provide Job Instruction

The team leader instructs those who are assigned to the job using the <u>Job Instruction approach</u> from Training Within Industry. Following this approach, the team leader first develops a job breakdown sheet for training by documenting the important steps, key points, and for critical steps, the reasons. The team leader then follows the Job Instruction steps: preparation, presentation, performance try-out, and follow-up. This learn-by-doing training ensures that the job performer knows the standard and performs it correctly.

Step 3: Follow Standard Work

Assuming that the standard and instruction were good, the result should be a stable, or statistically in control, process. However, the rest of the Plan-Do-Study-Act cycle is necessary since the job performer may need to be reminded of the standard, or he or she may think of a better way, or the standard may continue to produce anomalies.

Step 4: Monitor Control Points

As the job is performed, the job performer monitors the key input and output metrics to ensure the process is stable. As the organization matures, the method of monitoring shifts from more gross measures (like the amount of scrap) to include input variables that predict the outcome and can be control charted.

Step 5: Audit Standard Work

The team leader and higher-level managers or technical specialists perform multi-level audits of the job as part of their leader standard work. The team leader checks how the standard is followed and engages the job performer in a dialogue to reveal potential refinements to the standard. Higher level mangers check how well the audit process is performed. These audits reinforce the importance of following the standard and ensure compliance; equally important, they create a dialog with the job performer to uncover continuous improvement opportunities.

Step 6: Perform Fast Failure Analysis

Despite best efforts, an anomaly or <u>special cause</u> failure might occur. When failures occur, the team leader facilitates a simple 5-Whys root cause analysis. (See Chapter 13 and 14 for more on the 5-Whys). This "fast failure analysis" includes the following characteristics:

- Document conditions soon after the failure occurs, while the evidence is still fresh.

- Analyze the failure within a few days of the occurrence.

- Limit the number of failures analyzed each week based on the capability of the team – it's better to analyze a few anomalies well than many haphazardly. (Note: if your process exhibits many failures, then limit the quantity analyzed by setting a trigger point).

- Identify no more than three action items to correct the failure. (Note: it is better to implement a few actions quickly to enable fast cycles of learning than to create a long list that will take excessive time to complete or not be completed at all.)

- Visually manage the number of open failure analyses.

- List chronic problems or the need to reduce <u>common cause</u> <u>variation</u> (*i.e.*, the natural variation in the process) and prioritize, with higher level management, which should be assigned to a team for resolution.

Step 7: Perform Change Control

The team leader follows the organization's change control process and ensures that the improved standard is documented, job instruction is performed, and the improved standard is followed. Furthermore, in more mature organizations, a system exists so that the new knowledge is captured and shared organization-wide (known as *yokoten*).

One company that implemented this routine, Gerdau Ameristeel, achieved spectacular results. The company's rolling mills identified billets between cobbles (BBC) as a strong improvement goal. From a base index value of 100 in 2001, BBCs increased to 140 in 2002 and 231 in 2003, for a compound annual growth rate of 47% in the company's Jackson, TN mill.[16]

Despite the simplicity of the CI Routine, institutionalizing its use requires considerable effort. In typical organizations, the team leaders must learn new skills and change their behaviors; the front-line workforce must gain problem-solving skills; and higher-level managers must become skilled at coaching and auditing.

Several actions can help begin implementation of the CI Routine:

- Identify your key processes – those that have significant impact on performance and are currently causing problems.

- Define the leader standard work required for successful execution of the CI Routine, such as the weekly routine when the team leader will develop standard work, provide job instruction, and coach Fast Failure Analysis, and when higher level managers will audit and coach execution of the CI Routine.

- Display CI Routine status on visual management boards, including the status of job instruction, the open failure analyses and the performance metrics.

Transforming Your Organization

In this section, I will explain how to apply Kotter's eight steps to transform your organization, starting with the CI Routine as the foundation.

Establishing a sense of urgency

Kotter says that you need to convince at least 75% of your managers that the status quo is more dangerous than the unknown new way. Therefore, your leadership must make a fact-based case for urgent change and state that the organization's culture must change, using a strong statement such as, "We are not improving fast enough to remain competitive, and the cause is our current culture; therefore, we must change how each of us works, thinks and contributes to our competitiveness." Note that while this step must eventually occur at the highest level in the organization, it can begin at a departmental level.

Forming a powerful guiding coalition

Assemble a leadership coalition with enough power to lead the change effort. This group must include more senior managers and line managers than HR or Operational Excellence specialists. During a workshop, train the group and then engage them in the initial design of the CI Routine, including key process identification, leader standard work, failure analysis triggers, visual management and every other major element of the CI Routine. The group's members must be able promote the use of the CI Routine and to coach others in its application.

Creating a vision

This step actually begins during the first two steps; however, it separately recognizes that the vision will be shaped and clarified over three to 12 months or more. Kotter describes this rule of thumb: "If you can't communicate the vision to someone in five minutes or less and get a reaction that signifies both understanding and interest, you are not yet done with this step." You will return to this step after piloting the CI Routine. The next three steps prepare you to implement the pilot and then prepare you for a successful deployment after its completion.

Communicating the vision

Communication comes in both words and deeds. Meetings and newsletters help, but successful transformations require that you incorporate the message into routine activities, or "walk the talk." For deployment of the CI Routine, define the deeds that team leaders and managers must exhibit and establish a coaching and feedback process to ensure that the deeds are performed well. After initial application, identify success stories and weave them into the vision you have created.

Empowering others to act on the vision

Empowerment requires training and coaching, encouragement, and removing barriers to action. It will likely require changing systems or structures to create a culture of empowerment. For CI Routine deployment, develop training that specifically teaches the organization's version of the CI Routine. Classroom training is unlikely to change behavior, so plan for and provide coaching using a learn-by-doing approach. Lacking positive feedback, empowerment is anemic. Identify the inhibitors to using the CI Routine successfully – time, problem-solving skills, team leaders' analytical and facilitation skills – and remove them. Finally, change or develop the visual systems or databases for documenting anomalies and tracking their resolution.

Planning for and creating short-term wins

Short-term wins ensure that momentum for the change remains high and contributes to clarification the vision. Put the CI Routine it into practice in an initial application area and plan to provide support until the routine become habitual. Assess how it is working, capture success stories and refine how it is used and how you describe it. Cycle back to the preceding steps and refine the vision, communication methods and empowerment actions.

Consolidating improvements and producing still more change

The risk at this stage is declaring victory too soon. Old habits may return. At this point, raise the bar in the initial area and deploy the routine companywide. Raising the bar means to shift from gross triggers to statistically based control points and adding additional elements of Daily Management, such as the daily accountability process.

Institutionalizing the new approaches

Change sticks when it becomes "the way we do things around here." Kotter says you should show people how the new approaches, behaviors and attitudes have helped to improve performance and ensure that the next generation of management personifies the new approach. At this stage, you need to address systemic barriers such as hiring practices, performance appraisals and unwritten expectations placed on managers.

Conclusions

Global competition and increasingly complex processes prone to failure demand that organizations improve at a rate faster than the competition. Unfortunately, two-thirds of Operational Excellence initiatives fail to change the organization's culture. Typical initiatives focus on breakthrough projects and actively involve only a small percentage of the organization. The result is improvement in only a few processes and an inability to achieve the Transformation Tipping Point where the momentum for change becomes unstoppable. The Daily Management System is an essential ingredient of culture change, but because it requires fundamental changes in how managers manage and job performers think and problem solve, it is challenging to implement. The Continuous Improvement Routine is the core of the Daily Management System, and provides a straightforward first step in deploying a Daily Management System and achieving an operationally excellent culture.

Key Lessons Learned

1. Culture change is critical to sustaining continuous improvement.

2. Most companies fail to achieve the Transformation Tipping Point because they fail to: a) unequivocally declare that nothing short of a cultural transformation is acceptable, b) articulate the cultural True North and build ownership, c) engage a critical mass, d) change behaviors of leaders at all levels, and e) follow best practices for transforming culture.

3. The five characteristics of an operationally excellent culture include: a) accountability for crisp follow-through and execution, b) a rapid rate of process improvement, c) attacking process glitches and learning from them, d) developing the skills and capabilities of the organization to improve, and e) the entire workforce is engaged in the process.

4. A key enabler of culture change is the Continuous Improvement Routine, an excellent starting point for implementing a Daily Management System.

About the Author

Mike Bresko is president of Ascendigy Consulting, a firm dedicated to helping clients build excellence in management and process improvement. Mike began developing his expertise in 1986 as a member of Alcoa's corporate quality team which benchmarked companies for Lean and Total Quality practices, and developed and deployed approaches that eventually contributed to the Alcoa Business and Production Systems. Today, he focuses on the application of Lean, Six Sigma, A3 Problem Solving, and Lean Management Systems. An experienced executive, Mike applied this expertise as President, Alcoa Zepf and Global Manager, Alcoa Packaging Equipment. He has guided large-scale, world-class conversions applying Lean, TPM, Six Sigma, and Management Systems for clients in manufacturing, technology, service, and healthcare. For readers of this book, Ascendigy offers a quick, form-based assessment rating your current daily management system and suggests future steps to create a culture of Operational Excellence. To take advantage of this opportunity, e-mail Mike under the subject line of "Driving Operational Excellence Offer" and you'll receive the free assessment tool and instructions. For more information about Mike Bresko and Ascendigy, visit *www.ascendigy.com* or e-mail Mike at *mbresko@ascendigy.com*.

References

1. J. P. Kotter, "Leading Change: Why Transformation Efforts Fail," in *Lead Change— Successfully* (3ed), H. Sirken, et al. (*Harvard Business Review*, 2005): 2.
2. Separate surveys: McKinsey, 1998; PRTM Aerospace Survey, 2003; Aberdeen Group survey of 294 companies, 2005.
3. Association for Manufacturing Excellence. Survey of Manufacturing Leaders (2005).
4. N. P. Repenning, and J. D. Sterman, "Nobody Every Gets Credit for Fixing Problems that Never Happened: Creating and Sustaining Process Improvement," Sloan School of Management, MIT Center for Innovation in Product Development (2001).
5. Aberdeen Group survey of 294 companies, 2005.
6. S. J. Spear, *Chasing the Rabbit* (Reissued as *The High Velocity Edge*) (New York: McGraw Hill, 2009): 46-49.
7. M. Rother, *Toyota Kata* (New York: McGraw Hill, 2010): 11.
8. M. Gladwell, *The Tipping Point: How Little Things Can Make a Big Difference* (Boston: Little Brown, 2000): 12.
9. B. Walsh, "A Green Tipping Point," *Time Magazine* (October 12, 2007) *http://www.time.com/time/world/article/0,8599,1670871,00.html*
10. Ibid.
11. David Dubinsky, Daily Management: The foundation for High-Performance Organizations, Chapter 7 of this book.
12. D. Mann, *Creating a Lean Culture* (New York: Productivity Press, 2005).
13. Spear, 2009: 22-27.
14. W. E. Deming, *The New Economics for Industry, Government, and Education* (2ed) (Cambridge: Massachusetts Institute of Technology, Center for Advanced Educational Services, 2000): 31, 131-133, and chapter 4.
15. M. Warren, *The Training Within Industry Report*, 1940 – 1945, (2ed.) Originally published by War Manpower Commission, Bureau of Training, Training Within Industry, Washington, D.C. (1945): 248-249.
16. American Iron and Steel Institute, Globetrotter Meeting and Tour. (Gerdau Ameristeel, Jackson, TN, 2003).

Chapter Sixteen

Driving Results: Listening to the Voice of the Customer

Lorraine Marzilli Lomas

21st Century Marketing is a hot topic for discussion. The advent of the Internet and e-commerce marketing and information gathering techniques has both complicated and facilitated marketing initiatives, making it possible for even the smallest enterprise to go global – with all the logistical complexities entailed in the process. At the same time, the internet has made it increasingly easier and cheaper to gather information about your prospective customers. Savvy, successful companies who want to get to or remain at the top of the food chain must be able to determine the appropriate marketing communications mix and message for their products and services to reach and persuade those customers. To complicate matters further, the internet has created a sharper, more empowered consumer who has access to technology that facilitates research into alternative products and services.

The voice of the customer (VOC) is an in-depth, customer-centric process businesses go through to capture their customers' expectations, preferences, needs, desires and aversions. It is not only a market research technique that can provide a detailed outline of customer wants and needs in a hierarchical, prioritized format, but also a system to cultivate customer managed relationships. VOC works hand-in-hand with other Lean methodologies and Six Sigma tools to bring down marketing costs and eliminate waste and defects that can eat up a marketing budget without benefitting the bottom line.

This chapter will help you to:

- Understand the importance of integrating VOC into the overall business strategy.
- Grasp the basics of the VOC process.
- Learn what happens when everything goes wrong.
- Create a new level of trust by paying close attention to VOC.

The VOC Process: Why Being Customer-Driven Matters

Many Lean and Six Sigma initiatives concentrate on internal processes and procedures with a focus on eliminating waste and maximizing benefits to the corporate bottom line (the Voice of the Business). It is easy for the VOC to get lost in the technicality of the metrics used to institute improvement. No matter what industry you are in, if you lose sight of your customers' wants and needs, eliminating waste in your processes and procedures will do little good because your sales base and market share will dwindle into oblivion. In other words, if you lose sight of your customer, you ultimately lose sight of your profit base. Businesses are in business to a) serve customers, and b) make profit. If you neglect your customers, you neglect your profits as well.

VOC helps your change initiative teams identify, select and evaluate marketing projects that will drive results straight to the bottom line (increased sales) as opposed to top line (cost) savings. One study by NIST claims poorly designed VOC data collection systems and the lack of VOC tools cost U.S. corporations almost $100 billion per year in failed technology projects.[1]

Effective VOC processes, on the other hand, identify and distill problems, their cost/revenue implications and the root causes of those problems. The inherent dangers of not having an effectual and balanced VOC process include:

- Incorrectly set customer expectations

- Increased customer-caused defects (mistakes)

- Unnecessary re-engineering of product and processes due to misidentification of root causes

- An improper focus on customer dissatisfiers that neglects identifying what the company is doing right

- Implementing firefighting techniques to close the gap between customer expectations and product/service delivery

Successful VOC processes provide a comprehensive understanding of customer requirements. In turn, your organization will have a common language for your project team, critical input for setting design specifications for new products or services, a useful platform for product innovation and distinguish the best channels for the marketing mix.

Developing a Quality VOC Process

Before we can discuss specific metrics used to measure VOC, we first need a proper VOC process in place. What does that process look like? Ideally, a robust VOC process includes seven factors:[2]

1. Clear and identifiable ownership over the process;

2. Unified feedback and quality data collection;

3. A unified, single picture of the customer experience based on multiple sources throughout all levels of the customer experience;

4. The reporting process must be accessible, visible and actionable;

5. The process must identify the complete cost and revenue implications of the problem or opportunity under investigation;

6. It must identify what level of performance is acceptable to the customer; and

7. The process must track and report progress in a visible manner that is understandable to all stakeholders.

Simon Daisley, Managing Director, Future-Proof Consulting in the UK, outlines what he calls the Voice of the Customer Virtuous Circle:[3]

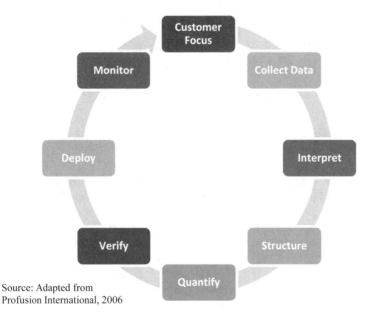

Source: Adapted from
Profusion International, 2006

Figure 16-1: VOC Virtuous Circle

Customer Focus

Frederick Reichheld, a renowned business strategist, once stated, "The only way to **earn** long-term growth is to build emotional and rational loyalty to your organization...You do this by having a crisp economic model that has customers at the heart of every decision you make."[4] If you want to establish and maintain customer focus, VOC should become the heart of your economic model.

Data Collection

The internet has opened up vast new realms in the data collection field, making it easier and cheaper to collect facts on customers and potential customers. The challenge in the 21st century marketplace is determining what information to collect and how best to capture it so that it accurately reflects the true voice of your customer. Internet surveys, web analytical tools, and customer loyalty/rewards systems are just a small sample of the new methods available for collecting information in the Internet Age. This is, of course, in addition to traditional methods such as personal interviews, telephone interviews, and direct mail surveys that attempt to gather facts on the total customer experience.

Interpretation

Interpreting the raw data that comes in may be one of the most challenging aspects of VOC. This phase involves not only identifying key customer requirements, but also interpreting current and future market trends. VOC helps you identify the key issues that concern your *current* clients, and hopefully, *future* clients as well.

Structure

Arrangement of the information allows you to identify patterns, distinguish themes and forecast trends. Structure works hand in hand with the interpretation phase, turning the raw data into a system that fosters repeat customers.

Quantification and Verification

Quantification of the data allows for meaningful measurement that translates across team members and departments so that everyone within the organization can understand the implications for present and future initiatives. This phase allows you to condense your information down to "hard facts" that your company can later act upon in a dependable manner.

Deployment

Once you have a sound, quantifiable foundation upon which to make educated and meaningful decisions for your company, you need to make the information accessible and comprehensible to decision makers across the organization. This involves pooling the knowledge learned into a single customer-managed relationship (CRM) system that allows rich analysis.

Monitoring

Because VOC is a continuous improvement process, it requires constant monitoring to determine a) where the organization is currently, b) where the organization is headed, and c) whether these positions are in line with organizational goals and strategies. As such, your organization should incorporate a company-wide communications program blended to furnish applications, equity, benefits and value in keeping with the ever-changing VOC.[5]

Qualities of Desirable VOC Metrics

There are numerous metrics used in marketing today to capture VOC. Some are better than others; all inherently risk some degree of inaccuracy through false reporting by customers. Nonetheless, in the initial stages of the process, gathering data is the top priority. In this endeavor, the focus is on collecting the data efficiently and effectively.

The main goal in choosing metrics for capturing VOC is to implement a method that accurately reflects the wants and needs of the customer. Before you decide which metric to use, you need to begin by first asking: What is a good metric?

A good VOC metric captures six qualities:

Credibility: Is the measure widely accepted within the marketing community? Is it based on a rigorous methodology with a good track record of results? What evidence is there that the metric is tied to hard financial results?

Reliability: Is the metric consistent across customer lifecycles? Does the metric provide consistency throughout different channels? Is it applicable to your industry?

Precision: Does the metric dive deep enough to provide valuable insight? Does it have multiple related questions to detect variation, shifts, and inaccuracy in customer feedback? Does it gather data that delivers a high degree of accuracy and insight?

Accuracy: Is the measurement correct? Does it measure the right facts? Does it drive results that are representative of the whole customer base, or just the squeaky wheels? Does it have an acceptable margin of error? Does it have a realistic sample size requirement that works in your situation?

Actionability: Does the metric lead to information you can act on? Does it have the ability to prioritize improvements according to expected project impact?

Predictability: Can the metric predict future customer behavior?

A lot of time and effort is spent planning the research and questionnaire design. In many instances, it is critical to get it right the first time. For instance, if your project involves a mass market mail survey, there's no going back once the survey is in the mail.

Another consideration is whether the project requires quantitative data, qualitative data, or a mixture of both. This often will depend upon the purpose of the study and what main questions are we attempting to answer. Market segmentation questions lend themselves to open-ended questions with a qualitative spin. These types of questions include:

- Who uses the product/service?
- Where is it used?
- How is it used?
- Why is it used?
- When is it used?

Outlining needs from Six Sigma's Kano analysis, on the other hand, lends itself to either (or both) quantitative or qualitative data collection. Determining satisfiers, dissatisfiers, attractors, must-haves, and delighters is easily translated into a Likert scale or other closed-ended questions that result in easily quantifiable and translatable data. Still, a qualitative component can also be built in to the research design to capture the unexpected (*e.g.*, "Which features do you like/dislike?") with open-ended questions, which can be more qualitative in nature ("What does 'quality' mean to you with respect to this product?").

Common Methods for Capturing the Voice of the Customer

VOC metrics all involve gathering data through a process of interviewing either current customers or the general market (current and potential customers). There are many ways to accomplish this data collection. Table 16-1 outlines eight of the most common methods along with a brief analysis of their costs, advantages and disadvantages.

Method	Cost	Advantages	Disadvantages
Mail Survey	Medium, depending on size of study	Responses are quantifiable. Allows for in-depth study using open-ended questions.	Response time is long and response rates are low.
Telephone Surveys	High	High number of contacts can be made in one day; data can be quantified and generalized.	Cost; response rates; lack of flexibility.
Internet Surveys	Low	If properly designed, data can be quantifiable and generalizable; Flexibility in changing study design and making corrections easily, cheaply and quickly.	Difficulty obtaining a representative sample of target populations; Requires technical knowledge to implement.
Focus Groups	Low-Medium	Customizable and flexible; can obtain in-depth responses; ideal for using visual or tactile mediums (ads, sample products).	Limited to qualitative data; may require travel to reach target populations.
In-person Interviews	High, depending on design and sample size	Highly flexible and customizable; can be designed for both qualitative and quantitative data collection; allows for visual and tactile mediums. Best for in-depth and/or lengthy surveys.	May require a lot of travel/time relative to sample size; Difficult to get target interviewees to travel or participate in long interviews.
Intercepts	Medium	Ability to use visual and tactile mediums; can gather both quantitative and qualitative responses.	Difficult to obtain target population response; data collection time can be longer than other methods.
Customer Complaints	Low	May expose process and product flaws not otherwise revealed by testing or other research.	Bias is inherent and results cannot be generalized.

Table 16-1: VOC Data Collection Methods

Many of these methods can be designed to focus on the general market (pool of random persons) or specifically on current customers, depending on the area or process under review. For instance, if you want to know what features should be built into your company's next new Smartphone, you don't want to limit your survey population to just current customers; you might want to differentiate between current and potential customers. Conversely, if you are looking to identify and improve specific problem issues in your technical support process, a general population survey will not help you in that endeavor.

Mail Surveys

Mail surveys can yield data at a much lower cost than telephone or interview survey methods. Time-of-day biases present in telephone surveys are not a factor in this survey type. The biggest problem seen in this form of data collection is response rate. An initial response rate is usually anywhere between 5-20%, well below any acceptable rate of reliability for generalization. In order to increase response rates, a high level of follow-up may be required, which increases expenditures.

One study conducted by Michigan State University looked at mail versus e-mail survey response rates and costs per response.[6] In short, the results of the survey showed that obtaining a 31.5% response rate for mailed surveys cost $10.97 per response versus a 29.7% response rate using a preliminary postcard followed by the e-mail survey at a cost of $1.31 per response. In general, mail surveys cost significantly more than electronic surveys. However, mailing still costs significantly less than in-person interviews.

Phone Surveys

Phone surveys still access a higher population than internet surveys, although the gap is closing quickly as more US homes gain access to the internet. Phone surveys, conversely, are subject to increased call screening through caller ID compared to the past, whereas, response rates are still lower than in-person interviews.

Internet Surveys

Internet surveys have gained in popularity because of their ease of implementation and low cost. Cyber-based surveys in the context of this chapter include surveys sent out by e-mail and surveys that are posted online. Data retrieved in this fashion is extremely difficult, if not impossible, to generalize; at the same time, increasingly sophisticated spam filters make it difficult to obtain appropriate response rates from e-mail surveys.

Focus Groups

Focus groups can take place face-to-face or online. Effective focus groups contain at least five people but no more than 15. The discussion is led by a moderator who asks pre-determined questions, and responses take the form of a discussion. The advantage of focus groups is that the moderator can probe further into the reasons behind satisfaction or dissatisfaction and even brainstorm possible solutions with the group.

Focus groups work well when introducing a new product or service in an area. When conducting in-person sessions, individuals in the group can be shown visual stimuli and can test out new products on site. The moderator can address a wide variety of topics in a short period of time and obtain qualitative, in-depth responses.

In-Person Interviews

Normally, data obtained from in-person interviews is not germane to the broad-spectrum population. This is often a result of convenience sampling or non-probability sampling to obtain interviewees. It is difficult to obtain in-person interviews with a truly representative sample of the study population. Therefore, in-person interviews are best used to obtain in-depth qualitative data where the questions being posed do not need to result in generalizable phenomena.

Intercepts

Intercepts consist of conducting interviews with random individuals in a public place, often a shopping mall. There is a growing body of companies specializing in conducting intercept data gathering. This makes it more convenient for companies to contract to harvest intercept data, as opposed to setting up their own temporary data collection site, which may be costly depending on the space and equipment needed to conduct the survey.

Customer Complaints

Obtaining data from customer complaints is inherently biased. For example, it would be difficult to generalize overall satisfaction with a product or service by sampling people who call in to report complaints. Tracking data from customer complaints can be particularly insightful and helpful in some circumstances, however. For instance, if 30 people call to report a problem with a faulty battery in their cell phone, this is indicative of a quality control problem that needs to be addressed. Additionally, if 25 of those 30 individuals report that they are still highly satisfied with the product overall, that can provide important information about the nature of that particular defect – that in essence, battery quality is an attractive or indifferent quality as opposed to a must-have or a one-dimensional quality.

A guideline to acceptable response rates, which vary by survey type, follows:[7]

- Mail: 50% adequate, 60% good, 70% very good

- Phone: 80% good

- E-mail: 40% average, 50% good, 60% very good

- Online: 30% average

- Face-to-face: 80-85% good

Case in Point: Microsoft Windows 7

One of the most visible uses of VOC currently can be seen in the Microsoft Windows 7 marketing campaign developed by Crispin Porter & Bogusky, an advertising agency based in Miami and Boulder (US): "I'm a PC and Windows 7 was my idea." The campaign for Windows 7 followed years of negative press after the debut of the Windows Vista operating system in January 2007, touting enhanced security features over Windows XP and better file sharing and media capabilities.[89] Negative pressure abounded: *PC World* rated it as the biggest tech disappointment of 2007,[10] and *InfoWorld* rated it as the second biggest all-time flop.[11] Criticisms were vast and varied, but mainly centered around three areas:

- Bulky system requirements and slow performance;

- Security features that annoyed the user more than they made the user feel safe; and

- Rampant incompatibility issues.

While the long-awaited Vista took three years longer to develop than originally planned, after being blasted by the press, the tech world and customers alike, Microsoft released Windows 7 in the fall of 2009, less than two years after the release of the much maligned Vista OS. Having failed to produce on its promises with Vista, Microsoft had to re-establish trust with its customers.

Well known for monitoring customer satisfaction and relying on VOC for product R&D, Microsoft had its finger on the pulse of its market when that beat started to splutter and fail. Compared to the six-year timeline for Vista, Microsoft replaced the problematic operating system in short order.

The Windows 7 campaign is designed to let PC users know that their voices were heard, and Windows 7 was designed (implicitly) to address the Vista shortcomings.[12] The ads feature actual Windows customers asking for certain must-have features like simplicity, fast response and less clutter. "Our customers co-create the product with us," said David Webster, general manager for brand and marketing strategy at Microsoft. "We're using the customers' voice to tell our story...You told us you want it simpler, we made it simpler. You told us you want it to boot faster, it boots faster."[13]

The result to date has been a resounding success. Reviews by PC World, Business Week and Fortune were big thumbs up over Vista. Webster also reports that initial feedback from customers was favorable on ease of use, value and brand identity.[14]

While Microsoft still has a ways to go to salvage its reputation after the Vista debacle, the new marketing campaign outlines the importance VOC plays in a company's bottom line. In the case of Microsoft, listening to the voice of the customer became critical in fixing problems and re-establishing customer satisfaction and loyalty.

Conclusions

The Voice of the Customer approach is central to business strategy. Companies that do not listen to what their customers have to say and incorporate customer needs and wants into their business strategy risk losing huge amounts of market share and revenue to competitors that do. The case of Microsoft neatly outlines what happens when companies do not deliver on the promises they make to their customers. As of July 2010, Windows XP still holds 62.55% of the operating system market share compared to 15.25% for Vista – a huge disappointment for Microsoft and an unqualified failure for its expected revenues from the product.[15]

The Microsoft case also demonstrates how maintaining a good VOC procedure can transform a failed project or product into a success. A company that listens to its customers and responds in a timely manner can salvage their reputation and retain customer loyalty. While the jury is still out on the Windows matter, the initial response seems to indicate that Microsoft Windows 7 and the VOC marketing campaign that goes with it will turn things around for the company. Windows 7 has already captured 12.68% of the OS market share in under one year.

To learn more about designing a company-wide VOC strategy and process, or to learn about specific tools and metrics to help you find and interpret the voice of your customers, contact Lorraine Marzilli Lomas at *lmlomas@rocketmail.com*.

Key Lessons Learned:

1. Listening to the VOC will give you a saleable product.

2. Understanding consumer perceptions will give you an edge in the market.

3. Having a strong VOC process in place can turn around a product failure and re-establish customer loyalty.

About the Author

Lorraine Marzilli Lomas is an innovative, out-of-the-box thinker, communicator, Lean Six Sigma Black Belt and marketing professional with an MBA in Information Technology and Knowledge Management. Currently studying for a Doctor of Business Administration (DBA) degree, specializing in Lean Marketing, she has a passion for organizational training and strategic maneuverings.

---

[1] John Goodman and Bruce Hayes, "A Robust VOC Process to Drive Better Six Sigma Results," Accessed July 5, 2010 from
http://www.isixsigma.com/index.php?option=com_k2&view=item&id=848:&Itemid=192
[2] Adapted from Goodman and Hayes. The authors included eight factors. The eighth factor, linkage to organizational incentives, was left out here for both space and applicability considerations. The topic of incentives that reward employees is beyond the scope of this discussion.
[3] Simon Daisley, "Voice of the Customer: The Oxygen of Business Success," Accessed July 5, 2010 from: http://gccrm.com/eng/content_details.jsp?contid=2068&subjectid=101
[4] Ibid.
[5] P. Kotler and K. Keller, Marketing Management (Saddle River, New Jersey: Pearson Prentice Hall, 2009).
[6] M. Kaplowitz, T. Hadlock and R. Levine, "A Comparison of Web and Mail Survey Response Rates," *Public Opinion Quarterly 68*(1) (2004), 94-101.
[7] Instructional Assessment Resources, "Response Rates," (March 8, 2010) *http://www.utexas.edu/academic/diia/assessment/iar/teaching/gather/method/survey-Response.php*

[8] A. Ricadela, "Gates Says Security is Job One for Vista," *InformationWeek News* (February 14, 2006)
http://www.informationweek.com/news/windows/microsoft_news/showArticle.jhtml?articl eID=180201580
[9] "Microsoft Launches Windows Vista and the 2007 Office System to Consumers," *PressCentre* (January 30, 2007) Microsoft New Zealand.
http://www.microsoft.com/nz/presscentre/articles/2007/jan07_windowsvistalaunch.mspx
[10] D. Tynan, "The 15 Biggest Tech Disappointments of 2007," *PC World* (December 16, 2007) *http://www.pcworld.com/article/140583-5/the_15_biggest_tech_disappointments_of_2007.html*
[11] N. McAllister, "Tech's All-Time Top 25 Flops," *InfoWorld* (January 21, 2008) *http://www.infoworld.com/t/platforms/techs-all-time-top-25-flops-558*
[12] S. Elliott, "The Billion Designers of Windows 7," *The New York Times Online* (October 21, 2009) *http://www.nytimes.com/2009/10/22/business/media/22adco.html*
[13] Ibid.
[14] Ibid.
[15] "Operating System Market Share," Netmarketshare (July 13, 2010)
http://marketshare.hitslink.com/operating-system-market-share.aspx?qprid=10&qpcal=1&qpcal=1&qpcal=1&qptimeframe=M&qpsp=136

Chapter Seventeen

Value Stream Mapping:
Learning to See Transactional Processes

Pamela D. Gladwell

Overview

Manufacturing processes have been reaping the benefits of various Lean tools, including Value Stream Mapping, for over 20 years. It has been only within the past several years, however, that transactional process areas have begun to apply the same beneficial techniques. Part of the difficulty in improving these types of processes is their inherent variability. Unlike manufacturing, transactional processes are not made up of machines, automation, robots or standardized parts. Transactional processes include things such as new product designs, patients, insurance renewals, purchase orders, new employees, help-desk tickets and software systems. In place of automated operation, transactional processes have people at the very heart of the systems – people who typically resist documenting and using standardized processes and procedures, and whose performance varies from operator to operator with no way to calibrate human performance to a set standard.

To make matters more complex, information also flows through these processes, which is often times critical to every step within the process itself. Transactional processes run across multiple departments with people who may or may not communicate well with one another, creating the potential for numerous holes in the system.

Given this scenario of managing processes in a transactional environment, it becomes apparent that we need a very powerful tool to help us drive improvements for these types of processes. This is where Value Stream Mapping comes to the rescue. Application of Value Stream Mapping will ultimately lead to reduced costs and improved customer satisfaction, while improving employee satisfaction and retention.

This chapter will help you to:

- Understand the basic Lean principles required for creating a Value Stream Map.
- Understand and apply the basic concepts of value-added vs. non-value added process step analysis.
- Understand how to calculate process efficiency.
- Create a Value Stream Map.

Basic Lean Principles Required for Value Steam Mapping

You don't have to be an expert in Lean to create a Value Stream Map. However, there are a few basic Lean principles you must understand in order to effectively begin using this tool. James Womack and Daniel T. Jones have done an excellent job of boiling Lean down into its most basic principles in their book, *Lean Thinking: Banish Waste and Create Wealth in Your Corporation.*[1] Womack and Jones summarized Lean into a list of five basic principles:

1. Value – Precisely Specify Value by Specific Product

2. Value Stream – Identify the Value Stream for each Product

3. Flow – Make Value Flow without Interruption

4. Pull – Let the Customer pull value from the producer

5. Perfection – Pursue to Perfection

Through reviewing the details of these five basic principles, we gain an understanding of the Lean basics, which enables us to analyze our own processes during Value Stream Mapping activities.

Value – Precisely Specify Value by Specific Product

Specifying value accurately is a critical first step in any Lean Six Sigma project, as well as a necessary part of creating and analyzing a Value Steam Map. If we don't understand what our customers value, we simply cannot do any type of meaningful process analysis. We must know and understand what the customer needs. Without this information, we can't define customer Critical-to-Quality (CTQ) requirements, which are the key measurable characteristics of our product or process. Without CTQs, we cannot set performance standards or specification limits that must be met in order to satisfy our customers. Clearly, without this information, we cannot measure process effectiveness and efficiency.

For various reasons, value is very hard for some businesses to accurately define. Some organizations get caught in the trap of thinking they already know what is best for their customers, so they create the CTQs themselves, with little or no input from their actual customers. People within these organizations are often heard saying things like, "Our customers just don't get it," or "Since our customers don't understand what they really need, we must define it for them." Another symptom of not truly focusing on what customers value is being too technology focused. These organizations often can be identified by their creation of complex, customized designs with sophisticated processing technologies favored by their company engineers. All too often, the resulting products are too expensive, contain features that are irrelevant and ultimately do not meet customers' needs.

The first step in creating a Value Stream Map is to obtain good customer (internal or external) data. (See Chapter 16 on Voice of the Customer for a discussion of gathering external customer data). Once we have established we have good customer value data, we can analyze the value of the steps that take place within the process under scrutiny. Be prepared to have some debate with respect to what is "valuable" as you analyze each process step. Something that amazes me every time I work with a team to create a Value Stream Map is the shock on their faces as they see the final map. I commonly hear statements like, "*That* is how we do this process?" or "I had no idea that was what is happening."

The tendency over time is the number of steps in a process increases as does the complexity, due to improper management. As a new problem or issue arises in the organization, processes are often times not carefully studied before extra steps are thrown in as ad hoc solutions to address the concern. So as things like new requirements, increased regulations and organizational structure changes, steps are added into processes without much thought or study of how they will impact the entire value stream. Over time, we wonder why we can't seem to keep up with customer demand or why our processes are so confusing and frustrating. As we analyze our value stream through the mapping process, our goal is to search out and eliminate any process step that doesn't add value to the customer. One technique that has been very effective in helping me to rid processes of steps that don't add value to the customer is to ask the following three questions for every process step.

1. *Does the customer care?*
   – Would the customer be willing to pay for this step to be done?

2. *Was it done right the first time?*
   – Steps like testing, reviewing, checking, revising, etc., are all classified as rework.

3. *Was there a physical change?*
   – Has the item that is flowing through the process actually physically changed? Is it different in some way?

While this might appear to be fairly strict criteria as you first begin analyzing your processes, it is important to remember we are on a journey of continuous process improvement and setting targets like these establishes a clear vision of what a truly optimized process will look like.

Value Stream – Identify the Value Stream for Each Product

By definition, the value stream is the set of all the specific actions required to bring a specific product/service through the three critical management tasks of any business:

- *Problem Solving Task*: From concept through detailed design and engineering to production launch

- *Information Management Task*: From order-taking through detailed scheduling to delivery

- *Physical Transformation Task*: Proceeding from raw materials to a finished product in the hands of the customer

We can simplify this definition by stating that a Value Stream includes all the steps from the point when the customer requests a product/service until the time they receive it. Given this definition, this would include the entire set of activities involved in creating and producing a specific product, from concept through actual availability, from the initial sale through delivery, and from raw materials produced right to the finished goods in the hands of the customer. This concept is important to your value stream mapping efforts because teams often times do not include *all* the steps of the process as required by this definition. The customer doesn't look at or measure their experience by individual departments; the customers feel the entire process as a whole, so this is how we must measure and evaluate ourselves.

Full, end-to-end value stream analysis often reveals significant waste, and it is an amazing eye-opener for any organization. An organization typically finds:

- Steps in the process that no one really understands the purpose for or even what (typically internal) customer that step is supposed to be serving. As an example, I have been in sessions where we found a detailed report was being generated weekly without identifying anyone who was actually using it.

- A number of steps linked to regulations, standards, or procedures where no one can locate the actual documentation in order to validate or defend the ongoing need for the steps. I participated in a team where we found an extensive amount of data being collected and stored in support of "export controls." However, as we kept pushing back on this very time-consuming task, we came to find out that the data being collected was not required, and worse yet, no one in the organization was doing anything at all with that data.

- Clear examples of the eight types of waste throughout the value stream. (See Chapter 14 for a detailed discussion).

Analyzing the entire Value Stream of an organization can be a very detailed and lengthy process to go through; however, it is an extremely enlightening and rewarding process. Since most of us don't have the task of analyzing the Value Stream for an entire organization, it is comforting to know that Value Stream Mapping can be used very successfully to identify the same types of issues in smaller subsets of processes within the organization as well.

Flow – Make Value Flow Without Interruption

The focus of flow is to keep whatever is moving through the process moving forward without stop. When the process stops or an item has to be reworked, this creates wait time and delays in the process (delay = waste). To uncover these occurrences in the process, we must record everything that is happening to our process item, whether an actual product, information or some type of service, as it travels through the process. And yes – I do mean *everything*.

One technique that keeps a team focused on getting all the details out is to have a strong facilitator become the item in question. At each and every step the facilitator should ask, "And then what happens to me?" This role play helps to make sure we capture every detail. This is a critical step in the mapping process, so we want the team to bring an actual completed transaction that has successfully travelled through the process from end to end. It is important to remember that we don't want to look at the process the way it is *supposed* to happen, nor do we want to see the way the process operates when all the conditions are perfect. To truly understand how this process currently operates, we need to have a true representative sample of what would be our typical situations on a typical day.

A common mistake in analyzing flow is to become focused on the people who are working in the process and whether or not they are "busy." This is not the purpose of value stream analysis. For instance, if a project manager is juggling 8-10 projects, is he or she really working on all 8-10 projects at the same time? The answer is no. As such, each time that project manager puts down Project #2, for example, to do work on Project #3, Project #2 sits idle. And, as we learned in Chapter 14, waiting = waste.

Creating flow can seem counterintuitive to an organization that is grouped by departments and divisions, as well as to a workforce that has become more focused on individual needs rather than the needs of the customer. The ideal process flow is single piece flow. Single piece flow is a Lean concept that tells us that the best way to setup a process is to always complete all the steps in the value stream all the way through to the end without stopping. When applying this concept, we avoid batching: a system where we collect a number of items going through a process until we have reached a particular trigger point before moving on to the next step.

For example, let's say we work in a department that processes and pays invoices for the organization's vendors. In this case, the vendor is the customer of this process. If we analyze our example process for flow, the wait time for the invoice going through this process typically runs anywhere from 0-14 days. Same-day processing creates zero wait. However, if our process dictates that invoices are batched and processed only twice per month, an invoice coming in the day after the processing day is going to wait 13 days before being processed. In and of itself, the wait time alone tells us the process is inefficient. It is even worse once we know it only takes five minutes to do the hands-on (value-added) work to complete this transaction. Then, in this case, the total end-to-end time for a five-minute process becomes 13 days. This is the type of thing that drives both internal and external customers crazy. Imagine the magnitude of multiple sub-processes each having this amount of wait time. Think about what happens to the end-to-end lead time for a value stream when there are multiple instances of batching involved.

To better understand how well our processes are flowing, we can utilize a technique called Process Flow Efficiency. In order to use this technique, we must clearly understand the concepts of value-added and non-value added. In addition to these two categories we must add a third: required non-value added. This is where we introduce process steps that are not meaningful to the customer, yet they are a necessary part of doing business.

> **Value-Added**: Essential processes that are necessary to deliver the product or service to the customer.

Required Non-Value-Added: Business processes that may not be meaningful to the customer, but which are an essential part of conducting business. Examples of Required Non-Value-Added steps are EPA reporting or Sarbanes-Oxley compliance.

Non-Value-Added: Also known as waste, these processes add no value from the customer's perspective and serve no critical business function.

There are just two basic formulas needed to calculate Process Flow Efficiency:

Process Flow Efficiency = Value-Added Time/Total Process Lead Time

Total Process Lead Time = Value-Added Time + Non-Value Added Time

Process Flow Efficiency Example:

A patient in a hospital needs to have a test performed (*i.e.*, X-ray, blood test, mammogram). The Process Flow Efficiency calculation would be built as follows:

Value-added time:

- Time to perform the test = 5 minutes
- Reading the results of the test = 10 minutes
- Results explained to patient = 5 minutes

Non-value-added time:

- From doctor writing order for test until order is entered into the system = 2 hours
- Patient waits for transport to testing area = 30 minutes
- Patient travels to test = 20 minutes
- Patient waits for transport back to room = 30 minutes
- Patient travels back to room = 20 minutes
- Waiting for expert to read the results = 2 hours
- Sit waiting for the doctor to read the results = 3 hours

Value-added time = 20 minutes
Non-value added time = 520 minutes

Total Process Lead Time = 540 minutes

Process Flow Efficiency = 20/540 = .04 or 4%

This example tells us that there is only 4% value-added activity in our process and we have plenty of room for improvement. It is critical to remember that customers are only willing to pay for value. Non-value added activity adds costs above and beyond what the customer is willing to pay for the product or service. In order to create flow, we must eliminate all non-value added activities from our processes. During our Value Stream Mapping activities, it is important to stay focused on the definitions we have provided thus far. I would recommend printing out a copy of the following key items and post them in the room where you will be doing the Value Stream Mapping: 1) The Three Questions to test for Value Add, 2) The Three Questions to test for Value Add and 3) The Eight Types of Waste (from Chapter 13). Getting rid of non-value added activities and wait time is the single biggest key to streamlining your processes.

Pull – Let the Customer Pull Value from the Producer

The Lean principle of pull tells us we only replenish an input or resource as it is used to fulfill actual customer demand. Implementing a pull system allows companies to create a steady, even beat across the entire process, where all the steps operate in harmony. In applying this principle to our Value Stream Mapping activity, we must start from the end of the process and work our way backwards. I find that it is helpful to have the facilitator ask the team something to the effect: "What had to occur just prior to this step to trigger its start?" In transactional processes, we often find this to be a very weak area. Process steps often end and have no triggers to initiate the next step in the process, which is a huge source of delay. Alternatively, we also find steps in the process where steps are triggered before they are needed, causing chaos, confusion and frustration for their downstream processes. This can lead to rework. As you walk through the Value Stream Map, seek to adopt and implement ways to create a pull system of process management as opposed to allowing a push system to determine the pace of the process.

Perfection – Pursue to Perfection

Perfection begins with the simple belief that perfection is achievable and within our reach. We must create and maintain a culture throughout the organization in which every individual has a passion for achieving perfection. The Lean principle of perfection is about ongoing continual improvement every day. There is no end to the process of continually striving to get better. This approach may seem frustrating to some; however, it prevents improvement efforts from ceasing at the first plateau. The key is to incrementally improve by constantly examining your processes for areas of waste and inefficiency. Lean Six Sigma is not a phase: it is a journey to perfection. Womack and Jones explain that when organizations clearly understand these principles, tie them together, and make full use of Lean techniques, they can chart and maintain a steady course toward becoming a Lean organization. The organization will continue to improve its processes every day, eliminating more and more waste with every project and making incremental improvements that bring it closer to perfection. It is important for everyone involved in the value stream mapping event to understand this concept of continuous, incremental improvement. Value Stream Mapping will uncover an overwhelming list of process improvement opportunities. We don't want our team to become frustrated by this list. They need to understand that a plan will be developed to systematically attack theses improvement opportunities based on their importance to and impact on the organization.

Creating a Value Stream Map

Armed with our Lean Basics, we are ready to understand how to create a Value Stream Map. So, what is a Value Stream Map? As discussed earlier, the value stream consists of all the activities an item must go through in order to design, order, produce, and deliver its products or services to customers. The Value Stream Map (VSM) is used to capture all those activities –not just the flow of work, but the flow of information and materials required to complete each step of the process. A Value Stream Map is very different from your basic process map.

Process Maps are typically:

- Functionally focused

- Incorporate a high level of detail

- Used to understand each process step

- Lacking in value judgments about the steps

- Come in two states: As-Is and To-Be process maps

- Created to reflect the "perceived flow" – the way the process *should* work

- A mingling of information and physical flows

Value Stream Maps typically:

- Have a great deal of detail

- Are focused on identifying cycle time reduction

- Become useful when wasted time is difficult to spot

- Cut across functional boundaries and multiple departments

- Use simple graphics or icons to show the sequence and movement of information, materials, and actions in the value stream.

Mapping a value stream for a transactional process (especially for the first time) might reveal some rather scary looking maps. Value Stream Maps are meant to help the team *see* what is currently going on in their processes. If I walked into a VSM session and saw a very simple, perfectly organized process on the wall, I would ask one of two questions:

1) "Do you really need to be working on this process?" or

2) "Do you really think you have captured what is really going on in this process at the appropriate level of detail?"

Two examples of real-life Value Stream Maps I have helped create are captured in Figures 17-1 and 17-2, below.

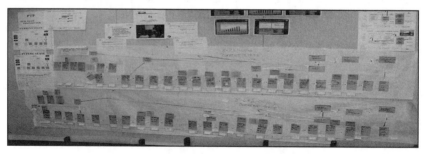

Figure 17-1: Linear Flow VSM

Figure 17-2: Spaghetti Chart VSM

Steps for Building a Value Stream Map:

1) Start with a High-Level Process Map

2) Identify the target product, product family, or service

3) Establish Scope of Activity

    a. start and finish (of the process)

    b. inputs and outputs (of the process)

4) Walk the process (backward and forward)

    a. use a real transaction

5) Fill in all the details for each step. Record <u>touch time,</u> <u>auto time</u> and wait time for every step. Identify rework, waste and root causes.

In order to see exactly how a Value Stream Map is created in real life, we will examine the following case study of an actual project I worked on in the past.

Case Study: Urgent Care Facility Improving Patient Handling Time

Background

An urgent care center feels their patients wait time is too long. The staff members have noticed increasing numbers of people waiting longer in the waiting room as time goes on. Although they don't have any real data or measurement systems currently in place, there are some obvious clues that something is wrong. The number of people sitting in the waiting room area is growing, and there are increasing complaints from patients indicating they feel the wait time is excessive.

The staff works long, hard hours. Employees are dedicated to their chosen field and to serving patients; however, many are becoming frustrated with their inability to serve patients effectively and efficiently. The gut-feel among the employees is that inefficient processes may be causing roadblocks and chaotic situations for both patients and staff. The staff easily notice several areas that could be improved; however, they have no idea which issue(s) will have the biggest impact on the overall problem.

UCC leadership formed a Lean Six Sigma project team and handed a draft charter to the team members. The charter indicated that the national benchmark performance is 90 minutes or less from the time the customer arrives (checks in) to the time the customer is treated and discharged. The team doesn't know how their customers currently compare to that benchmark, but they know they need to find out. The leadership team doesn't want to just meet the benchmark with this project – they would like to exceed it. They had also received information that there was as least one local competitor claiming to get patients through in 60 minutes or less. The leadership team wants this benchmark to be the target for the project team. The team is aware that customer satisfaction scores have dropped to the 40th percentile. While there are several other factors that drive the customer satisfaction score, the team knows that wait time is a major factor contributing to overall dissatisfaction.

The Center had been experiencing a growth rate of 5–6 percent annually and didn't want to risk losing any customers. The organization also didn't want the growth rate to slow. They were experiencing increased competition with surrounding area urgent care centers, who were driving down their throughput times and advertising their faster response times. So, the team needed to get this project up and running and the leadership wanted to see results quickly.

Creating a Value Stream Map Step-by-Step:

1. Start by Creating a High-Level Process Map

A high-level process map allows you to see the process as an overview of steps necessary to get the product or customer through the value chain. In this case, our map shows the steps and activities a patient goes through from the moment he or she arrives until the moment he or she leaves the facility. Process times are not assessed at this level.

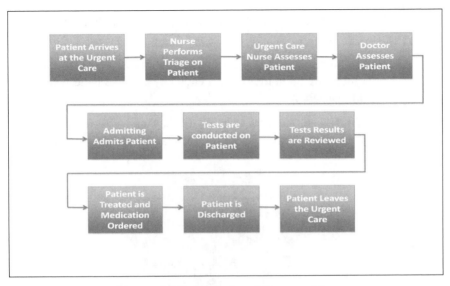

Figure 17-3: High-Level Process Map

2. Identify the target product, product family, or service.

This facility has patients that go through both the Urgent Care and the Emergency Room. The only "product" included in this case were the patients going through the Urgent Care. This requires that we actually analyze two different process scenarios if we included the Emergency Room Patients as well. For simplicity, we show only the Urgent Care patient value stream.

3. Establish the Scope of your Value Stream Mapping Activity

- Start - Patient arrives at the Urgent Care

- Finish – Patient leaves the Urgent Care

- Inputs – Patient (needing to be treated, symptoms)

- Outputs – Patient (treated, prescriptions, instructions)

4. Walk the Process (backward & forward)

- This process improvement team walked and observed the process for a day, writing down everything they observed happening and recording the flow of the steps.

- Multiple team members walked with several different patients to account for variations in the process, given that the experience of each patient can vary greatly.

- The team collected data by time stamping each individual process step.

- Observation data sheets were used to collect data about what was actually going on in the process each day to understand what was causing variation.

- Using this data, the team mapped all the steps of the process and recorded all the issues (using the red star bursts, shown below).

Figure 17-4: Sample Red Star Burst for Flagging Issues

- To make sure no steps were missed during the mapping, the team walked the process backward asking the question: "What occurred just prior to this step in the process?" This technique helps to flush out any additional details that might have been left out.

5. Fill in the Additional Details.

Record value-added touch time and non-value added wait time (inside the process box).

The final result is a Value Stream Map that clearly and visibly outlines all the steps of the process and shows the team exactly where the process is flowing and where it stops and why. At this point, the team can begin to take action on wastes that can make an immediate impact in the process.

Process Name:	
Patient Discharge Procedures	
Process Description:	
Preparing all the information and entering it into the Urgent Care Patient System in order to discharge the patient. Entering the order for the patient's medications	
Value-Added Touch Time:	3-5 min.
Non-Value Added Wait Time:	2-10 min
Total Process Cycle Time:	5-10 min

Figure 17-5: Process Box

Finally, the team can begin with a blank sheet of paper and draw a future state Value Stream Map based on how they could lay out the process differently in order to capture the best, most efficient flow.

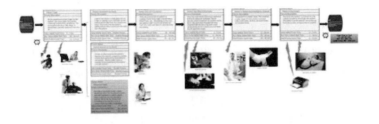

Figure 17-6: Future State Value Stream Map

Conclusions

Value Stream Mapping is an excellent tool for better understanding transactional processes. It provides a method of seeing how the process is flowing and where it gets hung up. It provides a way to truly *see* where all the waste, issues and wait time are occurring in the process so that the team can take immediate action attacking the problems and cutting time out of the process. These improvements, which will quickly lead to reduced costs and improved customer satisfaction, will also improve employee satisfaction and retention, another critical component often overlooked in Lean project analysis. To download a free copy of the excel template and the icons used to create this Value Stream Map, visit *http://www.pamgladwell.com* or *drivingoperationalExcellence.com*.

Key Lessons Learned

1. All Value Steam Mapping activities must begin with the knowledge of what is truly important to the customer and how it will be measured.

2. Value Stream Mapping must be done using real data based on how the process is actually occurring *today*.

3. A team of people must walk the process backward and forward in order to understand the variation that occurs within each type of transaction going through the process. This might require some data gathering over a period of time before the mapping session actually begins.

4. Use visual symbols relevant to your industry and transactional process to create a very visual Value Stream Map. The goal is to help everyone clearly *see* the flow of the process and an explicit picture is critical in achieving that goal.

About the Author

Pamela D. Gladwell, MBA, is a Lean Six Sigma Master Black Belt, author and instructor for Purdue University's On-Line Lean Six Sigma Program. Pam is the Chief Executive Officer of Performance Excellence Academy, LLC, headquartered in West Chester, Ohio. Pam consults with companies in the topics of change management, project management and Lean Six Sigma. She is a highly sought-after conference speaker and seminar leader. Her most recent experience includes roles as President of the Center for Quality of Management, Master Black Belt and Lean Six Sigma leader of GE Corporate Global Infrastructure Solutions, and Data Architecture Leader for GE Technology Services Group. As the Six Sigma Master Black Belt for GE-Capital Consumer Financial Services, Pam led the Executive Team in defining and prioritizing process improvement teams. She trained, led, developed, coached and certified a team of Black Belts and 450+ Green Belts through certification. She monitored Six Sigma goals and drove execution for meeting business objectives. As a result of the year's performance, Pam received the highest award within GE Capital – the Pinnacle Award.

Pam has a B.S. in Systems Analysis and a M.B.A. from Miami University in Oxford, Ohio. She earned the Charles S. Davis Award for Excellence in Graduate Study. Pam is currently pursuing her Ph.D. in Leadership and Organizational Change. For more information, or to contact Pamela in person, you can visit her website at *http://www.pamgladwell.com*.

---

[1] 2003. New York: Free Press.

Specific Tools

An architect's most useful tools are an eraser at the drafting
board, and a wrecking bar at the site.

– Frank Lloyd Wright

Chapter Eighteen

Lean Thinking Applied in Your Idea Development Lifecycle

Joann O. Parrinder

Overview

"Measure twice, cut once and have flexibility," are bits of wisdom my dad, a carpenter by trade, bestowed on me when he was helping me build a bookcase for my first apartment. The advice seemed simple at first, but became frustrating to implement as I tried to line up each metal bracket clip for the bookshelf I was building, in order to have that flexibility to adjust each shelf height. Thinking <u>Lean</u> is really what my father's advice was all about. Having flexibility was his way of saying *adding value*, and "measuring twice" was about reducing or eliminating waste in the process. Today, when you embark on a journey to develop an idea, this advice mirrors the <u>5S's</u> principle of Lean thinking (Figure 18-2).

This chapter is for anyone who ever had an idea to create something new or to improve something old. It is about learning how the 5S's are important in collecting your thoughts about your idea and communicating it to others involved in bringing your idea to fruition. While defining and capturing the essence of your idea, it is important to understand and align your idea's development lifecycle with that of your company's, your suppliers' and your customers'. This alignment focuses on key milestones that establish the baseline of your idea. We will also look at some examples and case studies to illustrate this importance.

This chapter will help you to:

- Learn how to think Lean when taking your idea from a thought to reality.
- Understand how the Lean principle of 5S's help in your idea development lifecycle.
- Understand the idea of the development lifecycle.
- Learn how to handle changes to your ideas.

The Idea Development Lifecycle Process

Figure 18-1 depicts the idea <u>development lifecycle process</u> of any product or service. Once the idea is initiated, it goes through several stages: concept, design, build, integrate and test, make or implement, verify for approval launch or release into production, and finally, production mode. These stages make up your development timeline complete with start and end dates or key milestones for each stage, with the final stage milestone being your Start-of-Production (SOP) date.

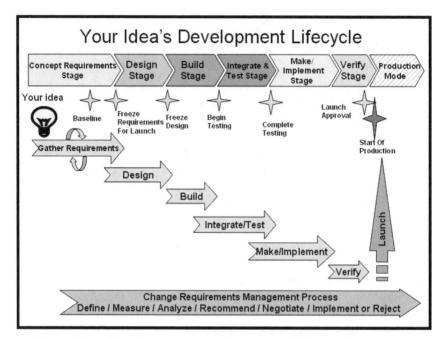

Figure 18-1: Idea Development Lifecycle and Change Management Processes

The 5 S's: Lean Thinking Applied to Idea Development

It happens. You have a thought, an idea for something new. Slowly, it transforms itself into a vision in your mind; something very specific takes shape. It may be a product or service. It may be a delightful tune, a fragrant smell, a loan approval or a simpler way to do something. This transformation from idea to a real product, service, improvement, method, or whatever its final form may be, has a systematic development lifecycle to ensure final quality.

Originally developed for Lean manufacturing, the 5 S's can be applied to the idea development lifecycle process as well. They help ensure that the final product, service or process *sustains* the original essence and integrity of the original idea as it goes through the development lifecycle process. (See Figure 18-2).

```
┌────────────────────────────────────────────────┐
│        Applying the 5S's in Developing Your Idea │
│                                                  │
│  The 5S's:              The 5S's to develop your idea: │
│                                                  │
│  • Sort                 • Sorting out and communicating your │
│                           idea from a high-level, big picture │
│                                                  │
│  • Set in order         • Setting up and organizing your idea │
│                           into features, functions and options │
│                                                  │
│  • Scrub and Shine      • Scrubbing your idea by documenting │
│                           to keep the good and remove what's │
│                           not needed                          │
│                                                  │
│  • Standardize          • Standardizing your idea's essence │
│                           by establishing its baseline       │
│                                                  │
│  • Sustain              • Sustaining your idea's essence while │
│                           allowing for changes to improve the │
│                           baseline                            │
└────────────────────────────────────────────────┘
```

Figure 18-2: Applying the 5S's in Developing Your Idea

Sorting Out & Communicating Your Idea

Once an idea is conceived, it must be transformed into words, pictures, flowcharts and criteria or conditions for operation and success as it matures through these stages. Often, ideas and concepts begin as vague forms in our minds that lack substance and formalization. By sorting out the various pieces – basic description, purpose, benefits and advantages – and communicating our vision, we begin to add critical substance that allows others to share our idea and play key roles in making it happen.

One way to do this is to distinguish between *needs* and *nice-to-haves*. What is a 'need' versus a 'nice-to-have?' A need could be a product with basic features or functionality, in the way that one of a remote key's basic functions is to open the driver side door of your car at the press of a specific button; it is a critical function that defines the product's basic purpose. If the need is a service, it could be like having your resume critiqued and professionally re-written for a position for which you are qualified and want to apply. A *nice-to-have* includes those things that, while not necessary to the basic task or purpose at hand, would still add value to your experience.

To illustrate, a remote start button on the electronic key would definitely be a nice-to-have, but it isn't critical to the key's function of locking or unlocking doors and trunks. For a resume service (Table 18-1), re-writing your resume for three different job positions is a nice-to-have in case you don't get the primary job for which you intend to apply, but isn't critical for the task at hand: winning the project manager job you so desire.

An Example of a Resume Service Requirements or Options	
Needs	**Nice-To-Haves**
• Critique current resume • Collect work experiences with start and finish dates, company, tasks, accomplishments • Write new resume for one position, e.g. project manager, that best uses the collection of work experiences • Write a cover letter that supports the project manager resume	• Re-write resume for a second position, e.g. IT project manager, using the work experiences that demonstrate this position • Write a cover letter that supports the IT project manager resume • Re-write resume for a third position, e.g. lean consultant, using the work experiences that demonstrate this position • Write a third cover letter that supports the lean consultant resume

Table 18-1: Needs versus Nice-to-Haves

The Needs vs. Nice-to-Haves chart allows you to sort out your idea's junk and eliminate waste. It is a format for later discussions on what process or product designs best fit the intended purpose.

Setting Up and Organizing Your Idea's Concept

As your idea matures through the development timeline, each stage has start and end dates and key milestones that signal stage completion. Unless you communicate the concept of your idea in sufficient detail, however, it will remain a figment of your imagination.

You may start with a sketch, a list of features, a flow diagram, a value stream, or some one-page visual of your idea. Each sentence represents and describes a feature, in detail, possibly a length of time to perform a service, a condition when something should happen or not happen and so forth. The purpose of this stage is to set out a list of requirements necessary to see your idea all the way through to actual production.

Through your conversations, presentations and discussions, you communicate what this product or service is and in sufficient detail so everyone will share the "vision" – the essence of your idea. This communication will be with your team, your management, your supplier and your customer or sponsor. When these efforts are effective, your people will have the exact same vision for your idea. You've now developed a team that can help you take your idea from concept to reality.

Scrubbing and Documenting Your Idea

This stage begins with formalizing your idea by writing it down and creating the requirements or <u>specification document</u>. This set of written requirements provides a permanent means to describe, explain, and communicate your idea to others. This process allows you to scrub your idea, clean it up, and refine it with the help of experts, novices, owners and anyone else who is a part of your team or interested in your idea. The value your idea brings to these people will also be written in the form of features, definitions of quality, operating instructions, test cases and implementation procedures, to name a few. The requirements document will go through several iterations as you develop and refine the description of your idea into its final form. Other questions equally as important when scrubbing and documenting your idea are:

When is the product or service needed?

When are additional units or services necessary?

What kinds of testing must be done to ensure a quality?

How much is the customer willing and financially able to spend?

What is the timetable for payment?

All are keys to aligning your customer needs and expectations with what your company can provide. The answers will help you to successfully design and deliver the most suitable and flexible solution possible that will not only satisfy, but also surpass, the expectations of your customer.

Standardizing or Establishing a Baseline for Your Idea

Once all of the requirements are documented and scrubbed for accuracy, it is then called a <u>baseline document</u> or specification. This document is labeled "Version 1.0." This key milestone is noted by all stakeholders or their representatives through signed approval, signaling their agreement to proceed with materializing your idea through the production phase.

If your idea is to be provided by a supplier, the baseline document is sent out in a Request for Quote (RFQ). The suppliers' responses are then evaluated for final selection. If your idea is to be created internally, such as a process improvement or a new service, the baseline document is distributed and your idea is presented and proposed to senior management for approval and funding. Whether it is supplier selection or funding approval, each step is a key milestone signaling that the concept stage is completed, and you are ready to start the design stage in the development lifecycle process.

Sustaining Your Idea's Baseline with Changes

Throughout the idea lifecycle, it is important to recognize that changes do occur. Therefore, it is necessary to establish a <u>change management process</u> very early in your idea development lifecycle. (See Chapters 7 and 8). Even as your idea is being organized, communicated and written down, changes occur as it is refined into its final form, the baseline. From the baseline document, all accepted additions, revisions, and deletions are integrated using the change management process: define, measure, analyze, recommend, negotiate, and implement or reject (Fig. 18-1).

Just as you did for your idea in the beginning, each change must be defined and written down: what it is, its purpose and its benefit to the baseline. Once established, the change can be measured and analyzed with respect to how it would be integrated into your idea without causing the idea to lose its essence. Other considerations include how to do it in a timely manner and maintain cost effectiveness. The recommended integration and its cost must be negotiated to determine whether the change will be accepted or rejected. If accepted, the change, as part of the negotiation, must have an approved date to implement – a key milestone for the release of any approved change.

This release date may either be the original Start-of-Production (SOP) date, or some date after SOP and released as an enhancement. Usually, the main roadblock to scheduling any change release is the length of time necessary to adequately develop and integrate the approved change into the overall solution to make it ready for release. This usually means the release date falls after SOP.

Stakeholders must be careful to ensure that at some point a key milestone is put in place wherein all baseline changes must stop so that your idea can materialize on time and with quality. Ignoring this will jeopardize the SOP date and will prove costly. After all changes are made to the baseline specification, the document is updated as Version 2.0 and represents what will be launched at the Start-Of-Production. Now the design can be fully developed and reviewed for accuracy with respect to the requirements.

Just as you freeze requirements, the design, too, must be frozen at some point and gain approval as the final design specification. This allows your idea to proceed to the next stage, the build stage.

Case Study: Think Lean by Reviewing Lessons Learned When Proposing Repeat Business

Monday morning, the first day of the month, started early for Mary Peters, Director of Sales for We-Can-Build-It Company.[1] When she arrived at her desk, her phone rang. Answering it, she found it was one of her clients, Tom Evans, president and owner of Evans Delivers Inc. calling.

> "Hi Mary, How are you? I just sent you an email for an RFQ for a build-to-print product that your company has done for us in the past. We are hoping that since your company has built this more than once, we could get a reduced price from your leveraged experience."

Mary was cautious about her answer because after reviewing the lessons learned of the last two jobs with Evans Delivery, Inc., Mary had learned that Tom's product engineering drawing prints at RFQ were revised numerous times, each time putting her company's manufacturing team through unexpected changes that increased costs and caused delays.

> "Tom, Good to hear from you. Regarding your RFQ, I see that you need eight units using drawing prints at revision 4.1 with the first two delivered ASAP. Then, the next two are to be delivered by the 24th and the remaining four by the 31st; is that correct?"

> "Yes," Tom said. "We were awarded new business and need our new delivery trucks upgraded. I have provided you with all of our requirements. So, when do you think I can have my first two sets?"

> "Tom," Mary replied, "First, let me tell you that we value our business relationship with you. However, I must inform you that we now have a new proposal process in place, even for repeat orders."

Mary went on to explain the approval process required her to create a proposal team consisting of herself, a program manager, a design and manufacturing engineer, a buyer and a financial analyst. The engineers then reviewed all drawing prints with the customer team to understand and verify the requirements in the specification document, noting all changes and obtaining the customer's signed approval. They used the drawings to create the bill-of-material (BOM) and process drawings. The buyer used the BOM to determine availability of all raw materials and component parts, pricing and delivery dates. The financial analyst compiled all the information for final pricing. The team program manager, who would be responsible for executing the work once awarded, established a schedule based on all feedback as to when the company could deliver the units. She incorporated this, as well as all risks, assumptions and constraints, into the solution proposal document. Once completed and distributed, a review session was held with senior management for approval before sales could deliver it to the customer for negotiation.

> "Once the customer has signed an approved contract, then our program team can move forward to complete any final revisions using the established procedure for managing changes and then execute the plan accordingly," Mary explained.

> "How long will this process take? I really need two of our new delivery trucks upgraded immediately." Tom sounded anxious.

> "I can call you later today to confirm, but I believe we can deliver a proposal to you by this Friday at noon," replied Mary.

> "Friday at noon will be fine! Looking forward to doing business with you."

The process in this story seemed straightforward. Let's review the facts of this proposed repeat business:

1. Start: Monday, the 1st, sales department received RFQ from Evans Delivery with a build-to-print request for eight sets of shelving and containers to fit into the customer's new delivery trucks. The work is similar to past work for this customer.

2. First delivery: a proposal delivery is due Friday, the 5th, at noon, which gives the proposal team less than four days to create the proposal and obtain management approval.

3. In the RFQ, the customer delivery dates are: two sets due "ASAP," two due on the 24th, and four due on the 31st.

4. In the RFQ, the customer provided the product's drawing prints, revision 4.1, which your research has found are different from the last two orders placed. From past experience, the customer's "minor" changes in design caused a delay in delivery by two weeks because a required fastener was backordered. Even minor changes need a formal change management process.

5. Since two sets are needed immediately, the buyer checks inventory, raw material, parts availability and prices. This helps determine when manufacturing can begin assembly and complete production of the first two sets, as well as determine whether the other customer delivery requirements can be met.

6. Mary can propose a firm date for the customer's immediate needs and confirm whether the other delivery dates are possible. If not, then she will propose alternative dates for customer approval.

With these requirements in hand, Mary meets with senior management on Thursday for a review.

After Mary's design engineer had reviewed the specs, the customer had revised the drawings to correct mistakes in the measurements provided. These revisions were captured and signed-off by the customer. With the corrections in mind, the buyer had determined there were enough resources available to deliver the first two sets on the 19th, the second sets on the 26th, and the remaining sets on or before the 31st, for a unit price that encompassed a 28% profit margin.

"Why can't we make the 24th for the second set?" asked the plant manager.

"Our customer requested a specific fastener and our supplier is only able to ship sufficient quantity to support delivery of the first shipment on the 19th. Due to popular demand, the supplier needs more time to produce and ship enough quantity for the remaining sets, which will add two additional days to our own delivery time," Mary explained. "We could expedite the shipment for an additional 15% markup in order to meet the 24th, but I would like to propose that option when negotiating with the customer."

The meeting concluded with Mary having senior management's approval. On Friday, Mary met with Tom to negotiate the proposal she had e-mailed beforehand. Tom thanked her and indicated his surprise that her company was able to complete a seemingly long approval process and still meet the proposal delivery date. He was also very grateful that the drawings and specifications had been reviewed with his team. His lead engineer had commented that their proposal process had prevented delivery delays due to incorrect measurements. Tom confirmed that as long as Mary's company delivered the second set by 8 a.m. on the morning of the 26th, his company would have enough time to meet his customer's delivery requirements without having to absorb the expediting charge.

In this case, making the proposal delivery on time was the first step toward gaining a satisfied repeat customer. Expectations were set and met by the company. By asking questions and verifying requirements before production, even with a repeat order, the process saved both companies time and money upfront.

Sustaining Your Idea through the Design Stage

As the concept stage approaches completion, your idea transitions to the next stage: design. In this stage, the baseline requirements begin to take shape, giving life to your idea and bringing it one step closer to the final outcome. This means there is sufficient detail to start laying it out and refining the requirements, where necessary, through the change management process. For a product, this means the design engineer can start on the schematics and/or mechanical drawings. For a computer program, the programmer can begin to create technical designs, algorithms, flowcharts and such. For a service, it means laying out what steps are needed, what skills are required, and what length of time defines a service unit. Once the design is approved, it is frozen and ready to move on to the build stage.

Sustaining Your Idea through the Build Stage

The build stage is when you begin to see the construction of the first units of your idea. For a product, you can see, touch, and operate it. For a service, you can begin to see the definition of the skills needed and the steps and procedures involved in executing the service. You can also plan for training, designate or hire employees to perform the service, and create a timetable for accomplishing the processes that make up your service. All these steps in the build stage transform your idea into its final form, which must not lose its essence. Everyone involved must study the design and ensure there is enough detail to mentally construct it to completion and ensure it is built accurately. This also helps the team understand and anticipate potential delays and risks. Constant monitoring and controlling the schedule, budget and scope, comes from mentally constructing the idea into its final form.

Sustaining Your Idea through the Integrate and Test Stage

After the first units or service procedures are completed, they must be tested and integrated with any upstream or downstream processes to make sure they work as intended. If a product requires software or must integrate with other products or systems, then it must be tested so that all these interactions work correctly to ensure expectations are met. For a service, you must execute scenarios in which this service will be executed to test performance quality and the time involved in executing each step of the service. All defects, mistakes or glitches – major or minor – are addressed. They must be documented, prioritized, and resolved in line with the baseline essence of the product or service.

Case Study: Timing is Key in a Just-In-Time Service by a 3PL

Another example involves a third party logistics (3PL) and warehousing supplier who makes a milk run every Monday morning at 10 a.m., picking up product from its customer, a manufacturing supplier. The 3PL transports the product via airplane and truck, then stores it in a warehouse in another country. The product waits for pickup from the Original Equipment Manufacturing (OEM) customer's supplier for ultimate delivery to the OEM customer's plant. This service is paid for by the OEM customer as part of its contract with the manufacturing supplier. If the manufacturing supplier is unable to meet the scheduled delivery due to a problem that causes a delay missing the pickup time, he then has to expedite shipping another way or pay extra for the 3PL to make a second milk run. Either way, this costs additional money to the manufacturing supplier for which he cannot bill the customer.

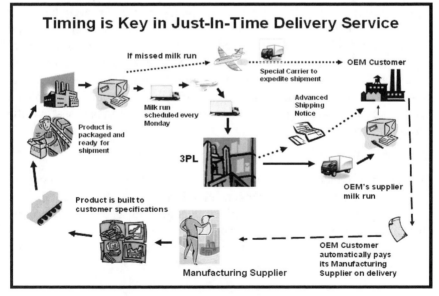

Figure 18-3: Thinking Lean in Just-In-Time

Likewise, the 3PL must ensure that the milk run happens as required at the manufacturing supplier's plants and has sufficient product when the OEM customer's supplier milk run happens. The 3PL may also make deliveries to the OEM customer for engineering test units, send advanced shipping notices and get the receiving department signature when delivering. Timing is everything to make this service work and make profit for the manufacturing and 3PL suppliers.

Sustaining Your Idea through the Make/Implement Stage

The make or implement stage deals with planning for making lots of your product available to customers or making sufficient resources available to provide your service or upgrade your process or software. For your product, this establishes the production operations stage, complete with proper and sufficient equipment, templates, operators, operator instructions and the like, to build a quality product. The process of making or implementing your idea must be reviewed and approved to ensure that it will be done each and every time in a consistent manner. That way, your idea will be repeatable, sustainable and quality-assured.

Sustaining Your Idea through the Verify Stage

Once established, your operations process must be verified for approval to go into production. The verify stage is where everything is checked to the requirements with measurements evaluated to acceptance criteria. The customer reviews the processes and results for acceptance or rejection. If rejected, it means that all defects identified and prioritized as "show-stoppers" must be resolved and re-verified to gain customer approval. Once approval is attained, the product, service or process improvement – namely your idea – can be launched or released into production. At this point, your project typically is considered completed and the project closure phase begins while your idea transitions into the production mode.

Sustaining Your Idea through the Production Mode Stage

While in production, the change management process continues to address all changes, enhancements or improvements for acceptance or rejection. All accepted requirement changes must be added to the baseline document and its revision number updated. The changes themselves will be processed as projects with scheduled implementation release dates.

Conclusions

In this chapter, we learned how important it is to understand and align your idea's development lifecycle by focusing on specific key milestones. Developing an idea through its lifecycle is Lean thinking using the 5S's. It means:

1. *Sorting* out and communicating your idea from high-level, big picture;

2. *Setting* up and organizing your idea into features, functions and options;

3. *Scrubbing* your idea by documenting to keep the good and remove what's not needed;

4. *Standardizing* your idea's essence by establishing its baseline, and

5. *Sustaining* your idea's essence while allowing a system for implementing changes to improve the baseline.

Thinking Lean can be used to plan and estimate the work for a business proposal in response to a customer's RFQ or to communicate and capture requirements for a new product, service, or process improvement. Thinking Lean involves asking questions to verify requirements: What, When, How Much, Where and Why. Aligning key milestones to establish a baseline, freeze changes made to the baseline and design to your company's, your supplier's, and your customer's development lifecycle process ensures you make the production release date. Always establish a change management process early because all great plans change and having a process to address those changes (*thinking lean*) makes success happen. You can download a helpful checklist by visiting *www.drivingoperationalexcellence.com.*

Key Lessons Learned:

1. Thinking Lean and doing it right the first time have several things in common: money, savings and profit.

2. Having a change management process during the idea development lifecycle is key to integrating changes that improve your idea while maintaining its original "essence."

3. Mentally constructing the final product, service, improvement or outcome in the minds of all involved ensures the essence of your idea is sustained.

About the Author

Joann O. Parrinder, MSIE, PMP, CPIM, CSCP, earned her bachelor's degree in Mathematics and Information Technology at Central Michigan University and her master's in Industrial Engineering at Wayne State University. Joann is a dynamic project manager and process leader with more than 20 years of experience and a history of successfully managing complex IT and engineering initiatives through all project phases and product stages. As a strategic and Lean thinker and a meticulous team leader, Joann has built strong business customer and supplier relationships and leverages a unique blend of management, engineering, and technology expertise in developing business solutions.

---

[1] Names of persons and companies have been changed in the case studies to protect client confidentiality.

Chapter Nineteen

Lean Six Sigma for a Leaner Supply Chain:
A Focus on Analytical Tools

Steve Cimorelli

Overview

This chapter is intended for business leaders, managers, Six Sigma sponsors and project leaders who are interested in learning how to *reduce costs* and *increase profits*. Companies around the world are broadening their application of Six Sigma beyond the realms of quality and design to drive improvements in virtually every business function.

While the case study outlined below applies lean principles to the areas of supply chain, production and inventory management, the *techniques* employed are applicable to any business process. The Six Sigma methodology presented here contributed more than $100,000 in combined improvements and provides an excellent framework to describe the lean processes involved.

This chapter focuses on several keys to success in applying the Six Sigma <u>DMAIC</u> process through an inventory management case study. The focus is on the DMAIC *process*, allowing the reader to think through how to apply the process steps to their own opportunities.

This chapter will help you to:

- Learn how to apply the DMAIC process
- Rate and prioritize potential projects
- Understand the benefits of using Creative Innovation tools
- Consider projects in your own companies that lend themselves to rigorous Six Sigma analysis

The Role of Six Sigma in Problem Solving

Problem-solving methodologies can be thought of as running along a continuum, beginning with simple, gut-feel types of approaches, moving towards more data-based analytical methods. As business structures and problems become more complex, companies must begin to collect data, look for patterns and trends, and ultimately apply structured statistical tools to isolate problem sources and design solutions. These statistical tools are the realm of Six Sigma.

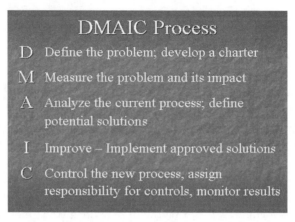

Figure 19-1: The DMAIC Process

DMAIC: Beginning with the End in Mind

The Six Sigma process seeks to improve processes by eliminating variation and defects, the opportunities for variation and defects in the *process*, and all non value-added activities. The DMAIC process begins with clearly defining the problem by way of a formula, called the 'Y-statement,' where the process output "Y" is a function of one or more inputs, or "X_n":

$$Y = f(X_1, X_2, X_3...X_n)$$

The DMAIC process is designed to provide a systematic method to reduce the number of key inputs down to a manageable set that have: a) a statistically significant impact on the process output, and b) a definable action plan. This "funneling effect" is illustrated in Figure 19-2.

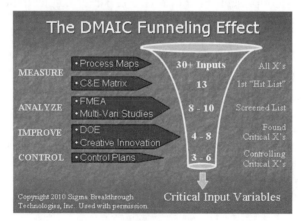

Figure 19-2: The DMAIC Funneling Effect

Case Study

In applying the DMAIC process, a real-world case study is provided, with the company name and identifying details fictionalized to protect confidentiality. The company is a global automotive parts manufacturer that supplements its product line with <u>branded</u> products purchased from multiple suppliers. Service levels for these branded products, as measured by on-time delivery, are significantly below that of other products. The company believes that supplier <u>minimum order quantities (MOQ)</u> and long <u>lead times</u> are contributing to lower service levels resulting in higher Backorders and Cancelled Orders.

Historically, the company's objective for Six Sigma projects has been to make a 50% improvement in the defined problem area. In this case, the team was challenged to make a 75% improvement through reduced backorders and cancelled orders, with an estimated combined cost savings and increased profits of $50,000. By the conclusion of the project, these goals were *exceeded*, reducing backorders and cancelled orders by 80% and driving more than $100,000 to the bottom line.

"Define" Phase:

The company's first step was to *define* the problem in the form of a Y-statement. The company saw the problem as poor on-time delivery of branded products. Company policy had been to limit inventory to no more than N months of supply. If the supplier's MOQ exceeded this value, they held customer orders until sufficient demand warranted placing an order and filling backorders upon receipt of the product.

This policy clearly contributed to poor on-time delivery (OTD). In the case of long-lead items, customers had to wait twice: first, while customer orders accumulated, and second, while the supplier's lead time transpired. The company also believed long lead times exacerbated the situation. The company's objective was to improve quality service on low-volume branded products with large MOQs, especially where those MOQ's exceeded N months of average monthly usage.

The next step in the process is to develop a <u>project charter</u>, defining the business benefits and timeframe for project completion. Following are the key elements of the project charter for our example company.

<u>Project Charter – Branded Product Service Improvement</u>

Objectives: Reduce service hits from XX/week to X/week (a 75% reduction) for branded products with supplier MOQ greater than six months of supply.

Benefits: 1.   Annual savings: $50K
             2.   Improved customer service, as measured by OTD
             3.   Reduce cancelled orders by 75%

Team: Six Sigma Belt, Master Black Belt, Sponsor, Process Owner and a 3-5 member cross-functional core group.

Schedule: The overall timeframe for a typical project is six months, but varies depending on complexity:

Measure: 4 weeks   Control: 6 weeks
Analyze: 2 weeks   Closeout: 2 weeks
Improve: 10 weeks

The team assigned to the project represents a truly cross-functional and top-to-bottom commitment by the company. The team is led by a fully trained belt (either a green or black belt) and the belt has access to an expert Master Black Belt who will coach and guide them along the way. Also included are the <u>process owner</u> and the <u>project sponsor</u>. These individuals are chartered by the organization to remove barriers and provide clout to ensure the project moves forward, and that process changes are fully implemented and sustained. (See Chapter 12 for more on the Project Charter).

"Measure" Phase:

The Measure Phase begins with two process mapping steps (see Figures 19-3 and 19-4). The first is a very high level 50,000-foot view, defining the process itself (center box), key inputs and key outputs. This step sets the process boundaries, clarifies the process itself, and identifies the outputs to be carried over into the C&E matrix, discussed next.

The second step is to dive down to the 5,000-foot view and document the sub-steps involved in the process. Note that all inputs and outputs from the first process map (Figure 19-3) must carry over to the second map (Figure 19-4).

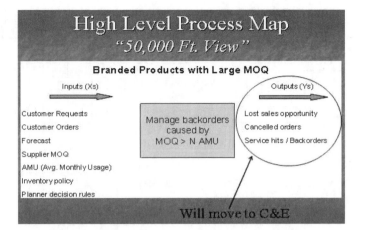

Figure 19-3: Process Map (50,000 Foot View)

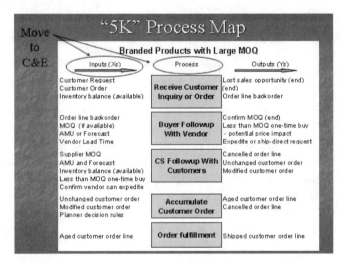

Figure 19-4 – Process Map (5K View)

The Measure Phase continues with a Cause & Effects (C&E) analysis, as illustrated in Figure 19-5. The team discusses each process step to determine the impact each one has on the three key outputs. Scores are normally assigned as: 0 (no impact), 1 (low impact), 3 (moderate impact) and 9 (high impact), with variation allowed in certain cases. On the top row, the team assigns numerical ratings to each key output (1 to 10 scale), based on the perceived importance to the customer.

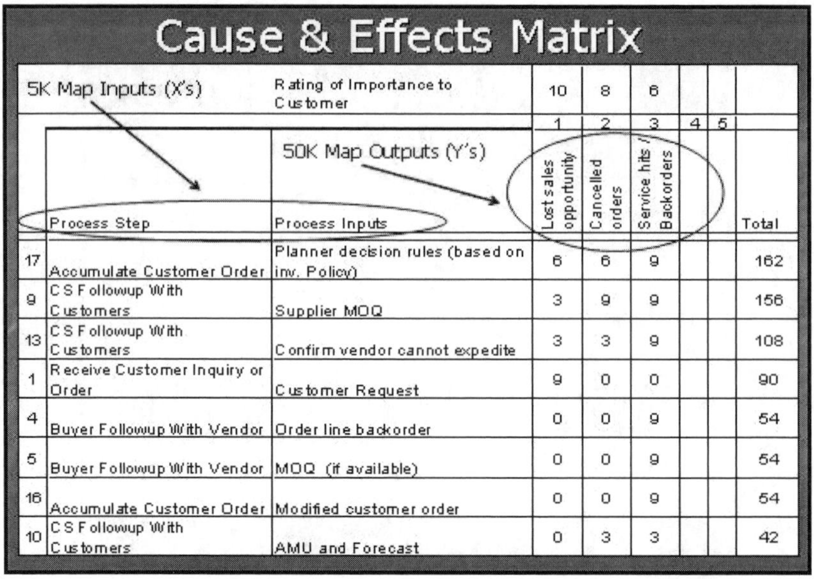

Cause & Effects Matrix

5K Map Inputs (X's)	Rating of Importance to Customer	10	8	6		
		1	2	3	4	5
Process Step	Process Inputs	Lost sales / opportunity	Cancelled orders	Service hits / Backorders		Total
17 Accumulate Customer Order	Planner decision rules (based on inv. Policy)	6	6	9		162
9 C S Followup With Customers	Supplier MOQ	3	9	9		156
13 C S Followup With Customers	Confirm vendor cannot expedite	3	3	9		108
1 Receive Customer Inquiry or Order	Customer Request	9	0	0		90
4 Buyer Followup With Vendor	Order line backorder	0	0	9		54
5 Buyer Followup With Vendor	MOQ (if available)	0	0	9		54
16 Accumulate Customer Order	Modified customer order	0	0	9		54
10 C S Followup With Customers	AMU and Forecast	0	3	3		42

Figure 19-5: The Cause & Effect Matrix

Totaling each row is done by multiplying each row's scores by their corresponding customer importance weight and summing to a total. The matrix is then sorted in descending order by total score, and the team decides where a natural break point occurs. Process steps above the break are deemed important enough to warrant further analysis. In this case, the scores dropped rapidly from a high of 162 to less than 50. The team decided that rows scoring higher than 50 warranted further analysis. Note that the C&E analysis has "funneled" the number of process steps down from nineteen to just seven.

"Analyze" Phase:

The Failure Modes and Effects Analysis (FMEA) shown in Table 19-1 is used to identify potential opportunities for the process to fail, the effect of each failure mode, and perceived root causes. For each row, a resulting effect is identified, and the team assigns a severity rating (SEV). Similarly, the team identifies potential root causes and assigns occurrence ratings (OCC). SEV and OCC range from 1 to 10, with 10 indicating the greatest severity or the greatest potential to occur. Refer to Chapter 21 for an in-depth analysis of how to perform an FMEA and assign appropriate rankings.

Process Step	Key Process Input	Failure modes	Effects	S E V	Causes	O C C	Current Controls	D E T	R P N
Accumulate customer order	Planner decision rules (inventory policy)	Orders accumulate until qty threshold is met	Customer waits beyond normal lead time	6	Decision Rule: Keep inventory below N AMUs	8	Inventory turns policy	7	336
CS follow-up with customers	Supplier MOQ	MOQ can't be reduced	Customer waits	7	Vendor constraint on MOQ	8	Evaluate low MOQ vendor alternative	6	336
CS follow-up with customers	Confirm vendor cannot expedite	Customer waits more	Customer unhappy; potential order loss	6	Vender constraint on Lead Time	8	Include in low-MOQ review	6	288
Rcv. customer inquiry or order in system	Customer request	Customer places order line – immediate backorder	Service hit & backorder	6	Inventory not available	8	Weekly BO report	6	288
Accumulate customer order	Planner decision rules	Customer cancels order	Lost sale	9	Waiting for orders to accumulate to threshold	5	Informal prioritization for OEM customers	6	270
CS follow-up with customers	Supplier MOQ	MOQ can't be reduced	Customer cancels order	9	Vendor constraint on MOQ	5	Evaluate low MOQ vendor alternative	6	270
CS follow-up with customers	Confirm vendor can expedite	Customer cancels order	Lost sale	9	Vendor constraint on Lead Time	5	Include in low-MOQ review	6	270

Table 19-1: Failure Modes and Effects Analysis

The team then identifies current controls in place to detect each root cause and assigns a detection score (DET), with 1 indicating the cause is certain to be detected and 10 indicating virtually no chance of detection. The three scores are multiplied together to arrive at a final RPN, or Risk Priority Number. For example, the first row scores are: SEV (6), OCC (8) and DET (6), for a total RPN of 288.

Finally, the FMEA is sorted and the team again determines a breakpoint for further analysis. In this case, the team decided on an RPN threshold of 270 or higher.

The team then had a decision to make, as lead time did not emerge from either analysis as a key X. The only quantifiable variable that did emerge, and for which data was readily available, was the Supplier MOQ. However, lead time data was readily available, and management continued to believe that lead time was a key factor despite the analysis. Therefore, the team decided to include lead time as a factor in the subsequent analysis using the ANOVA process.

<u>ANOVA – Analysis of Variance</u>

ANOVA testing is a process by which variables are subjected to statistical tests to determine whether or not a statistically significant effect on a process or outcome exists. ANOVA testing will show whether Lead Time and Lot Size had a statistically significant impact on backorders or cancelled orders.

Before proceeding to the tests themselves, the data first must be verified for accuracy and reliability. In our case study, the team obtained twelve months of historical backorder and cancelled order data, with each record containing relevant lead time and lot size details. Backorders were obtained from standard reports. The team chose a statistically significant sample and compared it to the live Order Management System (OMS) for consistency. A 100% match on all key elements was found, indicating that the report *accurately and reliably reflected* backorder history. Cancelled orders were put through a paired t-test to compare cancelled order quantities on matching records between two reports, as there was no OMS records. Again, a 100% match resulted, indicating that either of the reports could be relied upon.

Armed with reliable data, the team was ready to perform the required ANOVA tests. For each test, a null hypothesis (Ho) must be formed, stating the presumed innocence for each variable:

- Ho_1: MOQ has no impact on % Backorders
- Ho_2: MOQ has no impact on % Cancelled Orders
- Ho_3: LT has no impact on % Backorders
- Ho_4: LT has no impact on % Cancelled Orders

Conversely, an alternate hypothesis (Ha) is also needed, stating the potential "guilty verdict":

- Ha_1: MOQ has a statistically significant impact on % Backorders
- Ha_2: MOQ has a statistically significant impact on % Cancelled Orders
- Ha_3: LT has a statistically significant impact on % Backorders
- Ha_4: LT has a statistically significant impact on % Cancelled Orders

ANOVA tests generally follow a four-level process: 1) determine if the process is in control; 2) test if the data conform to a normal distribution; 3) test for equal <u>variance</u>; and 4) final ANOVA test (Fig. 19-6). At each stage, the roadmap specifies a particular statistical test be performed, based upon the results of the preceding tests. We will use the case study to illustrate several typical tests as we continue.[1]

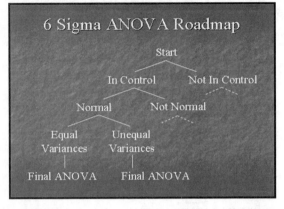

Figure 19-6: Six Sigma ANOVA Roadmap

Step 1: Determine if the process is *in control.* We first examine the baseline historical data, ideally presented in an Initial Moving Range (I-MR) chart of the number of customer order lines cancelled by week. As a general rule, if the data points remain between the upper and lower control limits (UCL and LCL), the process is considered to be in control, which is the case for this example.

Next, the data were segregated into two categories: 1) orders for parts having a supplier MOQ greater than 6 AMUs (the project scope), and 2) those having a supplier MOQ less than or equal to 6 AMUs (Fig. 19-7). The question we need to answer is, "Does MOQ negatively impact the company's ability to service customer orders for these products?" This can best be answered by studying the difference between the company's performance on orders that meet the MOQ criteria vs. all other orders. The ANOVA process is designed to help answer this question.

The I-MR chart also shows that cancelled order history is "in control" for all parts: those with both large and small MOQs. There *appears* to be a clear difference in performance between the large and small MOQ orders. It may seem reasonable to assume that the higher number of cancelled orders per week for large MOQ items and the greater amount of variation in this category is conclusive; however, further statistical analysis is required to conclude that the difference is *statistically significant.* This is a key difference between traditional problem solving and Six Sigma analysis.

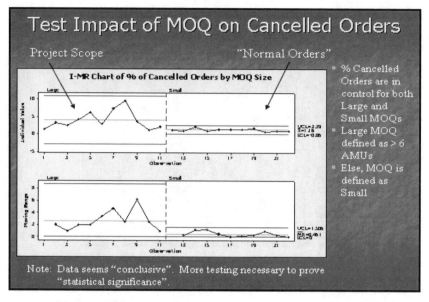

Figure 19-7: Revised I-MR Chart for Cancelled Orders

Step 2: Determine if the data in each category fit a normal distribution. Minitab normality tests serve to answer this question. The key determinant in each case is the P-Value. A P-Value greater than 0.05 indicates the data may be deemed normally-distributed and further analysis is applied.

Step 3: Test for Equal Variance. Passing the previous steps, the ANOVA roadmap indicates we now must use the F-test to determine if the variance between the Large MOQ and Small MOQ cancelled orders is statistically significant. The null hypothesis states the variances are equal (*i.e.*, there is no difference between the two). We look to the P-value to accept or reject this hypothesis. The P-value corresponding to the F-test is 0.000 (Fig. 19-8). Since this is less than 0.05, the test fails, and we can *reject the null hypothesis*. In other words, we conclude that the variances are statistically *unequal*.

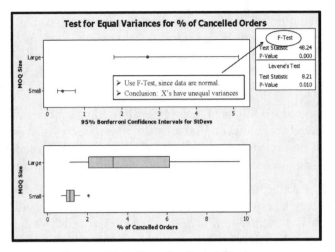

Figure 19-8: Test for Equal Variance

Step 4: <u>Final ANOVA Test</u>. Based on the unequal variance result, the ANOVA roadmap indicates a final one-way <u>ANOVA</u> test:

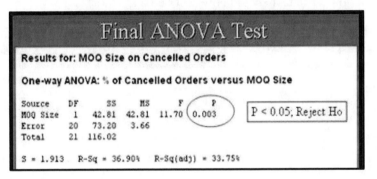

Figure 19-9: Final ANOVA Test for Cancelled Orders

The small P-value of the final ANOVA test indicates the null hypothesis can be *rejected* and replaced by the alternate hypothesis: MOQ has a *statistically significant impact* on Cancelled Orders. By following this rigorous analytical process, we can now reasonably state that MOQ is *guilty* of contributing to an increased level of cancelled customer orders.

The team then followed the same four-step process to test the impact of MOQ on backorders. The results indicated that MOQ also led to an increased level of backorders. The team will thus take these conclusions on to the "Improve" phase of the DMAIC process.

Before moving on, the team still had to deal with the issue of long lead times. The definition of long lead time is subjective and may differ by company, industry, region or other factors. In this case, the team decided to divide lead times into three categories: short LT (< 20 days), medium LT (20-39 days) and long LT (40+ days).

As before, the team followed the previously outlined process. The I-MR chart indicated that cancelled order history was in-control and P-values indicated a normal distribution. Following the ANOVA roadmap for a three-way test, the team applied Bartlett's test for Equal Variance.[2]

The small P-value (0.002) shown in Figure 19-10 indicates the null hypothesis can be *rejected* and replaced by the alternate hypothesis: Lead Time has a *statistically significant impact* on Cancelled Orders. Notice, however, which category has the significantly higher incidence of cancelled orders: It is **not** long-lead items, but *short lead time* items. This was a completely unexpected finding, contradicting the conventional wisdom among company leaders. The team was able to move on with confidence to address a root-cause finding, unencumbered by false assumptions. The team could now "act on fact."

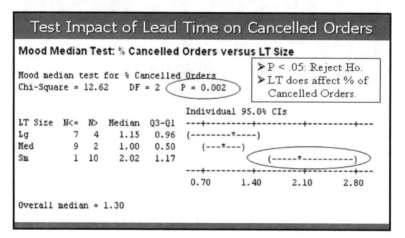

Figure 19-10: Final ANOVA: LT on Cancelled Orders

One final ANOVA test was required to address the final null hypothesis: Lead Time has no impact on Backorders. The large P-value of the test (.299) indicated this hypothesis could be *accepted*. In other words, lead time is *innocent* of creating backorders for branded products. Once again, this was a surprising finding to company leaders.

"Improve" Phase:

To ensure the team developed a robust set of improvement ideas, they applied a number of Creative Innovation tools, such as:

- Ideality Equation
- Itself Method
- Available Resources
- Pugh Concept Matrix

Applying each tool consumed one or more 90-minute team meetings. At the conclusion, ten new ideas had been generated, six of which were immediately actionable and incorporated into the project improvement plan. The Control Plan shown in Figure 14 in the next section describes several solutions the team put into action. Chapter 12 presents a variety of universal tools for use in the improvement phase of DMAIC.

The knowledge gained from previous steps provided the foundation for informed, fact-based discussions. Had the team attempted to jump straight into creative innovation solutions based upon earlier biases, assumptions or untested data, the "solutions" may well have been skewed, resulting in sub-optimal or even counterproductive solutions. For complex problems that lend themselves to the rigors of Six Sigma, it is critical to follow a structured DMAIC process before attempting to define solutions.

"Control" Phase:

The control phase is where solution ideas are clearly defined and made actionable. Each potential solution has a defined goal, measurement technique, sample size and frequency, along with a responsible person and completion date. Table 3 shows an excerpt of the case study control plan. The control plan has two main elements: outputs and inputs. The action plans are all associated with improving and controlling the key inputs.

As an example, consider the third row of the plan. The primary root cause is large supplier MOQs. Part of the solution set was to take advantage of a newly developed supplier willing to act as a 3PL, providing much smaller lot sizes to the company. The team developed a formal process by which candidate parts were reviewed for lot size reduction with the current supplier, and if necessary, be re-sourced through the 3PL provider. A specific goal was set to reduce the percentage of branded products exceeding the MOQ threshold.

Six Sigma Project - Control Plan

Project: Branded Product Service Improvement	**Orig**: mm/dd/yy
Process Owner: John Doe	
Sponsor: (Purchasing Director)	**Rev**: mm/dd/yy
MBB: (name)	

Process	Process Step	Output	Input	Goal (by date)	Measurement Technique	Sample Size	Freq.	Control Method	Resp. Person	Reaction Plan
Reduce Back-Orders on Large MOQ Branded Products	Customer Order	On-Time Shipment		N Backorders per week (dd-mm-yy)	Number of Back-Orders and Cancelled Orders	35	Wkly	I-MR	Purchasing Manager	Elevate to SCM Director
Reduce Cancelled Orders on Branded Products	Customer Order	Cancelled Orders		N Cancelled Orders per week (dd-mm-yy)	Number of Back-Orders and Cancelled Orders	35	Wkly	I-MR	Purchasing Manager	Elevate to SCM Director
	Buyer Followup With Vendor		Vendor MOQ	NN% of Branded PNs (dd-mm-yy)	Report of PNs with MOQ > NN AMUs	100% of PNs with Vendor MOQ > NN AMUs	Qtrly	Pareto Analysis: Reduce MOQ or move to new Supplier	Purchasing Manager	Elevate to Purchasing Director
	Buyer Followup With Vendor		Vendor MOQ	Avg. N/week or less (dd-mm-yy)	Report of Backorders "OK to place PO".	100% of PNs meeting criteria "OK to place PO"	Wkly	Weekly Report of orders meeting spec criteria	Purchasing Supervisor	Elevate to Purchasing Director
	CA Followup With Customers		Back-order	N backorder notifications per week (dd-mm-yy)	Report of BO's requiring customer notification	100% of Customer Order Lines Id'd as "follow up with cust."	Weekly	Weekly Report of orders meeting spec criteria	CS Manager	Elevate to CS Director

Table 19-2: Control Plan

The final element of the control phase is the Before/After Control Chart (Fig. 19-11). The chart monitors improvements over time, validating when the specified goal is achieved – in this case, a 75% reduction. Notice the four-week "after" window shows a significant improvement in the number of backorders. Over the weeks that followed, the team not only met the 75% reduction goal but exceeded it, achieving an 80% reduction in both backorders and cancelled orders and doubling the expected financial returns.

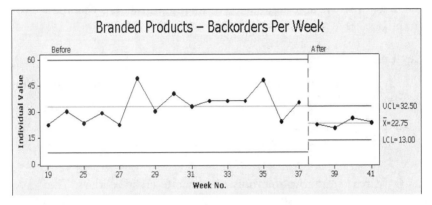

Figure 19-11: Before/After Control Chart

Conclusions

The primary intent of this chapter has been to present the DMAIC process in a way that helps you think through how Six Sigma can be used to improve your own business processes. To help "prime the pump", consider the following and think about what similar projects might exist in your own companies:

- Develop a production leveling system with a goal of achieving 70% improvement in demand stability through the supply chain.
- Minimize the occurrence and impact of unusually large customer orders.
- Optimize the benefits of sales specials while minimizing the negative impacts.
- Validate and improve the mathematical and statistical underpinnings of a theoretical inventory model.
- Identify and standardize global best practices for inventory categorization or other inventory management processes.
- Resolve specific customer complaints using Customer-Focused Six Sigma projects.

As you generate project ideas, enter them into a Project Hopper, similar to the C&E Matrix, allowing the matrix to calculate a weighted score for each project. The end result is a prioritized list of projects, ready for assignment.

More information on the processes discussed in this chapter, as well as supply chain topics can be found in my list of publications.[3] SCC Inventory Consulting offers a variety of Excel-based analytical tools: Demand Planning Analyzer, Inventory Optimizer, Kanban Workbench and other customizable solutions. For more information, visit the website products page.[4]

Key Lessons Learned:

1. ANOVAs often produce surprising findings. Be thorough, follow the ANOVA roadmap and take the time to do these well

2. Manage project scope. Six Sigma projects, because they follow a rigorous process, can easily take 180 days. Stay focused on your Y-statement.

3. Creative Innovation tools *do* generate creative ideas. They force you to ask questions you might not otherwise consider and help you to look at problems or processes from different perspectives and help you break out of paradigms.

About the Author

Steve Cimorelli is President of SCC Inventory Consulting, LLC.[5] He is a Certified Fellow in Production and Inventory Management (CFPIM), a published author and educator. Steve holds a BS in Engineering with 30 years experience in aerospace, industrial equipment and commercial manufacturing, distribution and supply chain management. He can be reached at *steve.cimorelli@SCCInventory.com*.

---

[1] The tests and corresponding graphs were all generated using Minitab, a statistical analysis software tool.

[2] Note that this is different from the F-test applied for the two-category MOQ test performed earlier. A Master Black Belt will normally guide the team through these details.

[3] *http://www.sccinventory.com/pubs.shtml*

[4] *http://www.sccinventory.com/products.shtml*

[5] *http://www.sccinventory.com/*

Chapter Twenty

Financial Impact Analysis of LSS Projects

Andres H. Slack

Overview

This chapter is intended for business leaders, managers, Six Sigma sponsors and project leaders who are interested in learning how to maximize the impact of their LSS projects, both before and during rollout. The current global economic situation dictates that companies spend their money wisely; wasted money spent on projects that do not actually impact the bottom line are no longer acceptable.

Financial Impact Analysis (FIA) provides a tool for executives and managers to estimate financial impact of proposed improvement projects *before* resources are dedicated. After rollout, FIA monitors the improvement process to track *actual* savings and revenue impact against targeted data. Financial Impact Analysis is a flexible tool that works well with other Lean Six Sigma metrics and provides a direct link between the project and the bottom line. This is a key consideration when soliciting buy-in for the project.

This chapter will help you to:

- Learn why and how Financial Impact Analysis is necessary to choosing and monitoring project improvement efforts
- Understand the prerequisites for performing FIA
- Understand the benefits of using FIA
- Learn step-by-step how to perform a Financial Impact Analysis on your LSS projects

Importance of Conducting Financial Impact Analysis

A Brief History

Six Sigma has firmly established itself as a highly successful process improvement methodology that appears to be here to stay for the long term. In contrast to transient business improvement initiatives, sometimes derisively referred to as "flavors of the month" (*e.g.*, quality circles, TQM, BPI, Zero Defects, and process reengineering), Six Sigma continues an unabated growth that began with its quiet birth at Motorola in the 1980's and its loudly trumpeted thrust into the world stage by General Electric's high profile launch in 1995. Other companies, such as Allied Signal, actually rolled out Six Sigma before GE, but their implementation was eclipsed by the sheer scale, massive investment

($450 million the first two years), and legendary status of GE's CEO, Jack Welch.

As Six Sigma has matured and as it gains a more varied practitioner base with wide-ranging areas of expertise, it has been influenced by other organizational performance improvement approaches. A notable change to Six Sigma has been the increasingly common inclusion of "Lean" (and, more recently, performance improvement approaches such as "Systems Thinking" and "Theory of Constraints") into its iconic DMAIC methodology. Lean was made famous by the Toyota Production System and is dedicated to improving efficiency and speed by eliminating non-value-added activities. This fusion of Lean and Six Sigma, which focuses on reducing process variation and eliminating defects, led to the coining of the term "Lean Six Sigma," or LSS.

Six Sigma has made several important contributions to the evolution of business improvement methodologies. These contributions include the introduction of a program architecture founded on strong senior leadership and buttressed by a core of "Champions," "Master Black Belts," and "Black Belts" who implement the program. Six Sigma also refined Deming's well-known PDCA (Plan, Do, Check, Act) methodology for problem solving into DMAIC (Define, Measure, Analyze, Improve, Control), with improved project management features such as formalized project reviews (tollgates) at the end of each phase. Six Sigma's DMAIC platform, with its methodical application of process improvement tools, proved very adaptable to the future inclusion into Six Sigma of other improvement approaches such as Lean, TOC, and Systems Thinking.

The Benefits of FIA

Perhaps the best known contribution of Six Sigma is the introduction of formal financial impact analysis as an integral part of the execution of each project. Only projects that can show financial benefit are considered for selection. It is this financial justification for each project that is widely credited with the broad acceptance and staying power of Six Sigma in American industry. This is because *financial impact analysis* is written in the language American managers understand and embrace. This "show me the money" feature of Six Sigma had been missing from prior business improvement methodologies (which had more of a "build it and they will come" philosophy), and this seemingly innocuous mutation of the Six Sigma DNA made all the difference when it came to the survival of Six Sigma among competing business improvement methodologies of this (the American) business ecosystem.

The emphasis on "American" in explaining the importance of financial impact analysis is not casual. In contrast to the USA, it is interesting to note how Japan readily adopted and socialized into their business culture Deming's variation-reduction statistical approach without the need for financial justification of each project. For one thing, in Japan – unlike in the USA – engineers are heavily represented in management ranks, so Japanese administrators understood at both the intellectual and gut levels the enormous promise of variation reduction and thus did not need "financials" to induce them to follow that course of action. Moreover, there is much greater emphasis on long-term business performance in Japan rather than the American short-term emphasis on quarterly financial results. This makes it easier in Japan for managers to make investments that have a long-term payoff horizon. For these reasons, the idiosyncrasies of American business culture make financial impact analysis at the individual project level a powerful facilitator for the adoption and retention of LSS.

Financial impact analysis plays an important support role in practices that have been identified as critical for successful Six Sigma programs. To use GE as an example, let's look at the role of financial impact analysis in three success factors that accounted for the spectacular triumph of Six Sigma in GE:

1. Top management's total commitment through highly visible, vocal and ongoing support (as a GE employee at the time of the Six Sigma roll-out, this author can attest to top management's commitment; this author was one of the hundreds of thousands of GE employees who witnessed Jack Welch – in person or on video – personally explain the importance and urgency of the initiative when it was rolled out in 1995).

2. Include participation in Six Sigma in all managers' performance evaluations. This is particularly significant in a company with a policy of "parting ways" with the managers performing in the bottom 10%.

3. Commit adequate organizational resources by deploying full-time black belts (trained Six Sigma professionals) to lead improvement projects. This can require a massive investment on the part of an organization (GE spent $450 million in the first two years of the deployment).

Senior managers receive reinforcement from the financial benefits derived from the LSS program to maintain their enthusiasm over the long term. It gives a valuable tool to upper management to justify to industry analysts, stock holders and to themselves, the expenditure of resources on the LSS program. Through the financial analysis of each individual project, GE was able to confidently track the ROI on their massive investment, thus validating the Six Sigma program.

With a formalized LSS financial analysis protocol, senior management can easily monitor the financial contribution of the LSS program, helping them remain engaged in the program. For example, financial impact analysis gives senior managers the ability to ask the "right" questions of the LSS program manager and take appropriate (or at least informed) management action. For these reasons, executives should have an on-demand dashboard for financial metrics.

Upper management is not the only group in an organization that appreciates financial measures. Middle and lower level managers can use financial impact analysis to give visibility to their financial contributions to the organization. They can also use financial impact of individual projects to get buy-in from process improvement team members and employees in general. Trustworthy financial analysis shows those affected that the disruption and effort associated with improvement projects are worthwhile. Virtually all employees want the company in which they work to prosper, and they willingly go the extra mile if they believe their effort will contribute to the wellbeing of the firm.

Another benefit of financial impact analysis is its value in justifying the existence (with its great expense) of full-time employees dedicated solely to LSS projects. These are mainly LSS Black Belts, but can also include full-time support staff such as a program manager or program coordinator. When times get tough, companies typically reduce cost by cutting payroll. Sound financial impact analysis provides a strong argument for the retention of salaried Black Belts and LSS support staff, and thus keeps the LSS performance improvement initiative alive in the organization, helping ensure the organization's long-term survival by giving it an advantage over competitors who scaled back or eliminated their improvement initiatives.

Calculating Financial Impact

The remainder of this chapter is devoted to providing a practical, rigorous approach to financial impact analysis of LSS projects. The goal is to provide a process that will readily gain acceptance by the various key stakeholders in the organization, namely, LSS practitioners, the organization's finance function and management.

First, a few operational definitions will help us get started:

Cost Avoidance, also referred to as **Type II** savings, or **soft savings** - consists of avoiding projected *new cost*. Example: reducing the cost of adding a new feature for a product or service.

Cost Reduction, also referred to as **Type I Savings**, or **hard savings** - consist of a reduction in an *ongoing cost*. Example: reducing the per-unit cost associated with providing a product or service.

Finance Subject Matter Expert (SME) - Critical to financial impact analysis is the involvement of a finance SME. To this end, LSS programs should include individuals from the organization's finance function, preferably those who engage in cost accounting or a related area as their primary role. The purpose of the finance SME is to help ensure that the financial impact analysis results are "real" dollars, not "PowerPoint" dollars. Finance SMEs do not need in-depth training in Lean Six Sigma. However, it is helpful to provide them with an overview of LSS so they understand the context of their role and the critical nature of their involvement in the program.

NPV, net present value - This is a favorite measurement in the world of financial analysis because it takes into account a) the time value of money, and b) opportunity cost. NPV is the sum of all future cash flows discounted by a specific interest rate to show the value of that cash flow in present-day dollars. The interest rate at which the cash flows are discounted represents the return of an alternative use for the money (another opportunity). Not pursuing the other opportunity incurs what economists refer to as an opportunity cost.

Revenue Generation - additional (incremental) net income directly attributable to a LSS project. Example: higher net income derived from increased sales resulting from the modification of a product or service.

Rough Order of Magnitude (ROM) - a "back of the napkin" calculation to estimate a ballpark figure, or very rough estimate, of a project's financial impact. In the earliest stage of a project, at the project identification and selection stage, the Black Belt or Project Sponsor reaches out to the Finance SME to generate this calculation. The ROM serves the purpose of minimizing resources devoted to proposed projects that fail to be added to the project portfolio by the organization's project selection process.

Nearly always, the project Black Belt or Sponsor will be much more familiar than the Finance SME with the process addressed by the proposed project. Therefore, the Project Sponsor or BB must take the lead in identifying all the variables that affect the financial impact associated with the process in question. The Finance SME will rely on the Project Sponsor or Black Belt (or other pertinent process experts) to provide sufficient information in order to generate the ROM figure or to be able to make an informed decision on the validity of the ROM. Often, the Project Sponsor or Black Belt generates the ROM and the Finance SME reviews it for obvious errors or omissions.

Eventually, the project under consideration will either be dropped or a full financial impact analysis will be required. This will occur either because the project was given the green light to proceed or because the selection process requires closer scrutiny of the financial impact in order to make a determination as to whether or not it should proceed.

Step-by-Step Guide for Financial Impact Analysis – Case Study

Background

The approach to financial impact analysis is quite simple: Establish a cost baseline or <u>reference cost</u> against which the cost of the improved process is compared. The delta, or difference, between the two is the financial impact of the project. The same applies for revenues: A baseline or reference revenue value is established and then compared to actual revenues after the improvements have been implemented. A defined length of time, usually one year after the implementation, is used for the comparison.

An example will be used to explain, step-by-step, how to carry out the financial impact analysis for a LSS project. For this example we will use a fictitious company, ACME Mortgage Co., and an improvement project with the descriptive name of "Cycle Time Reduction for Processing, Underwriting, and Closing of Loans."

At ACME Mortgage, loan officers submit loan application packages to the processing department in preparation for underwriting. Processing consists of running loans through Automated Underwriting Systems (AUS) for preliminary approval, collecting all required documentation, and conducting verifications of employment, assets, etc.

After processing, the loan is routed to the underwriting department where it is underwritten according to specific investor guidelines. The underwriting department issues a disposition on the loan: rejected, approved with conditions, or a final approval. Loans that do not receive final approval are sent back to the processing department for issue resolution. The final major step of the process is for the approved loan to go to the closing department where closing documents are prepared, closing instructions are generated and then sent to the closing agent.

For various reasons, mortgage loans are extremely time-sensitive, so speed is important in the flow of loans through the process. Taking too long to close loans results in added costs related to: 1) lost business due to clients cancelling their loan, 2) loss of income due to re-locking expired interest rates, and 3) loss of income due to re-pricing of loans when market interest rates go down.

The project at ACME Mortgage was very successful. The main goal of the project – to reduce loan cycle time from two weeks to four days – was also achieved, providing financial benefits related to the time-sensitive nature of mortgage loans, as previously described. In addition, overtime was significantly reduced for underwriters and processors, a planned office expansion was scaled back, and a courier service was eliminated. Each of these actions played a role in the overall financial impact of the project.

A Flexible Model for Every Team Member

Every LSS project has a variety of stakeholders who play a specific role and who have different requirement and objectives. The question for financial impact analysis then becomes: How do we capture all the contributions to the financial impact in a manner that serves these various stakeholder requirements? The execution method and the output of this analysis should incorporate attributes that satisfy each of the following stake holders:

- **Finance function**
    - o   Follows the cost accounting model
    - o   Uses a standardized format for all projects
    - o   Is auditable/verifiable
- **Senior leadership**
    - o   Provides confidence that the analysis reflects real dollars
    - o   Documents return on investment made on the initiative

- o   Enables easy and convenient access to a high-level summary of financial benefits

- **Process owner**

  - o   Provides visibility to the connection between the process and the company's financial bottom line

- **LSS team**

  - o   Provides a template that guides the team through the complexities of building the financial impact analysis

  - o   Ties financial analysis into the broader LSS project (problem statement, metrics, improvement actions)

- **LSS Program Manager/Coordinator**

  - o   Provides data suitable for IT systems to upload/download

  - o   Has an output (report) laid out and formatted so that it leads the reader in a logical sequence through the analysis and is easy to read and understand, with a one-page summary that can stand on its own

  - o   Provides a tool for tracking project metrics during the extended realization phase and connects them to the financial impact

  - o   Suitable for distribution as a best practice or as an example

A comprehensive spreadsheet populated with sample data is available at *www.drivingoperationalexcellence.com* as an example to help you with this process. You can also obtain a free, downloadable version of the file to use in your own financial impact analysis.

Executing the Analysis

Step 1: Identify costs or revenue streams to track

Note: Going forward, we will omit the word "revenue" in the interest of readability; however, unless otherwise specified, the same steps apply to the analysis of revenue generation as they do to cost savings.

With the collaboration of the process owner and finance SME (and others, as appropriate), the first step is to identify costs that are expected to experience a material change as a result of the prospective project. This includes costs that will *increase* due to project improvements.

Classify *cost reductions* as either Type I (cost reduction) or Type II (cost avoidance). There are cases in which both types of savings can be applied to one specific cost. This will happen if costs are reduced and future increases of that cost are avoided. In our case example, savings are achieved by reducing hours of overtime (OT), which is clearly a Type I savings. However, Type II savings also will be realized if there is a wage increase in the future because, by eliminating some OT we have also avoided some of the increased cost of the associated pay increase.

To illustrate, if a loan processing employee is paid $10/hr and project improvements result in a reduction of 20 hours per month, the savings are:

$10/hr x 20 hrs/mo = $200/mo (Type I savings)

If, six months later, the wages of this same position were increased to $12/hr, we now realize extra savings of $2/hr because we would have had to pay this amount if the OT had not been reduced.

$2/hr x 20 hrs/mo = $40/mo (Type II savings)

This example shows how Type II savings are very real. When conducting the project financial impact analysis, be on the lookout for Type II savings. Just be careful not to double count.

Do not include overhead costs associated with the LSS effort, such as the Black Belt's salary or (perish the thought) LSS consultants. These costs are captured globally by the organization's finance function in their analysis of the overall LSS initiative's financial impact on the organization.

Step 2. Establish the baseline cost for the costs identified in Step 1.

The baseline cost establishes a reference against which we can compare future costs and thereby capture the financial impact of LSS project improvement actions. The baseline cost is usually the historical cost, but not always. There may be no historical costs in cases where they simply were not stored, or in the case of a new process. One option in cases where there is no historical cost data is to measure the current costs and use that figure as your baseline.

Enter into the financial impact analysis template, month by month, the historical cost for the 12 months prior to improvement implementation, as shown in Figure 20-1.

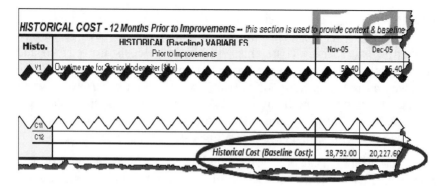

Figure 20-1: Historical Cost Baseline

Step 3. Develop a Cost Model

A cost model breaks down a cost into its component variables and the relationship between these variables. For example, for cost of overtime pay for processing and underwriting departments, a cost model could be constructed in the following manner:

> Variables: 1) Fully loaded hourly rate, and 2) Total hours of OT per month

The relationship between these two variables is straight-forward multiplication:

$$(1) \times (2) = \text{monthly cost}$$

This structure would be applied to each of the three categories of workers: senior underwriters, junior underwriters and processors.

Building a model for a given cost provides three benefits:

1. Clarity: it makes the cost more understandable

2. It adds credibility to the tie-in between project improvements and financial consequences

3. It extends the relevance of the analysis, *e.g.*, if a cost variable changes in the future, updating that variable allows comparison of actual costs to a more realistic reference value. The farther out a financial analysis goes, the less relevant historical costs become. Updating component variables as time progresses extends the relevance of the analysis.

HISTORICAL COST - 12 Months Prior to Improvements -- *this section is used to provide context & baseline*

Histo.		HISTORICAL (Baseline) VARIABLES Prior to Improvements	Nov-05	Dec-05	Jan-06
	V1	Overtime rate for Senior Underwriter ($/hr)	56.40	56.40	56.40
	V2	Overtime rate for Junior Underwriter ($/hr)	43.20	43.20	43.20
	V3	Overtime rate for Loan Processor ($/hr)	23.60	23.60	23.60
	V4				
	V5	Overtime Hrs for Senior Underwriter (Hrs.)	176.00	180.00	166.00
	V6	Overtime Hrs for Junior Underwriter (Hrs.)	151.00	173.00	178.00
	V7	Overtime Hrs for Loan Processor (Hrs.)	34.00	45.00	64.00
	V8				
	V9	Courier Workdays Evening Pickup Charge ($ per pickup)	70.00	70.00	70.00
	V10	Workdays per period (no. of days)	22	22	22
	V11				
	V12				
		COST CALCULATIONS Prior to Improvements	Nov-05	Dec-05	Jan-06
	C1	OT cost for Senior UW = (V1 x V5)	9,926.40	10,152.00	9,362.40
	C2	OT cost for Junior UW = (V2 x V6)	6,523.20	7,473.60	7,689.60
	C3	OT cost for Loan Processor UW = (V2 x V6)	802.40	1,062.00	1,510.40
	C4				
	C5	Courier Evening Pickup = (V9 x V10)	1,540.00	1,540.00	1,540.00
	C6				
	C7				
	C8				
	C9				
	C10				
	C11				
	C12				
		Historical Cost (Baseline Cost):	18,792.00	20,227.60	20,102.40

(Left margin label: HISTORICAL COST)

Figure 20-2: Component Variables at Work

Step 4.   Generate the Reference Cost

The reference cost is the cost to be compared head-to-head with the improved process's costs. Where the baseline cost is typically a historical cost, the reference cost is a projected cost into the future: It is the estimated value of what the costs *would be* if the improvements had not been made. It is the best estimate of what reality would be if the LSS project improvements had not been implemented.

The reference cost may or may not be the same as the baseline/historical cost. The reference cost will default to the baseline/historical cost if there are no anticipated significant changes unrelated to the project's improvement actions. This reference cost is derived from the cost model that was developed for establishing the baseline cost. This is typically carried out to 12 months after implementation of improvements, but may go out as far as five years.

REFERENCE COST - "As If" Cost, Assuming (as if) no Improvements were Implemented -- *Will be used as the*

Yr 1		VARIABLES Assuming No Improvements Were Made	Type I or II	Quick Hits	Nov-06	Dec-06	Jan-07
	V1	Overtime rate for Senior Underwriter ($/hr)	I		56.40	56.40	56.40
	V2	Overtime rate for Junior Underwriter ($/hr)	I		43.20	43.20	43.20
	V3	Overtime rate for Loan Processor ($/hr)	I		23.60	23.60	23.60
	V4						
	V5	Overtime Hrs for Senior Underwriter (Hrs.)	I		176.00	180.00	166.00
	V6	Overtime Hrs for Junior Underwriter (Hrs.)	I		151.00	173.00	178.00
	V7	Overtime Hrs for Loan Processor (Hrs.)	I		34.00	45.00	64.00
	V8						
	V9	Courier Workdays Evening Pickup Charge ($ per pickup)	I	75.00	75.00	75.00	75.00
	V10	Workdays per period (no. of days)	I	27	22	22	22
	V11						
	V12						
		COST CALCULATIONS Assuming No Improvements Were Made	Type I or II	Quick Hits	Nov-06	Dec-06	Jan-07
	C1	OT cost for Senior UW = (V1 x V5)	I		9,926.40	10,152.00	9,362.40
	C2	OT cost for Junior UW = (V2 x V6)	I		6,523.20	7,473.60	7,689.60
	C3	OT cost for Loan Processor UW = (V2 x V6)	I		802.40	1,062.00	1,510.40
	C4						
	C5	Courier Evening Pickup = (V9 x V10)			1,540.00	1,540.00	1,540.00
	C6						
	C7						
	C8						
	C9	Courier Evening Pickup Cost = (V9xV10) in $/mo.	I	2,025.00	1,650.00	1,650.00	1,650.00
	C10						
	C11	Proposed office reconfiguration budgeted cost	II				76,000.00
	C12						
		Type I Cost (Reference):		2,025.00	18,902.00	20,337.60	20,212.40
		Type II Cost (Reference):					76,000.00

Figure 20-3: Reference Costs

Step 5. Track Actual Costs

Track and record actual costs by following the cost model developed earlier. Additionally, make sure to include any new costs added by the project's improvement actions.

Caution: Typically, an individual LSS project financial impact analysis does not include LSS program costs (such as Black Belt salaries). Rather, the LSS program overhead costs are captured globally and are applied to the organization's overall financial impact analysis of the LSS program as a whole. Leave these costs out of the financial impact analysis.

The financial impact analysis is a dynamic document that must be updated as time progresses. Initially, all the Actual Cost figures will be projections. As each month goes by, however, these "projected" figures must be replaced with the actual data captured for the analysis.

The fact that these are true actual costs is indicated by the field "Projected/Verified" immediately below the actual cost entries (Figure 20-4)

ACTUAL COST - Actual Cost After Improvements -- *this section provides the actual costs for the period following implementation of improver*

Yr 1		VARIABLES After Improvements	Type I or II	Quick Hits	Nov-06	Dec-06	Jan-07	Feb-07	Mar-07
	V1	Overtime rate for Senior Underwriter ($/hr)	I		56.4	56.4	56.4	56.4	56.4
	V2	Overtime rate for Junior Underwriter ($/hr)	I		43.2	43.2	43.2	43.2	43.2
	V3	Overtime rate for Loan Processor ($/hr)	I		23.6	23.6	23.6	23.6	23.6
	V4								
	V5	Overtime Hrs for Senior Underwriter (Hrs.)	I		36	44	30	16	14
	V6	Overtime Hrs for Junior Underwriter (Hrs.)	I		78	34	42	66	18
	V7	Overtime Hrs for Loan Processor (Hrs.)	I		22	36	44	38	44
	V8								
	V9	Courier Workdays Evening Pickup Charge ($ per pickup)	I	75.00	75.00	75.00	75.00	75.00	75.00
	V10	Workdays per period (no. of days)	I		22	22	22	20	23
	V11		I		0	0	0	0	0
	V12								
		COST CALCULATIONS After Improvements	Type I or II	Quick Hits	Nov-06	Dec-06	Jan-07	Feb-07	Mar-07
	C1	OT cost for Senior UW = (V1 x V5)	I		2,030.40	2,481.60	1,692.00	902.40	789.60
	C2	OT cost for Junior UW = (V2 x V6)	I		3,369.60	1,468.80	1,814.40	2,851.20	777.60
	C3	OT cost for Loan Processor UW = (V2 x V6)	I		519.20	849.60	1,038.40	896.80	1,038.40
	C4								
	C5	Courier Evening Pickup = (V9 x V10)	I		1,650.00	1,650.00	1,650.00	1,500.00	1,725.00
	C6								
	C7								
	C8								
	C9								
	C10								
	C11	Proposed office reconfiguration budgeted cost	II				35,000.00		
	C12								
		Type I Cost (Actual After Improvements):		-	7,569.20	6,450.00	6,194.80	6,150.40	4,330.60
		Type II Cost (Actual After Improvements):		-	-	-	35,000.00	-	-
				Verified	Verified	Verified	Verified	Projected	Projected

Figure 20-4: Verified vs. Projected Cost

Step 6. Compare Actual vs. Reference Values for Each Period

This is the step where the realized financial gains are captured. The delta between the Actual and Reference Costs is the Gross Savings.

After Year 1, a decision must be made on how to treat the savings. The choice is between counting the gross savings of each year, or only the incremental savings (which can be incremental year-over-year or only over year one).

Usually, LSS programs will only consider the savings of Year 1, and second year savings only if they exceed those of the first year (incremental year-over-year).

Finally, to calculate the net present value (NPV) of the savings after the first year, a discount rate must be selected. The discount rate will be provided by the finance SME.

REALIZED SAVINGS

			Tot Yr1	Quick Hits	Nov-06	Dec-06
Year 1	Type I (Cost Reduction)	Reference Cost	243,276	2,025	18,902	20,338
		Actual Cost After Improvements	52,685	0	7,569	6,450
		Savings Yr | Mo.	190,591	2,025	11,333	13,888
	Type II (Cost Avoidance)	Reference Cost	76,000	0	0	0
		Actual Cost After Improvements	35,000	0	0	0
		Savings Yr | Mo.	41,000	0	0	0
	Verification	Projected / Verified		Verified	Verified	Verified
		Verified by (Finance SME Name)		J. Fitzpatrick	J. Fitzpatrick	J. Fitzpatrick

			Tot Yr2		Nov-07	Dec-07
Year 2	Type I (Cost Reduction)	Reference Cost	241,251		18,902	20,338
		Actual Cost After Improvements	8,325		694	694
		Gross Savings	232,926		18,208	19,644
		Incremental Savings Over Prior Yr (YOY)	44,361		6,875	5,756
	Type II (Cost Avoidance)	Reference Cost	0		0	0
		Actual Cost After Improvements	0		0	0
		Gross Savings	0		0	0
		Incremental Savings Over Prior Yr (YOY)	0		0	0
	Verificatio	Projected / Verified			Projected	Projected
		Verified by (Finance SME Name)				

INCREASED REVENUE

		Tot Yr1	Nov-06	Dec-06
Year 1	Reference Revenue	(1,618,271)	(90,558)	(104,769)
	Actual Revenue After Improvements	(1,150,505)	(69,489)	(79,810)
	Gross Delta Revenue	467,766	21,069	24,959
	Projected / Verified		Verified	Verified
	Verified by (SME Name):		JR Smith	JR Smith

		Tot Yr2	Nov-07	Dec-07
Year 2	Reference Revenue	(1,618,271)	(90,558)	(104,769)
	Actual Revenue After Improvements	(1,150,505)	(69,489)	(79,810)
	Gross Delta Revenue	467,766	21,069	24,959
	Incremental Revenue Over Prior Yr (YOY)	0	0	0
	Projected / Verified		Projected	Projected
	Verified by (Finance SME Name)			

Figure 20-5: Realized Savings and Increased Revenue

For the ACME Mortgage example, revenues were improved through reduced cancellations of mortgage loans prior to closing. Since revenue is actually being lost by these cancellations, Reference Revenue shows this as negative revenue. After improvements, there are fewer cancellations, which results in less lost income. Figure 20-5 reflects this improved revenue situation by showing a smaller loss of revenue. The comparison of these revenues (Reference vs. Actual) is shown in Figure 20-6.

ACTUAL REVENUE - After Improvements -- *this section provides the actual revenue following implementation of impro*

Yr 1	VARIABLES After Improvements	Nov-06	Dec-06	Jan-07
V1	Customer cancellations after submittal to Underwriting (units)	21	23	29
V2	Total loans in Underwriting (units)	1,145	1,435	1,231
V3	Avg gross pricing of cancelled loans ($)	3,309	3,470	4,341
V4	Avg gross pricing of NON-cancelled loans ($)	3,905	3,112	4,660
V5				
V6				
V7				
V8				
V9				
V10				
V11				
V12				
	COST CALCULATIONS After Improvements	Nov-06	Dec-06	Jan-07
C1	Percent of loans cancelled by customer while in Underwriting (V1 / V2)	1.834%	1.603%	2.356%
C2				
C3	Lost gross revenue from customer cancellations (V1 x V3)	69,489	79,810	125,889
C4				
C5				
C6				
C7				
C8				
C9				
C10				
C11				
C12				
	Actual Revenue:	(69,489)	(79,810)	(125,889)
		Verified	Verified	Projected

(left margin label: ACTUAL REVENUE)

Figure 20-6: Actual Revenue

Project Metrics and Financial Impact Analysis

It is important to include updated project metrics in the financial impact analysis report. These project metrics are the ones identified in the project charter and should not exceed three (see Fig. 20-7).

PROJECT METRICS

Metric Name / Description (From Project Charter)	Summary			IMPROVEMENTS REALIZATION		
	Baseline	Goal	Current 4/15/09	Nov-06	Dec-06	Jan-07
Cycle Time in Underwriting (Work Days)	10.00	4.00	3.89	5.25	4.75	4.00
Number of Discrepancies into UW with Initial Submission (Avg/Loan)	3.600	0.200	0.300	1.800	0.667	0.333
Loans resubmitted multiple times (%)	45%	15%	10%	33%	25%	15%

				EXTENDED REALIZA		
Year 2				Nov-07	Dec-07	Jan-08
Cycle Time in Underwriting (Work Days)				3.65	3.84	3.72
Number of Discrepancies into UW with Initial Submission (Avg/Loan)				0.268	0.380	0.373
Loans resubmitted multiple times (%)				20%	17%	15%
Year 3				Nov-08	Dec-08	Jan-09
Cycle Time in Underwriting (Work Days)				3.73	3.88	3.76
Number of Discrepancies into UW with Initial Submission (Avg/Loan)				0.263	0.410	0.376
Loans resubmitted multiple times (%)				21%	16%	17%

Figure 20-7: Project Metrics Worksheet

The reason project metrics should be included in the financial impact analysis is to ascertain and monitor the correlation between the project metrics and financial impact. If the project metrics head in the wrong direction, we would expect that related costs will be affected.

In order to make the financial impact analysis report a document that can stand on its own, it should also contain the following:

1. Project timeline (tollgate dates)

2. Key project personnel

3. Problem statement

4. Improvement actions summary

Structured this way, the financial impact analysis report provides all the relevant critical information related to a LSS project, with the notable exception of the control plan. A free copy of the template used here for generating the financial impact analysis and report is available at *www.drivingoperationalexcellence.com*.

Conclusions

Financial Impact Analysis is critical to project planning, execution and continuous improvement. Tough economic times have dictated that companies watch every dollar spent. Financial Impact Analysis is predictive in that it can estimate the financial impact of a potential project *before* money is spent making improvements, showing a direct link between improvement efforts and the corporate bottom line. It also works well with other metrics, ensuring that the project does not go off track during rollout. Finally, it will continuously monitor your improvement efforts into the future, ensuring your projects maintain an acceptable level of savings and impact revenue.

Key Lessons Learned

1. Knowing the impact of your LSS project *before* it rolls out ensures only the most cost-effective, highest impact projects are implemented.

2. Financial Impact Analysis is performed with the assistance of the financial SME and the results must be easy to read and understand for all stakeholders in the improvement process.

3. Financial Impact Analysis makes it easy to track expected project performance against actual project performance, providing an effective method for monitoring your improvement efforts.

About the Author

Andres Slack is a certified LSS Master Black Belt with an MBA from the University of Michigan and a bachelor's degree in electrical engineering from Florida International University. He currently works as a Lean Six Sigma consultant. Andres has extensive experience in logistics, manufacturing, and the financial industry. Companies he has worked for include Accenture, IBM, GE, and Emerson. His functional experience includes operations management, process improvement, organization performance excellence, Lean Six Sigma, quality systems, and logistics in manufacturing, financial services, and government sectors. For more information, contact Andres directly at *andresslack@hotmail.com*.

Chapter Twenty-One

Problem Solving Using Failure Mode Effects and Analysis

Steven C. Leggett

Overview

There is one over-riding, eternal question we always ask ourselves when implementing continuous improvement programs: How do we solve the problem? Unfortunately, this question is asked *after* we have already experienced the problem, and we are left hanging, wondering what to do about it.

Why not solve future problems *before* they show up at our customer's doorstep or *before* we have put costly resources into the process? Potential Failure Mode and Effects Analysis (FMEA) is an important tool for evaluation and process analysis to find and identify any potential irregularities and weaknesses in production and manufacturing processes. The advantage of using FMEA is that it addresses these potential failures before they ever make it into the actual process. FMEA uses past experiences with similar products or processes to design failures out of the system.

This chapter will help you to:

- Recognize the importance of implementing the FMEA process in your process and product design phase
- Learn the basic methodology for creating a FMEA project
- Identify potential problems *before* they occur or reach the customer

Prevention or Cure?

In the early 1980's, when Japanese automobile manufacturing hit the United States in the side of the head with its superior quality and efficiency, there was a recession. Japan had perfected their manufacturing processes while American companies dwelled in past successes that no longer applied to the current economic conditions.

Now the tables are turned and Toyota, the leading auto manufacturer in the world, has fallen. As of last February, over 10 million Toyota cars were affected by formal recalls.[1] The cost of curing the problem to date is unknown. Toyota's conservative estimates predict a loss of US$2 billion: about 56% for repairs and 44% in lost sales.[2] Independent analysts with JP Morgan and Deutsche Securities estimate the true range to be US$3.2-5.5 billion, including repairs, litigation and lost sales.[3] The damage to Toyota's reputation is not entirely quantifiable or even known at this point. Only time will tell the total impact of this enormous quality failure.

Prevention is the key success. You may think it is redundant, takes too many hours, too many personnel, it is not in the contract, and it costs a lot of money. As we have seen with the Toyota fiasco, it costs a lot more to cure a problem than it does to prevent one. What if Toyota would have prevented their failures? Where would they be today? Most likely no recalls, no high warranty costs, no tarnished image, greater operating capital and higher stock prices. As Ben Franklin once said, "An ounce of prevention is worth a pound of cure." Toyota has demonstrated this old adage poignantly.

So What is FMEA?

Continuous improvement systems have plenty of tools for you to put in your toolbox: DMAIC, value stream mapping, VOC, waste walks, cause and effects analysis, red-yellow-green charts and many others. While there are plenty of problem solving tools for you to work with, the challenge is figuring out which one are you going to use. Why not consider a *prevention* tool instead of a *problem-solving* tool? FMEA is just that sort of tool. Used upfront during the design process, FMEA works to prevent all possible failures from ever occurring. Put simply, FMEA is a tool used to eliminate failure modes (waste, errors, etc.) in product design (DFMEA) and process design (PFMEA) in the future.

FMEA is often misunderstood, and there are many interpretations about FMEAs and how they are applied. There are times when D/PFMEAs contain many errors or conflicting information or the failure mode was never thought of or incorporated into the original documents. Potential failure modes are added after the fact or after the failure occurred. Then the FMEA team scrambles to update the latest documents. On many occasions, the Quality/Engineering Manager or Quality Engineer is the entire FMEA Team and completes the required documentation just prior to the PPAP (Production Part Approval Process) submission deadlines. People need to understand that all FMEA teams should be cross-functional, multi-disciplinary teams.

An important characteristic of FMEA is that it is a process of determining failure modes based on *past experience*. If we know a certain component in last year's computer model had a 1 in 1,000 failure rate, we know that it will continue to experience the same failure rate unless we change something. While FMEA is something of an advanced brainstorming process, it is an educated one. The more we know about the components in our process or product, the better we are able to determine our failure rates.

As with most tools, FMEA is a process. It begins first and foremost by selecting a team. The team then a) detects the possible failure modes, b) assesses the severity, c) assesses the occurrence/probability of the failures, d) determines the detectability of the failure, e) assigns an overall risk priority number (RPN), and then f) takes action to eliminate or minimize the failure potential.

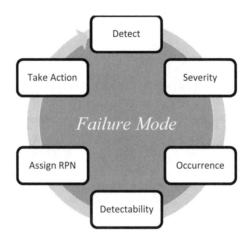

Figure 21-1: FMEA Cycle

FMEA Process Basics

Assembling the Team

FMEA is used mainly in process and product design; its focus is on manufacturing.[4] The process also relies heavily on engineers to help determine potential process and product failures. Consequently, your FMEA team necessarily will have a heavy concentration of technical people. You should gather your team from a representative cross-section of the company:

➤ Manufacturing

➤ Engineering

➤ Quality

> R&D

> Customer/Tech Service

Additionally, you can include representatives from both your customer and supplier bases. Maintenance, Purchasing, Sales and the IT department also may be areas from which you can gather potential team members, depending on the process or product you are addressing. A good FMEA team consists of four to six people working together, plus a team leader to facilitate meetings, track the FMEA process and make sure everyone is working together to achieve the goal.

The Deep Dive: Determining your Failure Modes

During the deep dive process, the FMEA team's questions, thoughts, documentation, lessons learned, and analysis of each line element, should be based on items that could potentially fail by their associated causes and/or mechanisms of failures related to the operation of machinery (process) and products. This analysis is based on past experiences and concerns regarding the entire operating production environment and performance of the machinery and products.

The team should begin by assembling all pertinent back-up information and documentation, both formal and informal, that can be used in determining potential failures in the product or process. Each member should have a full understanding of what the entire process is about and the goals it aims to achieve. Each team member should be trained prior to the start of the FMEA process as to what the machinery, process or product is expected to do or not do, under what specified conditions, and the required time period for which it is intended to function. These criteria should be available from sources such as design requirements, validation testing, performance testing, and contract and engineering specifications. This would also include possible federal, state and/or local regulatory laws. The FMEA team also should have access to process flow diagrams, blueprints, engineering diagrams and drawings, compatibility studies and reliability data.

As you can see, the deep dive into determining potential failure modes is much more than an educated guess. While past experience will many times unearth the most obvious potential failure modes, the team must also be open to heretofore unnoticed and unexperienced potential failures. For instance, if a new machine is needed for a process, the team will possibly have little to no experience with the process component. In this event, having a supplier representative on the team is recommended.

Failure modes can come in all shapes and sizes. A failure mode in a product could manifest as a poorly designed antenna in a cell phone or a poorly placed conductor on a microchip. In a process, a failure mode can be a machine that breaks down or produces defective parts, or even a gap in proper supply/inventory maintenance. In the healthcare industry, a Code Yellow (a missing patient) or a defective gauge on an autoclave can be serious failure modes that endanger patient safety.

The Heart and Soul of FMEA: Severity, Occurrence and Detectability

Once the deep dive has uncovered a host of potential failures, it is time to really go to work to uncover the core set of failure modes by assessing the severity, probability (occurrence rate) and detectability of each item on your FMEA problem list.

To help illustrate how this process works, we are going to follow a hypothetical FMEA team in an automotive manufacturing plant. The team is assembled to address a new braking system design they wish to implement in all new models. The team has assembled a list of potential failure modes in the new system based upon their past experience. In this example, we will limit our analysis to the system itself, not the process of production, for the sake of simplicity.

In a disc brake system, the main components are the brake pedal, the fluid line, the piston and slide pin, the caliper, and the disc or rotor. The driver presses the brake pedal, forcing brake fluid through the line, triggering the piston and slide pin to center and contract the caliper, which presses the brake pads against the rotor, creating friction and heat (released and cooled through vents in the rotor) to stop the car.

Severity

The first task for our team is to determine the severity of the various potential failure modes determined in their deep dive session. Table 21-1 outlines a sample ranking chart from the automotive industry. High severity rankings affect the overall operability of the system or whole product in question. In our example, a high ranking would lead to brake system failure and inoperability of the vehicle as a whole. Severity is looked at from both a customer and a machine operator or an assembler's viewpoint. If the defect affects both, the highest of the two scores is used.

Effect	Criteria: Severity of Effect (Customer Effect)	Criteria: Severity of Effect (Manufacturing/Assembly Effect)	Rank
Hazardous without warning	A potential failure mode affects safe vehicle operation and/or involves noncompliance with government regulations without warning.	May endanger machine operator or assembler without warning.	10
Hazardous with warning	A potential failure mode affects safe vehicle operation and/or involves noncompliance with government regulations with warning.	May endanger machine operator or assembler with warning.	9
Very High	Vehicle/item inoperable (loss of primary function).	100% of product may have to be scrapped or repaired in repair department with repair time greater than one hour.	8
High	Vehicle/item operable but at a reduced level of performance. Customer very dissatisfied.	Product may have to be sorted and a portion (< 100%) scrapped, or repair time is 30-60 minutes.	7
Moderate	Vehicle/item operable but comfort/convenience item(s) inoperable. Customer dissatisfied.	Product may have to be scrapped with no sorting, or incur a repair time less than 30 minutes.	6
Low	Vehicle/item operable and comfort/convenience item(s) operable but at a reduced level of performance.	100% of product may have to be reworked or vehicle/item repaired off-line but not at repair department.	5
Very Low	Fit and Finish/Squeak and Rattle item does not conform. Defect noticed by ≥ 75% of customers.	Product may have to be sorted with no scrap and a portion reworked.	4
Minor	Fit and Finish/Squeak and Rattle item does not conform. Defect noticed by 50% of customers.	Portion of product may have to be reworked with no scrap, on-line but out of station.	3
Very Minor	Fit and Finish/Squeak and Rattle item does not conform. Defect noticed by ≤ 25% of customers.	Portion of product may have to be reworked with no scrap, on-line but in- station.	2
None	No discernible effect.	Slight inconvenience to operation/operator, or no effect	1

Table 21-1: Severity Rankings

Occurrence

Next, the team will determine the occurrence/frequency rate, or the probability that a particular failure will occur. If known components are reused in a new system or process, determining the frequency will be relatively straightforward. However, if new components are used, the team will have to look at similar products or processes to make this determination. It is also important to remember that combining new components in a system or process can change the anticipated failure rates in other failure modes. For instance, a new brake pad material may cause more or uneven wear on a rotor; more or fewer pistons in the brake design can affect the performance of a caliper. A sample automotive frequency chart is outlined in Table 21-2, below.

Probability	Likely Failure Rates	PpK	Ranking
Very High: Persistent Failures	$\geq$ 100 per Thousand Pieces	< 0.55	10
	50 per Thousand Pieces	$\geq$ 0.55	9
High: Frequent Failures	20 per Thousand Pieces	$\geq$ 0.78	8
	10 per Thousand Pieces	$\geq$ 0.86	7
Moderate: Occasional Failures	5 per Thousand Pieces	$\geq$ 0.94	6
	2 per Thousand Pieces	$\geq$ 1.00	5
	1 per Thousand Pieces	$\geq$ 1.10	4
Low: Relatively Few Failures	0.5 per Thousand Pieces	$\geq$ 1.20	3
	0.1 per Thousand Pieces	$\geq$ 1.30	2
Remote: Failure is Unlikely	$\leq$ 0.01 per Thousand Pieces	$\geq$ 1.67	1

Table 21-2: Failure Mode Frequency Rate

We will take a look shortly at the importance of the interaction between severity and occurrence.

Detectability

Detectability involves assessing how easily a defect can be identified. As Table 21-3 demonstrates, high ratings indicate that defects of this nature can only be uncovered through manual inspection. The easier it is to recognize a defect, the lower the ranking. For example, a pinhole defect in a brake line may be nearly undetectable until it reaches the customer and brake fluid flows through the line for a time, resulting in a slow leak. Conversely, proper rotor thickness can be built into the production process through automatic gauging, making a rotor thickness problem nearly non-existent.

Rating	Detection	Criteria	Error Proofed	Gauged	Manual Inspection	Suggested range of detection methods
10	Almost Impossible	Absolute certainty of non-detection.			X	Cannot detect or is not checked.
9	Very Remote	Controls will probably not detect.			X	Control achieved with Indirect or random checks only.
8	Remote	Controls have poor chance of detection.			X	Control is achieved with visual inspection only.
7	Very Low	Controls have poor chance of detection.			X	Control is achieved with double visual inspection only.
6	Low	Controls may detect.		X	X	Control is achieved with charting methods, such as SPC.
5	Moderate	Controls may detect.		X		Control is based on variable gauging after parts have left the station, or go/no-go gauging performed on 100% of the parts after parts have left the station.
4	Moderately High	Controls have a good chance to detect.	X	X		Error detection in subsequent operations, OR gauging performed on set-up and first piece check (for set-up causes only).
3	High	Controls have a good chance to detect.	X	X		Error detection in station, OR error detection in subsequent operations by multiple layers of acceptance: Supply, select, install, verify. Cannot accept discrepant part.
2	Very High	Controls almost certain to detect.	X			Error detection in-station (automatic gauging with automatic stop feature). Cannot pass discrepant part.
1	Certain	Controls certain to detect.	X			Discrepant parts cannot be made because item has been error proofed by process/product design.

Table 21-3: Detectability Ratings

Risk Priority Numbers: Putting it all Together

Once your potential failure modes are listed and ranked in severity, frequency and detectability, it is time to put those numbers together to create a Risk Priority Number (RPN) to give the team a feel for the areas of greatest concern. The failure modes that have the greatest RPN values should be given the highest priority for corrective actions.

The formula is simple:

$$RPN = S \times O \times D$$

Where S is Severity, O is Occurrence, and D is Detectability

Table 21-4 illustrates how RPNs are determined in our example.

Failure Mode	Severity	Occurrence	Detectability	RPN
Pinhole defect in break line	9	3	9	243
Rotor thickness discrepancy	4	2	2	16
Improper brake line attachment	10	4	7	280
Slide pin sticks	5	9	9	405

Table 21-4: Sample RPN Score Sheet

Note that the highest ranking item on our sample list is not the one with the highest severity. An improper brake line attachment could lead to sudden disconnect and total break failure, whereas sticking slide pins can create uneven wear. A pinhole defect in the brake line causes a slow, gradual loss of brake fluid, causing brakes to feel "spongy," thus giving the driver warning that the brakes are not performing properly. However, left unrepaired, total brake failure can be realized. This problem, too, ranks below the slide pin problem in our example.

Creating an Action Plan

Once the failure modes have been ranked and ordered according to RPN, the team's task becomes one of designing ways to *prevent* these failure modes. This is where we will most likely need to really start digging down into the root cause of our failures in order to determine a proper action plan to prevent the problem from occurring in the future. A slide pin that sticks due to inadequate lubricant requires a different action plan than one that sticks due to inaccurate engineering calculations for proper pin size or pin slot size.

Cost may also factor into your action plan. You may need to get assistance from the accounting department and other members of the company in order to implement your plan if the costs are high. In the case of correcting the pinhole defect in the brake line, you may need to implement piece-by-piece testing at some point in the line prior to assembly. A new piece of costly equipment may need to be purchased. The team may also recommend that no action be taken. If you can determine there is a low probability that the defect rarely results in complete non-detection by the customer to the point of total brake failure causing injury or death, the cost of fixing the issue (at least in this manner) may outweigh the risk. Another solution could be to have the brake line manufacturer reduce the defect occurrence rate to comply with your company's standards for a category 1 occurrence ranking.

Not only must a set of actions be determined for each failure mode, but a person must be assigned to follow-up and follow-through on the plan, with a target date for completion of the action. Testing and monitoring will enable the team to ensure their corrective actions have been successful. Finally, the RPN scores of the failure modes can be revised to reflect the new risk assessment of the failure mode for future FMEA teams.

Conclusions

Toyota's accelerator problem has cost billions. There is no way to tell at this point just how much or how long the costs will go on. Once a defect has reached a customer, it is too late to fix the problem completely. The customer will always remember. While this may not always translate into lost sales or even a scarred reputation, it is easier and less costly to work to prevent or minimize the occurrence and severity of the defect than it is to fix it after the fact.

While many people shy away from performing FMEA due to confusion about the process or the need for gathering reliable, detailed information and documentation before the real process begins, FMEA is very straight-forward and easy to perform with the right information in the hands of the right team. The very basics of FMEA have been included here, but it is important to remember there is still much left for you to learn in order to hone your detection and deep-dive skills, apply ranking methods appropriately and choose the most effective action plans for the situation. For more information or assistance in implementing FMEA processes in your company, contact me at *steve-leggett@sbcglobal.net*.

Key Lessons Learned

1. FMEA is a tool to *prevent* problems before they happen.

2. Preventing failures before they happen is far less costly than fixing them once they have reached the customer.

3. The FMEA process is relatively straight-forward and easy to implement if you have the proper team and the proper information going into the process.

About the Author

Steven C. Leggett is a Senior Quality Improvement Coach for Lean Principles, LLC, which trains and coaches healthcare, automotive, aerospace and government and defense contractors in Lean and Six Sigma Problem Solving. Steve is a retired General Motors Senior APQP and Launch Supplier Quality Engineer. He was responsible for Cradle to Grave APQP functions, Lean Manufacturing, and warranty with respect to chassis components.

Steve has written and authored articles in numerous quality publications. He is the co-author of the *AIAG-FMEA Manual* (3ed) and the *MFMEA Manual* (1ed). He is the Chair of the *AIAG-PPAP Manual* (4ed), as well as a speaker at various local and national conferences. He has also won awards from ASQ Automotive Division for their Quality Professional of the Year 2003 and the AIAG Outstanding Achievement Award for 2002.

Steve is also a General Motors University (GMU) instructor and an Adjunct Professor of Metrology (Quality Systems) at Macomb Community College (MCC). He sits on the MCC Advisory Board for the Quality Systems and Technology Program. You can e-mail him at: *steve-leggett@sbcglobal.net.*

General References

SAE J1739, AIAG-FMEA, MFMEA, PPAP, APQP, MSA, SPC, ISO/TS 16949, and Juran's Quality Control Hand Book.

---

[1] Alan Ohnsman and Keith Naughton, "Toyota May Lose US Market Share, Drop Behind Ford on Recalls," *Businessweek* (February 11,2010),
http://www.businessweek.com/news/2010-02-11/toyota-may-lose-u-s-market-share-drop-behind-ford-on-recalls.html
[2] Tomoko Hosaka, "Toyota Recalls May Cost Automaker $5.5 Billion," MSNBC (March 16, 2010), *http://www.msnbc.msn.com/id/35893905*
[3] Ibid.
[4] FMEA has also become increasingly useful and applicable in construction, healthcare and IT industries. We will, however, maintain our focus here on the manufacturing sector.

Chapter Twenty-Two

Stop Guessing and Start Selling

Chuck Overbeck

Overview

Several years ago I was asked to attend a sales manager meeting in Dallas. The meeting had only one purpose: to improve our sales process. The meeting included management from both sales and marketing and we were to spend two days sequestered in a hotel conference room. Our hope was to emerge from that meeting with a better sales process that allowed the sales team to close more opportunities in a shorter amount of time. Everyone in the meeting knew there was room for improvement. However, we often disagreed on what the improvement should be.

At each step in the original sales process we would discuss what we thought to be the problem and recommend solutions. Not only was there debate on the solutions on occasion, there was debate as to the problem itself. Differences of opinion were frequently resolved by a majority consensus, after which we would move on. Ultimately, we left Dallas with what we all hoped would be an improved sales process. I say *hoped* because we didn't know if we had improved or not. I remember sitting on the plane flying home thinking, "I know we changed the process, but I have no idea if we improved it." In fact, we couldn't be sure we didn't make it worse. That little voice inside my head kept saying, "There has to be a better way."

There is in fact a better way. The solution is the result of almost two decades of sales and sales management experience combined with an Engineering and Lean Six Sigma education, as well as countless hours of developing and modifying these tools to better meet the unique needs and requirements of a sales organization.

This chapter is intended for practitioners of Lean Six Sigma who want to transition these principles to sales and for the sales professional who wants to improve using these proven methodologies.

This chapter will help you to:

- Understand the importance of having a clear sales objective
- Learn what it means to eliminate defects in the sales process
- Understand why you should use leading sales indicators instead of lagging indicators
- Establish an Ideal Customer Criteria

The New Sales Paradigm: Defining Selling as a Quality Process

Even among sales professionals who recognize sales as a process, the term is often used loosely. We accept there are steps needed to move an opportunity from start to finish, yet we resist the need to implement a standard practice. Ironically, the reason often given for this resistance is the expressed need to adapt to unique customers and situations. However, I have found very few sales people vary their process from prospect to prospect. The greatest variation within selling exists between the top performing sales representatives and those at the bottom. In other words, variation in selling accounts for variation in performance.

To establish a quality process for any department in a corporation, two things are required. First, clearly define the product of the process. Second, design the process to reduce or eliminate defects. A sales department must do the same thing.

Quality improvement initiatives all recognize that value is defined by the customer, and only the customer. Therefore, the product of a *Quality Sales Process* would be something the prospect determines to be of value. I have asked many sales professionals over the years, "What does your sales process produce?" The most common response to my question is, "a customer." Then I ask, "What *should* the product of your sales process be?" Some will respond with the same answer. Others know I am looking for something more and begin to ask me questions.

They are correct that I am looking for something more. After all, customers aren't paying you to be your customers. They're paying you for something else. That something else is the answer to the question.

The Quality Sales Process produces value for the customer. At the same time, it has to produce value for the organization selling the product or service as well. If it doesn't, why do it? When both parties benefit, it produces value to both over the long term.

The product of a Quality Sales Process is a "win-win" result.

An accurate, well-defined objective is the starting point in building any quality process, including sales. Our new knowledge of what we want to accomplish will provide focus in how we get there. Once we have our goal, we can begin the second step, elimination of defects.

To state the obvious, you can't eliminate defects until you first know what the product of your process is. Hence, we see the importance of defining the product of the Quality Sales Process. Once our product is defined, we can eliminate any activity that does not lead us to our desired outcome. We build our sales process around improving throughput and eliminating defects early.

To begin this journey, I will do something you've never seen in a book on selling. I will give you the mathematical principles and improvement concepts to ensure you increase your sales. When followed, these principles will improve the effectiveness and efficiency of a sales team. In short, sales representative can stop guessing and know they are going to sell more.

Do the Math

As I began my educational journey into quality and process improvement, I was introduced to the concept of <u>Rolled Throughput Yield (RTY).</u> The concept and equation are both very simple. The value lies in its implications. Understanding this simple concept forms the foundation for building a sales process of continuous improvement.

RTY is the understanding that the probability of getting something through a multi-step process is the product (multiplication) of the probability of all the sub-processes:

$$RTY = (p_1)\ (p_2)\ (p_3)\ (p_4)\ (p_n)...$$

Therefore, if I multiple the probability of the successful completion of every step from qualify to close, I will know the probability of closing a deal. For example, in a four steps sales process with the probabilities of success of 80%, 70%, 90%, and 60%. We know we have a 30% chance of getting the business.

$$p_{close} = (0.8)\ (0.7)\ (0.9)\ (0.6)$$

$$p_{close} = 30\%$$

This concept is straight-forward and there is a reason why it is important to your sales team. First, in sales we tend to only measure final results, <u>lagging indicators</u>. We know the p_{close} value, but not the values for the sub processes, our <u>leading indicators</u>. Because we fail to identify where in the sales process we need to begin our improvement efforts, our results can be less than desired.

In the above example, if we don't know the values for the sub-processes, we might try to improve step three, which is at 90% throughput. Imagine we can reduce the number of opportunities lost at this step by 50%. Now we have:

$$p_{close} = (0.8)\ (0.7)\ (0.95)\ (0.6)$$

$$p_{close} = 32\%$$

This represents an almost 7% improvement in throughput. But what if we understood all of the data and instead decided to work on step four? Making the same assumption about reducing the number of lost opportunities by 50%, the fourth sub-process improves from 60% to 80% and we now have the following:

$$p_{close} = (0.8)\ (0.7)\ (0.9)\ (0.8)$$

$$p_{close} = 40\%$$

This time, we improved throughput by 25% (verses less than 7% in the previous example). There are other factors to take into consideration. We could never have realized a 25% improvement by working on step 3. Even if we could make Step 3 perfect, it only allows for a 12% improvement to the total system throughput. Step 4 has a maximum cap of 50% total throughput improvement.

Understanding RTY gives a sales organization a crucial first step to understanding how to improve sales performance along with continuous sales improvement.

Selling is a Numbers Game, but Not Like You May Think

All too often when sales are down, managers will tell sales reps to get out and make more sales calls. "Sales is a numbers game." There is more truth to that than these managers often realize. There are two aspects to the so-called numbers game; the number of opportunities and the probability of closing those opportunities.

$$t_{close} = (p_{close})\ (n)$$

$$n = opportunities$$

The previous section on RTY addressed how the sales organization needs to approach improving the probability of closing deals. This section addresses what RTY can do to increase the number of opportunities. First, we need to identify constraints.

The two major constraints affecting sales professionals and organizations are time and money; time being the more limiting of the two. Therefore, if a sales team wants to be more effective at increasing its number of leads, it needs to find a way to free up time. Again, the answer is in the math.

Since order doesn't matter in multiplication (2x4=4x2), from a system probability perspective, the sequence of probabilities is irrelevant. In terms of production efficiency (t_{close}), this is not true. Order *does* matter. When it comes to improving sales outcomes, sales teams need to keep this fact in mind and develop their process accordingly. A sales organization's goal should be in front loading sub-processes with the lowest probabilities because this reduces the investment (time and money) in those prospects that will not close.

Fortunately in sales, we have a process step for doing this. It's called *qualifying*. When we qualify correctly, we minimize resources committed to fruitless opportunities. Sales reps are freed up to pursue qualified prospects, n. As n goes up, so, too, do sales, t_{close}. The sales person sells more and the company spends less.

The Science of Qualifying

Because of the subjective nature of qualifying prospects, many sales organizations do very little to formally define what it means to qualify. They would be better off taking Galileo's advice to "Measure what is measurable, and make measurable what is not so." What is subjective from an overall perspective can often be quantified to some degree when we look at its components. Prospect qualification is a perfect example for this.

Qualifying could simply be defined as the process of determining if a fit exists between the prospective customer and a product or service. Wikipedia defines a *qualified prospect* in this ambiguous way: "There is much debate in the sales profession as to what constitutes an actual 'qualified' prospect." Perhaps, this is where a sales organization should begin. After all, if we don't know what our prospect qualification process is to produce, how can we develop the process?

It is logical to begin with this question, "What do we hope to gain from the qualification process?" The answers to that question include:

- Determine the likelihood of a particular prospect to purchase.

- Prioritization of prospects.

- Determine if the customer has a need that can be met by the product or service.

- Identify potential problem areas.

- Evaluate the probability the prospect would be satisfied with the product or service and company.

- Determine if the prospect would be a desirable customer.

- If the prospect isn't qualified, determine the reason.

Once it is understood these outcomes provide value to the sales process, qualification can be approached with this end in mind. Value should drive our definition because it is the reason for having this step in the first place. Therefore, the *qualified prospect* is:

> *A prospect who possesses attributes common with satisfied and loyal customers and for whom our solution is a good fit.*

The three important aspects of prospect qualification are the customer, the solution, and the relationship. Explicit in the definition are the first two components, customer and solution. For the first we compare the prospect to a list of characteristics found to be common in the better customers. We should evaluate the prospect against multiple criteria to determine a reasonable fit. While this is subjective, as previously mentioned, it does not imply we cannot semi-quantify the process. For solution, it involves understanding the customer's needs and requirements and determining the effectiveness of a given solution in meeting those needs. The sales representative should evaluate an offering in terms of the product or service, the company, and customer support.

The final aspect, the relationship, is an implicit part of the definition. It comes from a long-term view of the sale. While the sales process is about a particular opportunity, gaining a customer is about developing and cultivating a relationship. Not all customers are capable of partnering with a supplier. This is not to say a sales person should walk away from these opportunities. However, the sales representative needs to be aware of the limited relationship potential and approach the prospect accordingly. Evaluation of the relationship potential will actually occur during the customer evaluation portion of qualification.

The Customer Yardstick

How do you measure whether a prospect is qualified? The same way you measure anything: against an accepted standard. The reason sales teams have a difficult time qualifying is that usually there is the lack of an established standard. It reminds me of Bill Cosby's account of Noah talking to God, "Right, what's a cubit?" Right, who are our customers?

Who are your customers? The answer to this question provides half the answer for qualifying. The other half is, who *isn't* your customer? Not everyone is your customer. Companies and sales people who don't realize this fail. This is why we have to qualify well. When we think everyone is a potential customer, we waste time and resources and accomplish nothing.

A few years ago, I developed a method to make the development of customer criteria more exact. It's based on the conclusions of Vilfredo Pareto, an Italian mathematician. He developed what came to be known as the Pareto Principle or the 80/20 Rule. By following this process, any sales team can develop an effective customer yardstick.

Define Your Customer

I have found this process works best when a group of sales representatives and managers participate in the exercise. Preferably there are more sales reps than managers, and the group should have between six and ten people. The facilitator should guide the discussion only. The goal is to have everyone participate.

A conference room with a whiteboard works great for these meetings. As people enter the room, give them a pen and pad of Post-It® Notes. Then follow these steps:

1. Draw a line down the middle of the whiteboard. On the left-hand side of the board write: Top 20% of customers. Ask everyone in the room to name common attributes of your best customers. As people list these characteristics, have them write them down on a Post-It Note and stick it to the left side of the board.

2. After the list has been exhausted, ask about the commonality in the 20% of customers who complain the most. This time, post the notes on the right side of the board under the heading "Bottom 20%." This is also a good time to explore common attributes among prospects who never purchase your products. Post these on the right side of the board too.

3. Next, we look for commonality on the left side of the board. For example, someone may have added, "Customers want the latest technology." Someone else may have posted "Thought leaders." Through a discussion, we might combine these two into one

attribute and call it "Forward thinking." After we do this on the left side, we do the same thing on the right.

4. Now, using the lists on the whiteboard and the Ideal Customer Criteria Matrix (Figure 22-1), we are going to develop the profile we will use to evaluate all prospects. Take the attributes from the left side of the board and write them down the left-hand column on the worksheet. The characteristics on the right are listed along the top.

5. Working down the first column of the matrix, compare the first item in the left-side column to the first item in the top row. For example, if the common attribute for the top customers were "Willing to pay for quality," and the first characteristic of the bottom 20% were "Make purchasing decisions on price alone," there would be a negative correlation between the two, *i.e.*, they cannot exist in the same prospect. Therefore, we enter a "-" in the corresponding box. If the second item in the column were "Willing to take risk," a "0" would be entered in the box because there is no correlation between the willingness to take risks and basing decisions on price alone. If the two attributes had a positive correlation, then a "+" would be entered in the box. An example of this would be from the left column, the customer is "Thought Leader," and along the top column, customers complain because "our solution is a closed system."

Customer Characteristics / 80/20 Revenue	80/20 Complaints	Make purchasing decisions on price alone	Want an open system					
Willing to pay for quality		-	0					
Willing to take risk		0	0					
Thought leader		0	+					

Ratings: Strong Correlation +, No Correlation 0, Negative Correlation -

Figure 22-1: Ideal Customer Matrix

6. Finally, look for the "-" symbols in the matrix. These provide a continuum upon which to evaluate prospects. In our example, a negative sign in the box that represents the interaction of "Willing to pay for quality" and "Make purchasing decisions on price alone," these two become the opposite ends of our criteria continuum. The reality is that very few prospects are at either extreme. Therefore, we may say anyone who is always willing to pay for quality gets a "5". Those who decide on price alone get a "1." This is the first metric in the criteria.

7. This process is then repeated for other negative signs in the matrix. Ideally, we are looking for between five and eight characteristics for our profile.

The ideal customer profile becomes the yardstick for qualification. When sales representatives evaluate all new prospects against it, they sell more. In effect, they are eliminating the defects from the process upfront. This isn't to say there is something wrong with the client, only that a good fit does not exist today.

Conclusions

While selling is a numbers game, there is much more to it than just sales dollars. Sales professionals can understand what works and what doesn't at every step by evaluating sub-processes. It's through a deliberate approach, which starts with better qualification, that sales organizations can eliminate defects early and focus efforts on true opportunities. Measuring leads to understanding. Understanding eliminates the guesswork.

Key Lessons Learned:

1. Measuring the sub-processes in a sales process leads to understanding and predictability of outcomes.

2. Eliminating un-qualified prospects early in the sales process frees up time to pursue true opportunities.

3. Qualification does not have to be subjective and arbitrary. By starting with the 80/20 Rule, a sales organization can understand who their customers really are.

4. Selling, like any other process, can be improved with Lean Six Sigma methodologies.

About the Author

Chuck Overbeck is the founder of Sales Sigma Consulting and the Sales Sigma Process. Chuck has over 18 years experience in sales and sales management. During that time, he has worked for Fortune 100 and Fortune's Fastest Growing Companies. He has successfully built sales teams, developed and implemented training programs for distribution partners, and has been involved in numerous product launches. He has made a career of delivering results and constantly looking for ways to improve the sales process. His ability to teach these principles has made those he mentored more successful in sales and in their careers.

Chuck is a graduate of the United States Military Academy at West Point. He is a former Infantry Company Commander and Army Ranger. He received his Six Sigma Green Belt and Lean Sigma training from Villanova University. He also received training in LeanSigma principles from TBM Consulting.

The Future

For tomorrow belongs to the people who prepare for it today.

– African Proverb

Chapter Twenty-Three

Challenges for the Future: Introducing Education to Lean Six Sigma

James H. Hardin

Overview

State and federal budgets are struggling to cope with the current economic crisis across the board. Foreclosure rates and home devaluation have undermined property tax revenues throughout the United States. Public elementary and secondary school expenditures are expected to increase 36% by the end of the decade.[1] Meanwhile, federal funding for targeted education programs is expected to drop by 5% from FY 2010 to FY 2011.[2]

Per-pupil expenditures continue to rise despite shrinking budgets. Total costs per pupil increased over 56% between the 1997-1998 school year and the 2006-2007 school year.[3] Figures show that while overall salary expenditures are increasing, they continually represent less of the overall education budget. Expenditures on employee benefits have increased, along with purchased services and supplies. Interest on school debt has also increased over 76%.[4] These figures don't even take into account the economic recession that began in December 2007.

The current economic situation has made it even more imperative for schools, like businesses, to operate at a higher level of efficiency to make their budgets stretch farther. We have seen throughout this book how applying Lean, Six Sigma, Operational Excellence and other strategies and methodologies has driven amazing improvement in businesses across industries, including non-profit organizations. Unfortunately, education lags behind the times in implementing organizational excellence systems and strategies. There is still a dearth of literature even available on the topic, let alone recommending application of these strategies.

This chapter will challenge you to:

- Drive your efforts toward making organizational excellence methodologies in education a part of your practice.
- Push educational systems in your area and across the nation to see the need to implement such strategies in their systems.
- See the need to implement such systems in education and become part of the future solution to the educational institution crisis.

Seeing the Future of Education through an LSS Lens

From my experience and the research I have conducted, more and more practitioners of Six Sigma believe the combined effort of Lean and Six Sigma increase the opportunity for larger gains while reducing the challenges of developing sustainable change. Businesses can expect a 10 to 30 percent improvement in their production when properly utilizing Lean Six Sigma. How would you like that much improvement in school climate, test scores, attendance or graduation rates? Probably, most of you would be astounded at a mere five percent increase in test scores across the spectrum in a single school term. Is this possible? Yes; however, this will never happen consistently unless there is total implementation of Lean Six Sigma system wide.

Education has a lot of stakeholders – more than the average business. The obvious customer is the student, who graduates with a diploma or degree from some institution and goes off into the workforce to live a wonderful life, assuming all of his or her requirements have been met. There are also the parents, who expect their children to graduate, leave the house and become financially self-sufficient so they, the parents, can enjoy their middle and retirement years without worry or further financial outlays. Colleges and graduate programs are also customers – they obtain their own customer base from students who graduate from high school and want obtain Bachelor's degrees. Further down the line are the businesses that depend upon educational institutions to provide a well-educated, intelligent workforce to employ in their organizations.

School boards and state, local and federal governments are also clients whose needs an educational institution must consider. Educational bodies count on government for budgetary allocations. No Child Left Behind requires demonstrated adequacy in student knowledge and performance and carries with it a host of requirements schools must follow that may or may not consist of value-added activities. Finally, the public in general can be considered a client of education. The degree to which the workforce is educated affects the overall economic performance of a nation.

With so many stakeholders and so much riding on how our educational institutions perform, it still amazes me to see education turning a blind eye to the improvements that can be realized by initiating Lean Six Sigma or Operational Excellence programs. In the following sections, I will outline how LSS can be applied to education to improve efficiency and outcomes (graduation rates, test scores, etc.) and decrease waste in operations.

Let's Talk about Lean and Six Sigma

As we've previously discussed, Lean is about eliminating waste in business processes. Lean was originally applied to manufacturing in a method known as Just-in-Time (JIT). In short, JIT turned manufacturing from a push process into a pull system where production is linked to customer demand and material replenishment requirements. JIT is a demand-supply model as opposed to supply-demand. As outlined in Chapter 14, Lean focuses on eliminating the 7M's of waste. These wastes are largely identified through Value Stream Mapping, as discussed in Chapter 17.

Six Sigma, on the other hand, is a set of specific improvement strategy tools and processes. The focus is upon identifying and removing defects. Six Sigma came out of Motorola Corporation in the 1980s, when one of the company's engineers, Bill Smith explained that an acceptable level of imperfection [for his company] was six sigma, which equates to producing a yield of products that are 99.99966% error free.[5] Today, Six Sigma has become so much more than an operating philosophy; it has become a goal, a metric, a methodology and a set of tools for eliminating defects. At its heart, Six Sigma embodies a methodology of improving quality (defect ratio) by gathering data, identifying then controlling variation, and improving predictability of business processes. Despite its focus on *eliminating* variation, many people forget that Six Sigma places a strong emphasis on value in waste reduction. Built into the philosophy is the recognition that there is some level of acceptable imperfection because there is a point at which the cost to fix a particular variation or waste becomes more costly than simply accepting it.

In education (as in any business) these practices have multiple implications and challenges. In Six Sigma, a defect is considered anything that causes customer dissatisfaction (See Chapter 16 on Voice of the Customer). The customers in education, as we have seen, are everyone from the student all the way up to the federal government. We are the only country in the world focused on educating *everyone*. Equal footing and opportunity for all, from top to bottom and bottom to top, is a necessary goal in order to improve, grow, learn, and enter that eternal journey toward success: the American Dream. Yet the variety of needs required by the overwhelming number of stakeholders often complicates and confuses the implementation of improvement initiatives. It is often easier to stay with the status quo than to figure out where to start and which customer to please first.

A second challenge we face is deciding where to apply our Lean Six Sigma efforts. Overwhelmingly, the focus is on test scores. However, this raises a whole host of issues:

- Which tests (metrics) do we use?

- Do they measure the right thing?

- Are the tests we are using as a nation measure the same thing (*i.e.*, are they comparable across states and across nations)?

- What do the results of these tests actually mean (*i.e.*, are they generalizable and applicable to something meaningful)?

For instance, in the United States, there are a host of secondary school aptitude tests used by different states: Iowa Test of Basic Skills (ITBS), Florida Comprehensive Assessment Test (FCAT), California Achievement Test and the Terra Nova test. Do these tests all measure the same thing? Do they rank results in the same manner? Does a student in Iowa who achieves a 94th percentile ranking on the ITBS have the same level of knowledge, skills and aptitude as a student in Florida ranked similarly on the FCAT? The biggest problem I see in "standardized" testing is the inability to define exactly what these tests measure. Do they measure actual knowledge? Do they measure "skills" or aptitude? Unfortunately, these tests are not unbiased for language or culture. It is difficult, for example, to determine whether a low-scoring Hispanic student lacks the knowledge, skills and aptitude measured by the test, or whether the low score results from a language barrier. If it is indeed the language barrier, the test obviously does not accurately measure what it intends to measure.

Because the focus in education is on test scores, many people do not or cannot look past this area to see the other areas in education where LSS methodologies can be applied to improve overall operational performance. Document management is a huge area in need for improvement within schools. In my experience, document management in schools is still cumbersome and inefficient. There are relatively few districts or universities that have a system-wide, freely accessible documentation system that is shareable – either across staff/faculty or amongst student clients. At the university level, for example, financial aid is separate from academics. Centralized systems eliminate the need to create numerous duplicate records and increase accessibility of information across departments.

Fundraising is also another area in which LSS practices can be applied. Do our fundraising efforts actually impact our bottom line? (See Chapter 10 for a discussion of Managerial Accounting and Chapter 20 for Financial Impact Analysis).

In deciding where to start with Lean initiatives and programs in education, the following chapters can offer some insight into the subject:

- Chapter 1: How to Get Started

- Chapter 2: What is Lean?

- Chapter 9: Project Selection

- Chapter 12: Operational Excellence in Non-Profits

Another consideration is how to apply LSS methodologies and tools to education. One metric used in education (for good or bad) is the standardized test. At the completion of certain grade levels, students are tested to determine their progress by analyzing the results statistically and applying the scores to a predetermined standard. Six Sigma would be six standard deviations from the mean. This translates to not more than four (unsuccessful) delta test scores per million attempts on a standardized test. Currently, No Child Left Behind does not define a specific level of success: States are allowed to define their own Adequate Yearly Progress. This has forced some states to lower their standards in order to ensure AYP is consistently achieved. In essence, this method of defining success in education is not aligned with the principles of Six Sigma: There is no consistent standard measure and NCLB actually creates a disincentive for true improvement in setting excellence goals (schools can be shut down if state standards are too high).

This focus on test scores as metrics of "good" education ignores everything else that makes up a quality education that produces intelligent, creative, healthy, well-rounded students. It also ignores the interconnectivity among educational processes: teachers, curriculum, counseling, physical education, extracurricular activities, and attendance, to name some of the more obvious. For example, if centralized document management is applied to a high school, teachers do not have to duplicate records (entries are made to a central system), more time is freed up for them to work on improving curriculum or helping struggling students, and students who receive extra help will have more incentive to stay in school and graduate, as well as improve their performance on standardized tests. As outlined in Chapter 3, Lean and Six Sigma are all about a *systems approach* to continuous improvement.

Applying Lean Six Sigma to Education

To improve the process of educating students, our goal is to improve every aspect of our responsibility in the *total learning environment*: staff, leadership, food service, transportation, attendance, child welfare, adult education and curriculum. However, increasing the quality of our products – students' level of learning and achievement (however that is measured) – to the point of 3.4 defects per million opportunities (DPMO) may seem unattainable. But what would you say to a ten, twenty, or thirty percent increase in student scores or graduation rates? What if your district sustained a 12 or even a five percent increase for three or four years in a row? What if fundraising and volunteer recruiting efforts achieved a 50% improvement in results? Imagine how much impact these results would have on a school's operational excellence.

Two methodologies are used in Six Sigma. DMAIC, which was explained in detail in Chapters 13 and 19, and DMADV, which stands for Define, Measure, Analyze, Design, and Verify. Notice the last two letter of each method differ: improve and control for DMAIC, and design and verify for DMADV. Many senior practitioners of Six Sigma believe DMADV is the stronger of the two applications. Their reasoning is because design and verify, when combined, produce new processes, products, and programs. An example of this methodology applied to education is instructive.

As a graduate assistant to the Dean of Education, I was asked by the school president to determine how Louisiana high school seniors chose which university to attend following graduation. We went through the standard Define, Measure, Analyze phases common to both DMAIC and DMADV. We discovered that a significant number used miles from home as the basis for their choice. This helped the president to *design* a massive recruiting program within a particular circle around the university, and in four years we could *verify* the campaign's success through metrics showing the university had more than doubled its student population and thus realized a tremendous increase in funding.

Let's go back and take a closer look at DMAIC. Define is used to pinpoint target areas for process growth or change. Measure is simply the use of one of many Six Sigma tools to collect and analyze data (the tool used is correlated with the data such as chi square, Anova, t-test, two tailed t-test, risk analysis and the f-test). Sometimes this is not so simple because reliability and validity of the information and data can distort the picture or scenarios. Always look at the situation from outside the box. The Analyze phase uses the information from the measure step to signal relationships between data, qualified information, and the target, goal or objective. For example, is there a correlation between learning style and teaching style? Another example could be whether there is a relationship between attendance and grades, or attendance and school activity involvement. The Improve phase of DMAIC is used to perfect the process or product. If there is a relationship between learning and teaching styles, we identify and make improvements (change). Perhaps we focus continuing education efforts for our teachers on learning new teaching methods and styles, or we tailor tutoring and reading assistance programs to adapt to the learning styles that work best with each student. Control activities are used to implement and regulate performance and success. One good example is to monitor, not supervise, the total activity and involvement of students and staff in all areas, using positive reinforcement for quality achievement. Monitoring student achievement on standardized tests is the most obvious control measure used in education today. Unfortunately, without a LSS system in place, when the red flags go up, schools are at a loss as to how they can identify and tackle the problem.

DMADV in Detail

The DMADV design is used for developing new programs, services and products as opposed to simply improving those already in existence, which can provide a better fit and approach to some educational problems. For example, a school has defined an area in need for improvement: student academic achievement as measured by GPA. GPA can be considered one indicator of expected performance on standardized tests, *i.e.*, if a student has a low math GPA, his or her performance on the mathematical section of the SAT is expected to be low. We accordingly develop a project goal of increasing GPA by 20% school-wide. There are many alternatives for how we might do that; we must analyze these alternatives to figure out which methods of improvement will provide the greatest level of impact for the cost.

In the real world, this can be difficult to achieve without implementing an LSS system organization-wide. For instance, we may need to first improve our fundraising and volunteer recruiting efforts in order to attain the financial base and staff we need to implement any new program. In the alternative, we need a LSS system in place to analyze a reorganization of the school budget to make a new system or program possible.

In our ideal example, however, we will assume that LSS is applied system-wide and we already have achieved sufficient financial and staffing goals to implement a new tutoring program designed to help students increase their grades.

In DMADV, we now need to *design* a process, service or program that will meet the needs of our various customers. Some of the common problems we face in education are students with English-speaking deficiencies, ADD and ADHD, behavioral disorders and a whole host of other problems. However, what many of these students have in common is the need for a particular learning style that adapts to their situation. Most, if not all, need some degree of individualized attention and one-on-one assistance. For students with ADD and ADHD, an appropriate teaching style could be to incorporate more visual or auditory teaching methods as opposed to text-book learning. For ESL students, an English language program may do more to enhance a student's comprehension in the classroom than any other method.

For this example, we develop three different pilot programs with a small test student population to study. One program will offer ESL classes to students dedicated solely to improving English language proficiency among non-native speakers. A second program is designed to incorporate more audio and visual teaching methods into the classroom. The third program will offer one-on-one tutoring to designated students using community volunteers in an after school setting within specific subject areas (reading or math).

Finally, the DMADV method requires that we *verify* the design performance of our new services. In this example, we would need to compare our participants' current GPA to his or her past GPA. This may not be quite so straightforward as it looks on the surface. For instance, those receiving one-on-one tutoring in math cannot be verified by looking at overall GPA, but only on their GPA in math-related coursework. However, we would want to measure ESL students' progress by their overall GPA, since improving English skills would impact all areas of learning. Another problem we face is comparing the results of our pilot programs with the overall progress of the general population, as well as measure it against a control population of students with low GPAs who did not participate in any of the programs.

Moving toward a Lean Educational Environment

It is also important to remember that, in Six Sigma, the customer determines what about a product (education) has value. Any part of education that is not adding value to product is wasteful and must be eliminated in order for it (the waste) to not interfere with the value stream – the process of developing and delivering a higher quality product.

Lean identifies three different categories of waste: time and materials (resources), unevenness or variation (test performance amongst and between particular classes or groups of students), and overburdening workers or systems. (See Chapters 1, 2 and 14). All employees are expected to think critically about their job and make suggestions on how to eliminate waste and to participate in <u>kaizen</u> events (a process of continuous improvement which involves brainstorming sessions to repair problems).

One method we can employ in an academic setting is the Just-in-Time philosophy, where waste is eliminated by providing needed supplies, materials and products exactly at the time necessary to be used (developed) for the next action to occur. Two examples are eliminating excess inventory and ensuring all students are in their class, seated and on time when classes begin.

Rather than push the product (leading, learning, teaching, developing) down the line (through each grade level/subject/activity), all products (leadership, students, staff) are "pulled" through the system by demand or recognized need. Leaders, teachers, staff, and especially students do not participate and learn until they are ready. Lean stresses the idea that "quality" cannot be inspected or supervised into manufactured products, but must be built into the production process.

However, in education, we are working with individuals as our ultimate output or product. Can education be compared to a manufacturing process? Of course it can. We are building the future of our country through education. We are striving to build stronger, better qualified individuals who live better lives than they would either without an education or without a quality education. The end result of the process, or the finished product, is called Jidoka in the manufacturing setting. In education, this would consist of the successful completion of a grading period, school term or graduation. Unacceptable variations (defects such as a student's inability to learn or unacceptable budget gaps) must not pass each station (grade level, unit, area of concentration or school building) until it is fixed, repaired or mastered. Lean educator practitioners use the <u>Five Whys</u> to trace problems to their source and resolution, to drill down to the *root cause* of the difficulty. (See Chapters 13 and 14 on the 5 Whys).

Education, with all its complexities, is not exempt from its duties to improve service quality through Lean and/or Six Sigma strategies, methodologies and tools, simply because it claims to be so much more different than other industries. Many other industries – healthcare, non-profits, service and information technology – all once made the very same claim: "You can't apply a manufacturing methodology to us!" Yet, over the past decade, LSS practitioners have proven them all wrong and have adapted these flexible strategies to almost every economic sector imaginable, including the federal and state governments.

Education is the foundation for all other industries and areas of life, and we *must* begin to implement these strategies to improving our service performance in this area. If we do not address efficiency at the most primary and basic level – education – we endanger our way of life and our economy. Without educated workers, Lean businesses cannot function, and this will ultimately have a significant, widespread impact on our nation as a whole.

Conclusions

I have seen little research from public education at the present time. This must change soon, as stronger accountability and millions in financial support are endangered. This change also must occur if our quality of life is to continue. This is something that must be addressed now. Simple, proven and effective methods are at hand to improve education without increasing taxes. If your school district spends fifty million yearly and could find a way to eliminate just one million from its operational expense, do you think you would be interested in knowing more about Lean Six Sigma and how it can be applied to education?

This chapter has introduced an explosive set of tools and strategies that have been used on a very limited basis in education to date. They have been available for many years, but have been applied most frequently to manufacturing and to engineering challenges. Now it is time to "re-engineer" education. A volcanic eruption of success in education can be developed when Lean Six Sigma is properly utilized. My purpose has been to develop an understanding of some of these key tools and methodologies and demonstrate how they can be applied to that most important institution: education.

I encourage leaders and LSS practitioners and consultants to push for implementing Lean and Six Sigma in our educational organizations. We need to create new tools and adapt old tools, methods and strategies to the educational setting. Education needs to become leaner, meaner and more effective so that we, as a nation and as individuals, can succeed.

If you would like more information and want to know more about Lean Six Sigma in education, e-mail me at *jhardinc@yahoo.com* or go to Flat Rock Consulting at *www.leansixsigmaatwork.com.*

About the Author

James Hardin holds a B.S. in Health, Safety, Recreation, Physical and Elementary Education. His educational background also includes a Master of Education in Guidance and Counseling, Specialist in Education in Counseling and Administration (with a published thesis) all from Northwestern State University. He is a graduate of the National Superintendent Academy (AASA/George Washington University), and he is a Lean Six Sigma Black Belt (Villanova University). James has had a very wide range of work experiences, including service as a school district administrator for twenty-four years. James recently retired for the second time, after over forty years in education.

Acknowledgments

Recognition is given to the following individuals for their mentoring and support in my growth. Ron Crabtree, president of MetaOps and Karen Young of Strategic Solutions that Work, along with other instructors at Villanova. Recognition is also given to George Eckes for the brilliant examples he uses in his lectures at Villanova.

---

[1] NCES. (2009). *Projections of Education Statistics to 2018* (37 ed). U.S. Department of Education, Washington, D.C.
[2] U.S. Department of Education, Fiscal Year 2009 – FY 2011 President's Budget State Tables for the U.S. Department of Education (2010)
http://www2.ed.gov/about/overview/budget/statetables/11stbystate.pdf
[3] NCES, *The Condition of Education 2010* (Washington, D.C.: U.S. Department of Education, 2010): Table A-34-1.
[4] Ibid.
[5] R. Raifsnider, and D. Kurt, Lean Six Sigma in higher education: Applying Proven Methodologies to Improve Quality, Remove Waste, and Quantify Opportunities in Colleges and Universities (Xerox Corporation, 2004).

Conclusion

Taking Continuous Improvement into the Future

Ron Crabtree

The First Step of a Long Journey

The last pages of this book are not an ending; in fact, they are just the beginning. For those of you who have yet to take your first steps into LSS/OpEx or even the idea of continuous improvement, the first step is always the hardest. Your decision is a simple one: continue as you are, or set out on a path that will help ensure your organization has a place in the future. For those of you who have already taken those first steps, we have outlined a comprehensive set of strategies, methods and tools that will take you down that road further and help you avoid some of the potholes along the way. Some of you may simply have strayed – we hope you are back on the right path.

One of the messages we hope to convey is that continuous improvement is exciting to those who practice it. Change – the *right* change, at least – can inspire hope, creativity and productivity among people throughout all levels of your organization.

"Exciting?" you ask, "How so?"

If I were to tell you that buying an electronic medical records system with voice transcription capability would cost $20,000 for your five-doctor practice, you might balk at the idea. What if I tell you, however, that this one purchase would eliminate $30,000 in yearly transcription costs, free up one hour of each doctor's day, eliminate the need for one staff member dedicated to filing patient records and notes, and reduce mistakes and errors in treatment by 20% (thus reducing malpractice costs), how would you feel then? Probably pretty excited.

And that is just one problem tackled in a relatively small office. Now expand those implications to a larger, multinational company with multiple processes and supply chains. Hard savings and cost avoidance can reach into the millions.

Now *that* is something to get excited about.

These types of results with LSS and OpEx aren't just academic, either. General Electric (GE) former CEO Jack Welch used Six Sigma to reinvent his company. His four-year plan to produce nearly defect-free products, services and transactions seemed ridiculously unattainable. In 1996 when Welch unveiled his Six Sigma plan, GE's annual revenues totaled a little over $70 billion (1995).[1] At the end of those four years,

GE's 2000 earnings had almost doubled to $130 billion, and net earnings had gone from $6.5 billion to $12.7 billion.[2]

That is just the beginning of the story. Welch's protégé at GE, James McNerney, went on to become CEO of 3M company, taking with him Welch's rigorous Six Sigma principles and programs. Over his four-year tenure at 3M, Welch systematically slashed personnel in developed countries (US and Europe) and increased 3M's presence in developing countries. The company went from net sales of $16.1 billion in 2001 to over $20 billion in FY 2004.[3] More importantly, McNerney more than doubled net earnings of the company during that same time.

Yet, this is still not the end of the story. McNerney went on to become CEO of Boeing in mid-2005. When he took over running the company, Boeing had revenues of $53.6 billion and net earnings of $2.57 billion.[4] In 2007, before the onset of the recession, Boeing reached total revenues of $66.4 billion and net revenues of almost $4.1 billion. Furthermore, Boeing has weathered the recession far better than most companies. Their revenues continued to rise to $68.28 billion (2009). While the company's net revenue dropped to $1.3 billion, a significant factor of this resulted from substantial increases in R&D investment – almost double that of previous years at $6.5 billion.

These are just a few of the most prominent success stories in the world of Lean Six Sigma. Whether you are a multi-national conglomerate or a small business, continuous improvement programs offer these same opportunities to all enterprises. Can you get excited about doubling your net earnings, whatever level they might be at today?

The question today's business owner, manager and executive needs to ask themselves is, "Can we afford *not* to institute a rigorous continuous improvement program like LSS or OpEx?" In a recessionary economy with declining government space contracts and a troubled airline industry, Boeing managed to grow revenues and invest significantly in R&D. Can your company say the same?

If you've dabbled in LSS or OpEx and your projects aren't producing the results you expected, you should ask yourself whether you've integrated these systems into the very bedrock of your company culture, indoctrinated your employees in the process and the benefits, and fully bought into the commitment necessary to create sustainability.

In the proceeding chapters, you have hopefully learned several invaluable lessons about continuous improvement methodologies, strategies and tools:

- Continuous Improvement is not a "quick fix" firefighting method of solving problems.

- It requires buy-in from all levels of the enterprise, from line worker to CEO.

- LSS tools need to be implemented within a system that adopts Lean thinking.

- There is a methodology for managing change that is critical to project and strategic success. If you don't manage change, change will manage you.

- Project selection is a critical component of LSS/OpEx; there are several tools and methods for accurately prioritizing and selecting projects that impact your bottom line.

- Continual measuring and monitoring are critical components of sustainability.

These are just some of the lessons we've hoped you gleaned from our discourse. Go back and re-read the book; I guarantee you will find even more pearls the second time around that you missed on the first read.

I also encourage you to contact the experts who have dedicated considerable time authoring these chapters, and who have dedicated their lives to implementing and leading the type of change that drives straight through the heart of an enterprise down to the bottom line. If continuous improvement is not in your heart and never makes it to your bottom line, there is a big disconnect somewhere in the pipeline that you need to look for. LSS and OpEx are about driving change that creates solutions for success, now and into the future.

We continue to face an increasingly globalized economy. Creating a system of continuous improvement that spans multiple countries, cultures and languages is a daunting task. There are many opportunities for disconnects, as Toyota has proven. However, systems like LSS and OpEx are approaches to continuous improvement potentially flexible enough to address these considerations. The key is to remain focused on the end goal: providing value to your customer by eliminating waste and defects and promoting value. This is the heart and soul of continuous improvement.

Recessionary periods also present unique challenges. The temptation for companies to reduce "unnecessary" costs may lead executives to cut continuous improvement programs. Unfortunately, I have seen the results: quality suffers and costs increase through defects, recalls, decreasing value (from the customer viewpoint), lost sales and sales opportunities, and ultimately a focus that devolves into implementing more traditional "cost-cutting" strategies. Throwing out Lean initiatives in the interest of cost cutting is short-sighted and harmful. By following and maintaining LSS and OpEx programs through the difficult times, your organization will weather a recessionary storm better than your counterparts.

Finally, we, as a group, challenge you to take continuous improvement into all industries and throughout all levels and departments in your organization, whether you are a small business or a large multinational. Challenge yourselves to be creative and take LSS and OpEx into heretofore unknown territories. Explore the full set of capabilities these systems offer to improve and grow your organization into a first-class 21st century enterprise capable of sustaining change even into the next century.

---

[1] SEC Annual Report 10K450, 1996.
[2] SEC Annual Report 10K450, 2001.
[3] SEC Annual Report 10K, 2001-2004.
[4] SEC Annual Report 10K, 2009.

Glossary of Terms

Activity-based costing – costing model that identifies organizational activities and assigns cost according to actual consumption

Affinity diagram – a brainstorming tool used by project teams to generate ideas regarding potential causes or solutions to a problem

ANOVA (Analysis of Variance) – process by which variables are subjected to statistical tests to determine whether or not they have a statistically significant effect on a process or outcome

Balanced Scorecard – tracks business organizational functions in the areas of financial, customer, internal business process, and learning and growth

Baseline cost – establishes a reference against which we can compare future costs and capture the financial impact of LSS project improvement actions; usually the historical cost, but not always

Baseline document –the version-controlled specification document outlining all the requirements for an idea that is scrubbed for accuracy and signed off by all of the stakeholders

Branded product – usually a purchased product, labeled as one's own with permission from the original supplier

Business case – the compelling statement of the urgent need for the project and any consequences if the problem is not resolved

Business strategy – a document that defines the vision, mission, objectives, performance metrics and targets and overall master work plan to achieve the future state direction of the business

C&E (Cause & Effects) Matrix –tool used to quantify the impact process inputs have on primary process outputs

Catchball – participative approach to decision making in which information and ideas are thrown and caught back and forth, up and down throughout the organization; the purpose is to build consensus around the best approach for achieving an objective

Cellular design – work design that maximizes flow; work flow is organized in a manner that minimizes time, effort and resources and increases quality and throughput

Champion – senior level manager assigned to support and approve resources and tollgates

Change Management Process – the process of stages that address and integrate all additions, revisions, and deletions to the baseline document; these stages are define, measure, analyze, recommend, negotiate and implement/reject; judicious approach that aids in transitioning people or organizations from a current state to a desired future state

Common cause variability – natural or random variation that is inherent in a process over time

Constraints – limitations or bottlenecks that prevent a business from achieving its goals

Control charts – graphical tools used to monitor performance variation in a process

Control plan – documentation of the measures that will be monitored to ensure a new process will be kept in control for the long term

CTP (Critical Thinking Process) – the intellectually disciplined process of actively and skillfully conceptualizing, applying, analyzing, synthesizing, and/or evaluating information gathered from or generated by observation, experience, reflection, reasoning, or communication, as a guide to belief and action

Critical to Quality tree – a mapping tool used to identify measureable characteristics of customer requirements to the drivers of specific needs

Design of Experiments – a method of simultaneously testing the effects of multiple factors on process outputs

Development Lifecycle Process –the stages that an idea for a product, service or improvement goes through – from conception through development – to be launched into production or implementation; these stages are: concept, design, build, integrate and test, make/implement, verify and launch or release into production mode

Discount rate – annual rate at which future values are diminished so that they can be compared to values today

DMAIC – the five-phase Six Sigma methodology for improving performance of processes in organizations; Design, Measure, Analyze, Improve and Control

DMADV – a variation of the DMAIC process, sharing the first three elements of Design, Measure and Analyze, but its difference lies in the last two phases: *Design* and *Verify*

Enabling processes – processes that do not directly contribute to the value of a product or service, but which are required to do business (*i.e.*, filing taxes, complying with regulations)

Fishbone diagram – a cause-and-effects matrix of a problem with associated categories detailing the potential causes

Five Why's – a root-cause analysis tool used to find the basis for problems in the quality of products and services

Five (5) S's – a lean manufacturing principle that stands for Sort, Set in Order, Scrub and Shine, Standardize and Sustain

FMEA – acronym for Failure Modes and Effects Analysis, a matrix tool used to identify potential failure modes in a product or process along with effects and causes of each failure

Gate review – review of all end-of-line defects at the point where the next step is getting the product or service to the customer

Gemba walks –Gemba walks refer to structured tours, typically by management, of an area or operation of where work is performed; the purpose is for workers and managers to observe the place where work is performed to understand and identify what is really happening

Goal statement – a statement outlining the results of the project with reasonable expectations of when deliverables can be expected

Granular statement – a concise statement describing the finer details of a problem

Guiding principles – definitions of the most important work practices, behaviors and rules that combine to form the foundation of the Lean culture an organization is trying to create and sustain

High Performance Enterprise – organizations that are more predictable, controllable, innovative, flexible and able to grow profitably and sustainably in both good and bad times; organizations that are totally aligned to beat their competition

Hoshin kanri – Japanese term for policy deployment; the driver and infrastructure of hoshin kanri center on the cascading of executive management's strategies throughout the organization; **also known as Strategy Deployment**

Ideality Equation – subset of the Ideal Final Result (IFR) technique where the ideality equation, Ideality = Sum of Benefits / (Sum of Costs + Sum of Harms) indicates that the solution improves (i.e., it rises towards ideality), through any combination of: increasing benefits, reducing costs or reducing harms

IFR – acronym for Ideal Final Result; 1) the solution to a problem, independent of constraints of limiting mechanisms; 2) a set of creative innovation tools used to analyze potential solutions to a problem from fresh perspectives or paradigms

Indirect costs – costs for activities or services that benefit more than one activity, process or project; often difficult to estimate or trace direct benefit; *e.g.*, rent, utilities, legal costs

Input factors – the elements of a process that are manipulated in a DOE to determine the causes of the experimental results

Integrated Enterprise Excellence (IEE): developed by Forrest W. Breyfogle III, this 9-step business management system provides a roadmap for the creation of an enterprise process system in which organizations can significantly improve both customer satisfaction and their bottom line; IEE is a structured approach that guides organizations through the tracking and attainment of organizational goals by integrating enterprise process measures and improvement methodologies with tools such as Lean and Theory of Constraints (TOC) in a never-ending pursuit of excellence.

Itself Method – a means of expressing the IFR as if the problem could solve itself; examples include self-cutting grass (genetically modified grass that breaks itself above 3 inches), parts that order themselves to maintain desired inventory levels, and word processing programs that self-correct typing errors

Job Instruction approach – a 4-step process within TWI that teaches supervisors how to train job performers to do a job safely and correctly and ensures the performer understands and follows the standard

Job Methods approach – a 4-step process within TWI that teaches supervisors how to develop best-practice standard procedures for a job

Just-In-Time (JIT) – manufacturing philosophy implemented by Taiichi Ohno at Toyota's manufacturing plants; JIT reduces waste by supplying required materials only when the process needs them – there is no batching of supplies

Kaizen –a tool used to analyze a process for rapid, continuous process improvement

Kano model/Kano needs – a diagram of customer satisfaction into categories, including attractive qualities (nice-to-haves, delighters), one-dimensional qualities (satisfiers), must-be qualities (dissatisfiers), indifferences, and reverse qualities

KJ – a Voice-of-the-Customer process developed by Japanese anthropologist Jiro Kawakita to summarize large quantities of data. The technique generally follows a six-step process: 1) agree on an issue; 2) write and understand facts using clear, concise statements (obtained through interviews); 3) group similar facts; 4) title the groups – summarize again; 5) lay out groups and show relationships between groups; 6) vote on most important second-level issues and draw conclusions

KPI (Key Performance Indicators) – critical measures that determine the status of a process or operation; KPI are usually brief, succinct and visual, and allow anyone in the process to make a quick determination

Lagging indicators – economic or financial indicators that confirm (after the fact) a previous trend

Leading indicators – economic or financial indicators that indicate a change in measureable financial factors evident before a trend begins

Lead time – 1) a span of time required to perform a process (or series of operations); 2) in a logistics context, the time between recognition of the need for an order and the receipt of goods. Individual components of lead time can include: order preparation time, queue time, processing time, move or transportation time, and receiving and inspection time. (APICS Dictionary, 12th Edition)

Lean –a manufacturing operations management principle and continuous improvement methodology designed to reduce or eliminate waste in order to increase process speed and improve quality

Levels – operating parameters of the input factors set at distances far enough apart to show significant differences in the performance of the factors

Lot size – the amount of a particular item ordered from a plant or a supplier issued as a standard quantity to the production process

MOQ – acronym for Minimum Order Quantity; the smallest amount of product that can be ordered from a supplier

Non-siloed – organizational silos that are broken down so that scorecards, strategic planning, and business improvement efforts are addressed from an overall system point of view.

Non-value added – processes or activities that do not add value (attributes or features a customer is willing to pay for) to a product or service

Opportunity cost – the alternative opportunity that is forgone because of a particular decision or course of action

Organizational silos –with organizational silo management, there can be much misdirection and/or wasted effort relative to enterprise-as-a-whole benefits; *e.g.*, silo goal setting/achievement and process improvement efforts.

Pareto Chart – chart containing both bars and a line graph where individual values are presented by bars and the cumulative total is tracked by the line

Pareto Principle – (a/k/a the "80-20 rule") – principle that states that for many events, 80% of the effects come from 20% of the causes; applied to sales, this means 80% of your sales come from 20% of your customers

PDCA – Plan-Do-Check-Act; a four-step problem-solving process used in process improvement; described in Chapter 5

Percent less than – data plotted on a selected probability plot coordinate system to determine if a particular distribution is appropriate (i.e., the data plot as a straight line) and to make statements about percentiles of the population

Performance Management Architecture –refers to the design and implementation of how an organization defines, measures, manages and executes the performance of an employee's job

Problem statement – a concise statement defining the magnitude of process failures and their impact on the quality of products and services

Process Flow Efficiency - a measure of the overall efficiency of a process based on a comparison of the Value Added Time versus the Total (Value Added Time/Total Process Lead Time)

Process Mapping – method and technique used to analyze all the steps used and/or required to move a product or service through the manufacturing or delivery process to the end customer.

Project Charter – a one-page document outlining the purpose, financial impact, goal, scope, milestones, and resource needs to complete a project

Project scope – the boundaries around the problem process identifying where the project team's investigation begins and ends

Pugh Concept Matrix – a tool used to evaluate solution alternatives against an existing baseline by: 1) ranking solutions to identify strengths and weaknesses, 2) attacking each weakness to generate new or hybrid solutions, and 3) ranking the new solutions; steps are repeated through several iterations until a dominant solution emerges

Pull system – a system that communicates real-time needs from downstream operations and replenishes those materials in the exact quantities when requested; pull systems typically consist of bins, inventory cards, boards or other visual cues used to signal the need for material replenishment precisely on time.

Push process/system – traditional system of manufacturing where production is based upon a production plan that is based upon *expected* orders and not *actual* orders

Qualifying – process whereby a pool of potential customers are matched to a specific business by comparing them to a base set of criteria determined to reflect a good prospect for a sales team

Reference cost – the estimated value of what costs *would be* if an improvement had not been made

Required Non-Value Added Work – see "enabling processes"

Rolled Throughput Yield – the understanding that the probability of getting something through a multi-step process is the product (multiplication) of the probability of all the sub-processes

Satellite-level – a term and methodology developed by Forrest W. Breyfogle III used to describe a high-level IEE business metric (*e.g.*, profit margins and revenue growth) that has infrequent sub-grouping or sampling so that short-term variations will result in control charts that view these as common-cause variability.

Scope creep – going beyond the originally agreed upon boundaries of the project scope

Screen main factors – an experimental design used to identify the input factors that have a significant impact on the outcomes of a process

Short interval performance boards – white boards, flip charts, computer screens or documents that visually display and define the expected level of performance for an operation versus the actual level of performance achieved within a specified period of time

Sigma level – measurement of how far a sample or data point is away from its mean, expressed statistically as a standard deviation

Single Piece Flow - the ideal state where parts are manufactured (or transactions are completed) one at a time and flow throughout the value stream as a single unit

SIPOC – acronym for a high-level process map with 5 to 7 essential process steps and associated suppliers, inputs, outputs and customers

Six Sigma – continuous improvement methodology using data and statistical tools with a focus on reducing defects and variation

Spaghetti chart – a visual that maps how people, information and/or materials travel spatially through a process

Special cause variation – any variation in a process that can be explained by one of the 6 M's; variation in a process from a cause that is not an inherent part of that process

Specification document –the written document of all the requirements that define and describe a product, service or improvement

Sponsor – the person who determines if a LSS change project exists or not; this is usually a senior manager in the organization, who serves to provide resources, remove roadblocks, and review progress

Swim lane – a process mapping tool in which each entity involved in the process is assigned a horizontal lane; all process steps are aligned on the map according to the entity having primary responsibility

3PL (Third-Party Logistics) – a firm that provides multiple logistics services for use by customers, preferably in "bundles"; 3PLs often provide transportation, warehousing, cross-docking, inventory management, packaging and freight forwarding

30,000-foot-level – a term and methodology developed by Forrest W. Breyfogle III that creates a time-series tracking chart to provide a high-level -level view of overall process performance. In IEE, this reporting tracks project or operation metric responses with an infrequent sub-grouping/sampling plan so that short-term variations result in charts that view these perturbations as common cause variability. This metric has no calendar boundaries and the latest region of stability can be used to provide a predictive statement for the future.

Throughput accounting – accounting approach that is cash focused and does not allocate all costs to products or services sold (*e.g.*, overhead), but only those costs that vary with output

Time value of money – the idea that money received today is worth more than in the future because of lost interest

Tollgates – deliverables in each phase of DMAIC essential to the decision to move forward in the Six Sigma project

Training Within Industry (TWI) – a series of methods developed to improve production during WWII, later adopted by Toyota

Transactional Process – any non-manufacturing process operation, *e.g.*, Engineering, Help Desk Management, Human Resource Management, Marketing, Sales, etc.

Value-added – activities, actions and processes that add value to a product or service in the eyes of a customer (*i.e.*, the customer is willing to pay for the additional action, activity or process)

Value Chain – a chain of activities that adds value to a product or service at each step of the process

Value Stream – all the actions and information flows required by a current process to bring a product or service from concept to end user or customer; the goal of a value stream is to satisfy the customer

Value stream mapping - a Lean tool (flow chart) of the total set of activities step-by-step and how much time each step takes as a process unfolds; may also include inventory and work in progress

Variation – any measureable fluctuation in the characteristics of a product or service

Variability –lack of uniformity; statistically, the degree to which differences exist in a set of scores, with the standard deviation used to describe the amount of difference in a sample

Voice of the Process – the data generated by the process

Voice of the Customer – collection of data that reflects the wants, needs and desires of your customer base

Waste – non-value added activities exemplified by the "eight wastes" encompassed by the acronym DOWNTIME

Waste walk - an event organized to focus on a specific area to identify process waste

Zero Defects Mentality –intolerance for mistakes/defects; the belief that it is possible to create an organization or individuals that will *never* produce defects in anything it does/they do; leads to a blaming, fearful culture